Literary Criticism and Cultural Theory

Edited by

William E. Cain
Professor of English
Wellesley College

A Routledge Series

Literary Criticism and Cultural Theory

William E. Cain, *General Editor*

The Politics of Melancholy from Spenser to Milton
Adam H. Kitzes

Urban Revelations
Images of Ruin in the American City, 1790–1860
Donald J. McNutt

Postmodernism and Its Others
The Fiction of Ishmael Reed, Kathy Acker, and Don DeLillo
Jeffrey Ebbesen

Different Dispatches
Journalism in American Modernist Prose
David T. Humphries

Divergent Visions, Contested Spaces
The Early United States through the Lens of Travel
Jeffrey Hotz

"Like Parchment in the Fire"
Literature and Radicalism in the English Civil War
Prasanta Chakravarty

Between the Angle and the Curve
Mapping Gender, Race, Space, and Identity in Willa Cather and Toni Morrison
Danielle Russell

Rhizosphere
Gilles Deleuze and the "Minor" American Writings of William James, W.E.B. Du Bois, Gertrude Stein, Jean Toomer, and William Faulkner
Mary F. Zamberlin

The Spell Cast by Remains
The Myth of Wilderness in Modern American Literature
Patricia A. Ross

Strange Cases
The Medical Case History and the British Novel
Jason Daniel Tougaw

Revisiting Vietnam
Memoirs, Memorials, Museums
Julia Bleakney

Equity in English Renaissance Literature
Thomas More and Edmund Spenser
Andrew J. Majeske

"You Factory Folks Who Sing This Rhyme Will Surely Understand"
Culture, Ideology, and Action in the Gastonia Novels of Myra Page, Grace Lumpkin, and Olive Dargan
Wes Mantooth

"Visionary Dreariness"
Readings in Romanticism's Quotidian Sublime
Markus Poetzsch

Fighting the Flames
The Spectacular Performance of Fire at Coney Island
Lynn Kathleen Sally

Idioms of Self-Interest
Credit, Identity, and Property in English Renaissance Literature
Jill Phillips Ingram

Idioms of Self-Interest

Credit, Identity, and Property in English Renaissance Literature

Jill Phillips Ingram

Routledge
New York & London

Routledge
Taylor & Francis Group
270 Madison Ave,
New York NY 10016

Routledge
Taylor & Francis Group
2 Park Square,
Milton Park, Abingdon,
Oxon, OX14 4RN

Routledge is an imprint of Taylor & Francis Group, an Informa business

Transferred to Digital Printing 2010

International Standard Book Number-10: 0-415-97842-4 (Hardcover)
International Standard Book Number-13: 978-0-415-97842-2 (Hardcover)

Library of Congress Cataloging-in-Publication Data

Ingram, Jill Phillips.
Idioms of self-interest : credit, identity, and property in English Renaissance literature / Jill Phillips Ingram.
p. cm. -- (Literary criticism and cultural theory)
Includes bibliographical references and index.
ISBN 0-415-97842-4 (alk. paper)
1. Economics in literature. 2. English literature--Early modern, 1500-1700--History and criticism. 3. Authors, English--Early modern, 1500-1700--Political and social views. 4. Self-interest. 5. Credit--Moral and ethical aspects. 6. Obligations (Law) 7. Debtor and creditor. 8. Property in literature. 9. Social control in literature. I. Title.

PR428.E39I64 2006
820.9'3553--dc22 2006019290

ISBN10: 0-415-97842-4 (hbk)
ISBN10: 0-415-87939-6 (pbk)

ISBN13: 978-0-415-97842-2 (hbk)
ISBN13: 978-0-415-87939-2 (pbk)

Visit the Taylor & Francis Web site at
http://www.taylorandfrancis.com

and the Routledge Web site at
http://www.routledge-ny.com

for
Robert

Contents

A Note on Texts

I have regularized the capitalization and punctuation of titles and modernized the spelling in some of the passages quoted here.

Acknowledgments

This study has benefited from questions asked by audience members at the Sixteenth Century Studies Association conference, the Shakespeare Association of America meeting, and the Early Modern Cultural Studies Association meeting, where I delivered portions of it as talks.

An earlier and shorter version of Chapter Two appeared as "Economies of Obligation in Eastward Ho," *Ben Jonson Journal* 11 (2004):21–40. Portions of Chapter Four appeared in *Early Modern Culture* V (Winter 2006). I am grateful to these publishers for permission to incorporate their material here.

I am grateful to my advisors at the University of Virginia who guided me through the early stages of this study: Gordon Braden, Clare Kinney, and Katharine Maus. Many people have offered much-valued encouragement and commentary during the course of this project, including Margaret Ferguson, Theresa Krier, Lois Potter, Anne Lake Prescott, Cristina Cervone, Andrew Escobedo, Nicole Reynolds, Tom McAlindon, Kevin Gustafson, Paul Halliday, Patrick Griffin, Andrea Laue, Heather Morton, Elizabeth Bridgham, Ronda Chollock, Tonia Jeray, and Zack Long. I would also like to thank Max Novick at Routledge for his patience and helpfulness in editing the manuscript. Malcolm Smuts provided early encouragement, as did other members of the fall 2000 Folger Institute seminar, "Defining the Court's Political Thought." Thelma Crafton provided a model of integrity and wit: her memory continues to inspire. Michael Phillips and Susan Phillips have been wonderfully supportive and I am forever indebted to them both.

I thank Claire Ingram for the great joy and "all the untidy activity" she has brought into my life this last year. Above all I am thankful for the keen and judicious eye of my husband, Robert Ingram, whose steadfastness, patience, and advocacy have meant everything. Without him, nothing would have been possible.

June 5, 2006
Athens, Ohio

Chapter One

Introduction

The speaker of Shakespeare's *Sonnets* implores the fair young man to remember him after his death:

> But be contented when that fell arrest
> Without all bail shall carry me away,
> My life hath in this line some interest,
> Which for memorial still with thee shall stay.[1]

This suggestive vision—in which death the jailor arrests and imprisons the speaker without bail—prods the young man to participate in the speaker's redemption simply by remembering him in the lines of poetry left behind. The "interest" that the line holds for the speaker's life is manifold. In the first instance, it gives him a deathless and continual residence in the young man's mind. But it also implies a legal right of possession. Since his life has an interest, or a share, in the line of poetry, a part of him lives on; the verse, as an entailed estate on which the speaker has a legal claim, is suggested to his potential heir as a partial replacement for the living poet once he's died. The poem is offered as solace for its reader, but ultimately the "interest" is more centrally the speaker's own self-interest. By highlighting his worth as something enduring in the lines after his death, the speaker enriches both the poem's worth and his own value in his reader's eyes.

The speaker's self-interest is not the unbridled, aggressive drive many sixteenth- and seventeenth-century writers condemned as malevolent and antisocial. Commercial self-interest, according to some contemporaries, led inexorably to unethical or criminal actions. "Private interest," wrote the author of *Britannia Languens or a Discourse of Trade* (1680), "leads men into Cheats, Thefts, and all those other base merciless and execrable Villanies, which render the Actors Criminous, and odious by the Sufferings and

Injuries they bring upon others."[2] Behind this argument lay the Christian humanist emphasis on a social rationality of trust in preference to self-interest. Thomas Wilson's *Art of Rhetoric* (1553) counseled, "For if I should . . . follow gain without respect to the hindrance of mine even Christian: why should not . . . every man for himself, and the devil for us all, catch that catch may?"[3] Henry Carey thought self-interest a synonym for faithlessness: "the self-interested and perfidious heart of man."[4] But the speaker of Shakespeare's sonnets asserts an "interest" that is neither villainous nor perfidious but is instead comforting and mutually beneficial for both the young man and himself. The notion that the speaker would pursue his self-interest—in this case offering the poem as a memorial to his life—is natural.

This book examines these idioms of self-interest in English literature of the late sixteenth and early seventeenth centuries. It is concerned, in the first instance, with recovering and analyzing the various languages used to articulate self-interest in the period's literature. More importantly, this project of literary archaeology demonstrates quite clearly that self-interest was not—as we have been taught to believe—understood by most early modern English men and women as, in and of itself, a bad thing.

"Interest" had been used since the fifteenth century to describe one's economic stake in property or commodity. In 1523 John Fitzherbert employed it to describe property rights: "Their title and interest grew by inheritance."[5] The word usually referred to a right of legal possession, as when in *2 Henry VI* the Duke of Somerset said to Henry VI: "All your Interest in those territories is utterly bereft you."[6] The legal meaning of "interest" was diluted by a second term that pointed to a general advantage, in the sense of political power.[7] Sir Geoffrey Fenton's 1579 edition of Guicciardini's history of Italy employs this sense of the term when describing the motivations of the French and other nations attempting to invade Italy in the late fifteenth century: "Carried with ambitious respects touching their interests and desires particular."[8]

These competing vocabularies—of private economic interest or purely personal gain, considered unethical, and of legitimate property right—suggest a faultline in early modern notions of self-interest, but one that would close. By the dawn of the seventeenth century, conceptions of personal advantage became numerous and complex, contradictory and fluid. How was the drive of self-interest scrutinized and judged in this period of economic expansion in London? Many early modern authors continued to portray the self-interested merchant as greedy and selfish, yet not all depictions of self-interest were censorious. Indeed, while the self-serving lawyer or monopolist continued to fall victim to playwrights' and poets' satirical pens, contemporary pamphleteers aggressively defended self-interest in the name of commercial growth.

This defense of self-interest is a subject about which modern literary criticism is curiously silent. Yet more attention must be paid to the process by which the early modern market began to accommodate notions and practices of self-interest. Increasingly during the late sixteenth and early seventeenth centuries, economic agents with a wide range of motivations began to assimilate practices and languages that legitimized personal profit and advantage; likewise, they began to temper conventional vilifications of usury, prodigality, and risky enterprises. Sermons, casuistry manuals, parliamentary debates, legal tracts, and personal diaries were but a few of the media engaged in this interpretive discourse. Ironically, even radically hostile puritan characterizations of "dangerous" economic greed helped speed the accommodation of self-interest as a virtue rather than as a vice. By familiarizing their audiences with the comic archetypes with which to interpret market changes, puritan sermons and pamphlets actually helped early moderns to accept, exploit, and enjoy the figures they represented.[9] Of particular concern to this study is the methods by which poets and playwrights both gauged the conceptual shift regarding self-interest and advanced it in their own works.

Previous examinations of self-interest have either missed or ignored the extent to which this accommodation took place or the significance of its beginnings in the late sixteenth century. Many have argued that until the late seventeenth or the early eighteenth century most English thought self-interest was harmful.[10] To be sure Mark Kishlansky's study of the emergence of adversarial parliamentary politics has identified the legitimation of self-concern in political life.[11] Andrew McRae has likewise traced the shift in representations of rural community in England from those of stability in the fifteenth and sixteenth centuries to those valuing individual enterprise and property in the seventeenth century.[12] Nonetheless, economic historians and literary critics continue to define non-political, private interest as symptomatic of extreme individualism that was an anti-social force through the mid-seventeenth century.[13] This book elucidates the fallacy of that particular argument.

I

Long before commercial markets emerged in England, self-interest was the subject of political debate. Fifth- and sixth-century Sophists agreed that people gathered in political association for the self-interested reason of mutual defense. "[E]very living creature loves itself," Cicero wrote, in *De finibus*, "and from the moment of birth strives to seek its own preservation."[14] The idea that self-interest could serve as a legitimate foundation for the political order survived in the contract theories and found their most stark and notable formulation in Thomas Hobbes' *Leviathan* (1651). Hobbes argued that man's most powerful drive was self-interest, a radically aggressive urge which leads him to excess and, left unchecked, ultimately to destruction. Only submission to absolute authority allows humans to live peacefully together and to enjoy the benefits of society. The absolute authority of the sovereign and state law, Hobbes argued, was necessary to force people to keep their covenants and to resolve disputes. In effect, Hobbes made the legal enforcement of contract the only feasible glue of human society. Without absolute unquestioned authority, passions would overcome reason and lead to quarrels, and the destructive centrifugal force of ambition and market competition would leave society in a state of each man at war with another.

Many early moderns, however, rejected the argument that self-interest had to be harnessed so strictly. Instead, private interest had to be balanced against the state's interest. Those state interests, according to the political language of *raison d'etat* or *ragion di stato*, stressed a pragmatism that benefited the state or the sovereign, though not always their subjects. The source of the term *ragion di stato*, Francesco Guiccardini, also provided the term "interest" for this new kind of politics. In *Ricordi*, first published posthumously in 1576, he writes:

> If [men who preach liberty] thought they would be better off under a tyranny, they would rush into it post-haste. For self-interest [*interesse suo*] prevails in almost all human beings, and those who recognize the value of honor and glory are few.[15]

While much of Guicciardini's own work was loosely based on Cicero, with an ethical emphasis on duty to the state, the "new humanism" of the late sixteenth century supplanted Cicero with Tacitus. In a well-known piece of Tacitism in the early seventeenth century, the Bolognese author Virgilio Malvezzi argued that "men will always be more moved with private interest, than with public profit."[16] The debate between states' interest and individual interest developed throughout the seventeenth century, first in political tracts on republicanism leading up to the Civil War and then with Marchamont Nedham's tract *Interest Will Not Lie* (1659).[17] Rejecting the Hobbesian notion that self-interest is inherently destructive, Nedham suggested that one could apply to men the principle that states act in their self-interest: fundamentally, that men base their decisions on their own self-interest.

But such theories emerged in the half-century and more before Nedham advances his thesis. The most vocal contemporary challenge to the negative definitions of self-interest came, predictably, from merchants, tradesmen, adventurers, and others with a vested interest in commerce. Some argued for the virtue inherent in honest trade—Thomas Tusser, for instance, championed trustworthiness and moralistically claimed that profit was the benefit of good husbandry in *Five Hundred Points of Good Husbandry* (1573), first published in 1557 as *A Hundreth Good Points of Husbandry*.[18] The additions to Tusser's 1573 edition are noteworthy for their focus on instructions to farmers in what one critic sees as Tusser's recognition of a new rural "dynamic economic system."[19] When Tusser advises in his poem "The Ladder to Thrift," "To get by honest practice,/and keep thy gettings covertly," he is at once supporting the notions of honest, diligent husbandry and a self-interested profit motive.[20] He both echoes the Christian doctrine of upright, honest dealings, and encourages aspirations of the farmer to, by "keep[ing] [his] gettings," eventually rise to a higher social strata. In other writings the Christian ethos of the "calling" is linked with the profit it can bring. William Scott's *An Essay on Drapery* (1635) invokes medieval and puritan arguments regarding man's duty to work: he calls for *sancta avaritia*, asserting that "He cannot be a good Draper which is not first a good man," and "honesty without wisdom is unprofitable."[21] In Scott's essay, one modern critic has noted, "self-interest is not, *a priori*, an evil."[22] Encouragement to seek one's own profit is given moral grounding and often described as an aspect of civic responsibility and neighborliness. Invoking Cicero on the natural sociability of men, Lewes Roberts, merchant and captain of the City of London, contended, in 1641, that "we are not borne for our selves in a saying no less ancient then true," while defending merchants' activities as inherently sociable.[23] In response to fears that personal interest would lead to dishonest practices, many writers highlighted just dealing. Scott, for instance, subtitled his *Essay on Drapery* "Trading justly, pleasingly, profitably," implicitly prioritizing justice over profits. John Wheeler, secretary of the Merchant Adventurer's Society, defended the merchant in *A Treatise of Commerce* (1601) as merely a friendly neighbor with good communication skills:

> It is almost unpossible for three persons to converse together two hours, but they will fall into talk of one bargain or another, chopping, changing, or some other kind of contract . . . The Prince with his subjects, the master with his servants, one friend and acquaintance with another, the captain with his soldiers, the husband with his wife, women with and among themselves, and in a word, all the world choppeth and

> changeth, runneth and raveth after marts, markets, and merchandising, so that all things come into commerce, and pass into traffic (in a manner) in all times, and in all places:[24]

As Everyman, the merchant is stripped of his threatening force as alien, exploitative other.

But merchants were not the only ones to raise their voices in defense of self-interest. Arguments for it later took the form of a social pragmatism based on notions of social order and stability. Mid-seventeenth-century pamphlets on enclosure reasoned that the pursuit of self-interest not only was "natural," but also that it produced economic and social benefits for the lower orders. The minister Joseph Lee argued in *Considerations concerning common fields* (1653) that self-oriented motives lead to ultimate good for the community because private farming yields more than farming in common, and those making profits are enabled to make weekly contributions for relief of the poor.[25] In a subsequent pamphlet Lee asked rhetorically, "May not every man lawfully put his commodity to the best advantage, provided he do it without prejudice to others?"[26] Indeed he went so far as to contend that the "advancement of private persons will be the advantage of the public."[27] Lee reasoned that the profitable farmer is more able to contribute to charity, and that his successes will enable him to employ the poor who need work. Thus he gave the profit motive a moral backing, joining in the rising number of voices by the mid-seventeenth century who celebrated the godly improver of the land who contributes to a growing market economy.[28]

The premises of such arguments, however, were not entirely novel. In 1623, Edward Misselden suggested that it was appropriate for merchants to seek their private gain, their *Privatum Commodum*, "in the exercise of their calling."[29] And as early as 1581, Sir Thomas Smith, prompted by the inflation crisis, posited self-interest as an acceptable force in *A Discourse of the Commonweal of this Realm of England.*[30] In the *Discourse*, Smith presented a series of discussions between a Knight, a merchant, a husbandman, a capper, and a doctor. Smith highlighted the husbandman's independence and responsibility for decisions affecting his land. Men naturally "seek where their advantage is," he argued, and so farmers, instead of being subject to restrictions addressing the hardships caused by enclosures, should be given "liberty to sell . . . at all times and to all places as freely as men may do other things."[31] The *Discourse* expresses a conception of society in which self-interest contributes to national prosperity and common well-being. The doctor, presented as the voice of authority, reflects and comments upon the grievances of the other speakers. He stresses that "men may not abuse their own things to the damage of the Commonweal."[32] Smith used his dialogue both to highlight and criticize the conventions of the traditional agrarian complaint, and to develop an appreciation of economic individualism, in support of a sense of personal gain that was both morally acceptable and materially beneficial to the nation.[33] Edward Misselden expressed this relation in terms of private gain as inseparable from public gain: "Is not the public involved in the private, and the private in the public?" and "What else makes a Common-wealth, but the private-wealth?"[34]

These defenses of economic self-interest clearly anticipated Bernard Mandeville and Adam Smith who, in the century after Hobbes, would characterize self-interest as a given quality of human nature, though without Hobbes' harshly negative judgment. Smith's famous passage on the self-interest of butchers, bakers, and other tradesmen suggested that "self-love" and profit were the primary motivations in entering the market to buy and sell. The propensity to "truck, barter, and exchange," which Smith saw as the foundation of commerce and the division of labor, was driven by individual desire.[35] Private interest carries benefits to others besides the initial self-interested agent. The sonnet-speaker's "interest," in the form of the poem, will serve the young man as a pleasing memorial; Misselden's merchants' wealth benefits the commonwealth; and Smith's bakers provide bread for hungry consumers. We must carefully trace the development of this more salutary understanding of self-interest in the late sixteenth and early seventeenth centuries. In order to sketch the contours of this shift in the creative literature in the period, however, we must draw upon the recent work of historians. When we, as literary critics, place fictional economic behaviors in the context of actual historical ones, the detailed examinations of economic and social historians such as Craig Muldrew and Keith Wrightson become essential to such a project. Their work has shown that individual self-interest in sixteenth- and seventeenth-century England was not, either in practice or in perception, primarily a socially threatening force.

III

Many economic historians have traditionally understood self-interest as an anti-coagulant of community. On this reading, selling for profit on the market encouraged a self-interest that eroded communal cooperation. Max Weber and R. H. Tawney, for instance, thought markets were instrumental in dissolving the communities of medieval Europe and in creating the structural conditions for modern individualism.[36] Christopher Hill valorized the communitarian Diggers' opposition to enclosure on grounds that the Diggers stood squarely against selfish, hence destructive, economic individualism characteristic of the market.[37] These scholars and many others claim that it was the emerging market in the sixteenth century that led to self-interested rational economic behavior.[38] C.B. Macpherson goes so far to suggest that England had become an individualistic market society by the seventeenth century in which property and the capacity to labor were both alienable.[39]

This argument that self-interest destroyed early modern communities was a scholarly shibboleth until Craig Muldrew eviscerated it in his pioneering study of early modern English economic behavior. The traditional model to explain early modern economic man assumes that marketing gave rise to profiteering and elevation of self-interest over communal duties and obligation. Yet, as Muldrew shows quite clearly, the ability of the community to absorb and process individual interest was already highly developed in this period. In his analysis of hundreds of records concerning credit disputes in the sixteenth and seventeenth centuries, Muldrew finds that increased market competition, rather than dissolving communities, strengthened communal ties.[40] Most buying and selling was done on credit, creating large credit networks in the process. These networks were so entwined and extensive that moral factors were introduced which stressed cooperation.[41] Individual profit and security were best achieved with the direct cooperation of one's neighbors. Muldrew posits that early modern markets constituted a "moral economy," but one that nevertheless was composed of "individualistic contractual relations."[42]

Muldrew's account complicates our understanding of market relations in seventeenth-century England in a number of important ways. By conceiving of economic transactions in a community-oriented framework, he finds the neoclassical model insufficient. It is misguided, he contends, to think of the market in early modern England as guided by "invisible hand": we must attend instead to the ways in which individuals operated not merely as profit-driven, rational agents, but also as social participants sharing communal notions of trust. Muldrew suggests as a replacement for the term "capitalism" (as a disinterested, rational system), "creditism," meaning an economy not based on alienable "capital" but instead on social "credit." The market operated as an "economy of obligation."[43] His revisionist account rejects Marx's explanation of credit relations as based upon distrust and alienation. Ethical responses to market conflict, Muldrew finds, in fact intensified as a result of an explosion in credit transactions.

Muldrew's evidence for this increasingly "ethical" economy of obligation is, in part, the rise in debt litigation. The rise in the number of credit transactions meant the expansion of the contractual legal culture so that as litigation increased, so did the importance of all types of courts. The crucial feature of this juridical society was public dispute resolution, a practice that expressed its members' desire to live in a state of communal relations with their neighbors to such a degree that reciprocal trust, mutual hospitality and civic duty could be maintained. This type of resolution was centered on the concept and process of reconciliation, and as such involved the settling of disputes after they had occurred, first by informal and then by legal means, to effect the "negotiated community." Muldrew finds that the poor and disenfranchised actually begin, in this period, to utilize social and legal structures to address their condition. Far from rejecting Marx's analysis of problematic inequalities in accumulation that emerge with the rise of the market economy, Muldrew sees such differences, but finds that the poor had access to legal means of addressing such inequalities:

> while the expansion of the market led to a relative swelling of the ranks of the poor, because of credit it also led to the expansion of a contractual legal culture in which responsible members of households who engaged in economic exchange were given a great deal of moral autonomy in their economic agency—which they certainly used in King's Lynn where they took their betters to court. The powerful justificatory force of contract did nothing to address the increasing inequality of accumulation, but it did give the poor equality of access to right.[44]

This legalism, he stresses, is intensely personal, so that the emphasis is on "trust" rather than self-interest. Thus Muldrew counterposes "the idea of self-interest" against that of "trust":

> The structural changes which might have taken place in economic practice to create a more utilitarian marketing culture where the idea of self-interest could have come to be seen as a more coherent locus of the interpretation of economic exchange and communication than trust now need to be investigated.[45]

Muldrew muses about a cultural shift in which "self-interest" overtakes "trust" as a locus of interpretation. What happens, however at the moments in which the notion of self-interest first confronts the trust-based economic culture? It is this structural change to which this book attends. It is not the case that one collection of beliefs and practices came to replace the other. Moments of "self-interest" could, after all, operate in accordance with the social theory of trust and contract. When we look to creative literature of the period we find individual characters testing out such moments. But in Muldrew's "economic epistemology" of the period, individuals are first and foremost members of households, which were all dependent on one another "in a social field of material security, in which household wealth was seen primarily as a social relationship."[46] While in much creative literature of the period, individuals sometimes operate as "members of households," it is more often the case that they function as independent agents, making decisions that highlight their very vulnerability, separateness, and agency as individuals. Thus the preoccupation of fictional literature with subjectivity makes it an especially fruitful field to scan for this testing.

IV

Recent studies of "inwardness" and "interiority" have explored the emergence of the subject in Renaissance England and the techniques of personal resistance that presume personal interiority.[47] When considering the market, however, public actions and utterances, indicating participation in communal matrices such as credit networks, take precedence over interiority. It is obviously not in the interest of the individual, no matter the financial and political pressures, to jettison notions of communal trust. In early modern literature, self-interest is thus often asserted mildly, fitting itself into a communal context. Often authors represent subjects as reacting in inventive, novel ways when faced with vexed social situations in which their social "credit" is skewed and their self-interest is not adequately accounted for. Thus the ways in which the individual proposes readjustments in his or her relationship to the collective, rather than either rejecting broader communal interests or accepting a position of subordination, warrant close attention.

In identifying these novel behaviors, I recover early moments in a larger cultural shift toward the acceptance of explicitly self-interested responses. Such general shifts in political or social thought are traceable through "languages" or "idioms."[48] Idioms—theological or legal languages, for instance—discharge various political and intellectual functions, contain implications, and convey modes of assumption and ambiguity. In the drama, for example, assumptions can be expressed by way of contrasting characters' behaviors or sets of decisions, one implicitly more attractive than the other. In some cases sympathetic characters echo or mimic the actions of questionable characters, in the process distorting the function of those actions. Jonson, Marston, and Chapman, in *Eastward Ho* (1605), deploy idioms of personal credit to dramatize virtuous characters borrowing economic behaviors from devious characters. Those good characters in turn lend credence to self-interested, risk-taking, entrepreneurial practices previously thought irresponsible. Shakespeare and Sir Francis Bacon steep *Timon of Athens* (1608) and the *New Atlantis* (1627) in credit and legal discourses to critique paternalistic systems that deny the expression of self-interest. Aemilia Lanyer and Isabella Whitney employ languages of economic credit and of property rights to assert, through their poems' speakers, their own claims to credit and patronage networks. The very vocabulary of credit is highlighted, in plays such as *The Merchant of Venice*, to signal approval for characters willing to risk, or to "hazard," in order to get ahead. A similar cultural valuation for the merchants' hazardous undertakings in their business ventures and their travel is expressed even in religious writings, where Lancelot Andrewes speaks, in his sermons, to the biblical principles behind such a valuation.

To locate such values as expressed in these idioms, we cannot look solely to the manifest content of the literature, but sometimes must investigate the latent aspects of narrative and dramatic form. Douglas Bruster, who locates such latent moments in the drama, provides a valuable example for a method with which to examine the ways Renaissance authors confront social change in the intensifying market economy.[49] More recent work has focused on specific economic practices, such as that by Theodore Leinwand, who pairs fictional texts with actual economic practices (e.g. mortgage payments, or the use of venture capital) in order to trace emotional and psychological responses to economic crises.[50]

This book's primary aim is to illumine the ways in which economic agents altered the language of self-assertion. For evidence, it examines a wide range of early modern English texts (including commercial handbooks, legal statues, casuistry manuals, female legacies, and pamphlets on trade) and genres (including city comedy, tragedy, elegiac poetry, satirical poetry, and utopian prose narrative).

Why not leave investigation of this cultural shift in the meanings of self-interest to historians? Most obviously because literary analysis enables a kind of close reading of the constructions of self-interest that is not the historian's forte. More importantly, literary texts are themselves historical evidence, but evidence to which historians have paid insufficient attention. Defenses of self-interested actions in poems, or implicit approval of self-interested behaviors by way of plot-lines in the drama, for instance, provide one cultural script through which attitudes towards self-interest were changed: in this sense we conceive literary works as a type of social action. In dramatists' and poets' nuanced defenses of characters' (and speakers') self-interested actions, are what J.L. Austin terms "illocutionary acts," or words as deeds.[51] In this study of self-interest, we distinguish the speech-acts from their effects. For example, when the speaker of Isabella Whitney's "Wyll" describes debtors' prisons and her own lack of credit in London, her utterance is an action—it complains, or has the (illocutionary) force of complaining about being denied credit. The effect of her utterance is the (perlocutionary) consequence of her complaint: perhaps she will succeed in obtaining credit, have some influence on poor laws, or convince other female writers to more vigorously pursue credit networks in London's competitive financial environment. Language, reckons Austin, does not merely "reflect" social attitudes but, as action itself, changes social attitudes. Thus, Quentin Skinner employs Austin's theories to describe the effect when early capitalists appropriated the evaluative vocabulary of the Protestant religion. The capitalists' appropriations increased the acceptability of capitalism and helped, Skinner argues, to channel its evolution in specific directions.[52] The merchant, for instance, tailors his projects to make them answer to the pre-existing language of moral principles, incorporating capitalist practices into a normative religious language. By invoking a term such as "religiously" and using it to describe freedom of trade, for example, he applies the term in such a way that not only describes his behavior but serves to evaluate it.[53] We can capture the historicity of evaluative concepts by tracing their changing applications. In stressing "actions" of self-interest I emphasize the concept, rather than strictly the term, "self-interest." Although I acknowledge early uses of the term "interest" in political and economic contexts to set the parameters of my project, it is largely the implicit behaviors of self-interest that I locate throughout the book.

In these novel descriptions of self-interest we can find examples of what Skinner calls "rhetorical redescription."[54] Skinner borrows the concept from Quintilian, whose *paradiastole* to Book IV of *Institutio Oratoria* describes the process by which an action is assigned different motives to make it more appealing. A given evaluative description is replaced by a rival term that serves to place it in a positive moral light. One example Quintilian offers of such redescription, a concept originated by Aristotle in the *Art of Rhetoric*, is particularly relevant to early modern market culture: "prodigality must be more leniently redescribed as liberality. . . ."[55] In London's expanding market culture, liberality—in the form of charity—allowed citizens to fulfill a civic duty while at the same time serving their own self-interest. The charity of London's aldermen, for example, in provisioning the city, controlling the markets, administering poor relief, and licensing alehouse keepers, provided communal benefits while also serving to consolidate the aldermen's power.[56] In the process of consolidating that power, however, such figures would have to employ some entrepreneurial, risk-taking behavior in order to, for instance, maintain order or mobilize the benevolence of the wealthy. Thus the scheming and self-serving manipulations of the "prodigal" get redefined as skillful and judicious "liberality."

V

Hints of such shifts emerge in literary genres traditionally thought to critique the pernicious materialism of prodigal characters in London's market culture, namely, the genre of city comedy. City comedy prodigals, typically interpreted by literary critics as marginalized figures who threaten the "settled social fabric" in which they operate, have alternately been considered as "outsiders" serving as "scapegoats" for behaviors that the nobility (the "insiders") would otherwise feel for their own prodigality.[57] The avaricious lender and projector Sir Giles Overreach in Philip Massinger's *A New Way to Pay Old Debts* (1621), for example, is ostracized, driven mad, and serves as one such scapegoat. The literary *paradiastole* of prodigality is more explicit in *Eastward Ho*, where the virtuous thrifty Golding models his behavior on the prodigal Quicksilver. The conservative Golding not only adopts the risk-taking, theatrical behaviors of the prodigals, but he then incorporates those prodigals into the unified community at the play's end. In such cases, thrifty, virtuous characters incorporate the reckless energy of the prodigals to negotiate successfully the "clash of idioms" inherent in city comedy.[58] In *Eastward Ho* the idioms merge instead of clash. In using the prodigals' behaviors to draw the prodigals back into mainstream civic and economic channels, characters such as the alderman Golding achieve the "negotiated community" that Muldrew observes.

As certain idioms of self-interest emerge, other outdated practices—like paternalism—that constrain self-interest fall away, or are exposed as insufficient. Paternalism was as a strategy of estate management for farmers who would, as a means of control, nurture relations with their tenants.[59] The reciprocity it entailed was one of *unequal* obligations. Rather than giving social subordinates a sense of empowerment in improving their economic situations, paternalistic systems worked to keep power inequalities in place. But the growing force of economic self-interest and the increasing number of credit transactions among tradesmen and farmers alike made them increasingly dissatisfied with such unequal obligations. The inadequacy of the paternalistic system in the emergent market economy was commensurate with its inability to recognize the conflict and insubordination self-interest sometimes produces. We see such inadequacy registered in dramatic texts such as *Timon of Athens* and the *New Atlantis*. Paternalism aimed to quash the recognition of self-interest on the part of subordinates by suggesting that their needs were already provided for. In *Timon*, Shakespeare portrays the denial of self-interest as resulting in the eruption—embodied in Timon himself—of an ultimately anti-social drive harmful to society. Texts such as *Timon* suggest that the constant recognition of self-interest is preferable to its repression.

The late sixteenth and early seventeenth centuries also witnessed individual authors reflecting on their own economic agency. Female writers writing in autobiographical modes, for example, were not encouraged to assert a desire for economic success or literary fame. They would be challenging, for one, the injunction to be "chaste, silent, and obedient."[60] When expressing their own economic agency (while also questioning the conditions of that agency), they often had to do so in coded terms. One of the ways in which they began to do this was to develop their own idioms with which to position themselves as economic agents. One such idiom, in this case a genre, was the "mother's legacy," dying mothers' bequests and last words to their children, hugely popular works which also served as one of the few acceptable outlets for women to publish their writing. Elizabeth Grymeston's *Miscelanea, Meditations, Memoratives* (1604), Dorothy's Leigh's *The Mother's Blessing* (1616), and Elizabeth Joscelin's *The Mother's Legacy to her Unborne Child* (1624) were bestsellers, with Leigh's reaching twenty-three editions between 1616 and 1674.[61] But the very feature that protected these writers from being charged with improper activity—the legacy was a literary form which remained ostensibly private, containing the intimate words of a mother to her children—also limited the illocutionary force of the texts. The act of those texts was not necessarily to assert their authors as agents in the public market economy.

For that assertion, we can look to the work of the writer Isabella Whitney who, in her "Wyll and Testament" (1573), borrows from the female legacy tradition, but places her poem in a far more public and explicitly market-oriented context. She does so by using elements of the satirical mock-testament genre that traditionally implicated general cultural formations that led to the testator's "death." She also added elements of the female complaint, a genre that traditionally presents "effects" suggesting "causes" for the speaker's emotional distress, in a quasilegal formulation. In her case, the distress is economic—her speaker has been denied access to London's credit networks. By employing these mixed genres not only to articulate her economic agency but also to gesture to—and implicate—the causes of her financial disadvantage, Whitney offers a public and communal authority for her private financial distress. At the same time she places herself within a credit network—offering the poem as a means to increase her social credit and her viability in the market culture. When we place Whitney's poem alongside works such as Aemilia Lanyer's "The Description of Cooke ham" (1611), another work considering loss of economic credit (in terms of patronage), we can understand them as textual interventions attempting to redescribe the self-interest of female writers as viable, identifying themselves as economic agents. By implicating systems that in effect forestall or bar their speakers from commercial and social networks, such authors call for an opening of those networks, essentially attempting the "negotiated community" that aldermen, for example, can effect more explicitly.

My analysis focuses on such "negotiated communities" and employs Austin's speech-act theory to examine social acts and public utterances understood by a community of speakers. In London's emerging market economy, that community was composed primarily of credit relationships. The ways in which members of that community understood the very word "credit," however, was polyvalent. In the drama of the period 1590–1640, for example, we can discern the ways in which "credit" was used both to endorse and to disgrace others' actions regarding debt. We also see how Skinner's "rhetorical redescription" applies to the shifting valence of the word "credit" when used in the context of reputation, separate from its meaning as the ability to assume debt. When we examine closely the ability of characters to achieve credit, we find that it is most often the result of gaining communal respect. While this association appears to be self-evident, it is the process of winning that credit that reveals some unexpected contours of character development and evaluation. Tricky or wily characters whose ruses come to be believed are granted a measure of respect for their wittiness. A character who can make others believe him, inspiring in them a measure of trust, is commensurate with a character with the skill and connections to achieve loans, thus he is "credited" on both accounts. Often we see such a character as one who is willing to take risks, specifically to "hazard" his reputation, for the prospect of personal gain. By tracing a series of such characterizations across a broad range of plays and prose "characters" in the period, we can analyze this particular aspect of the valuation of self-interest as it develops in fictional literature. By focusing on the vocabularies of "credit" and "hazard" in *The Merchant of Venice*, we more clearly understand the ways in which characters such as Bassanio and Portia negotiate these vocabularies to their advantage. Further, we gain insight into the nature of that social advantage, as the communal acceptance of self-interest is reflected in the development of the society's shared terminology, its agreed-upon vocabulary of what counts as respectable "credit."

One aspect of that shared terminology is the moral or ethical valuation of such terms as "hazard." In Lancelot Andrewes's Cambridge lectures, for instance, the moral, and more specifically, the biblical basis for merchants' enterprising ventures and hazardous activity is given as a justification for profit and for their economic self-interest. The lectures were widely known and circulated in note form from the 1580s to the 1630s, but not printed until 1650.[62] Andrewes and other writers reflect a shifting attitude towards risk and chance, one that in the middle ages was more negative and more singularly associated with gambling. But even concerns over gambling began to change in the early seventeenth century, as a result of mercantile activity that legitimized the calculation of chances in endeavors, such as the development of probability theory. While the prohibition remained against anyone attempting to calculate chances that instead only God could determine, the need to measure risk in merchant enterprises legitimized instruments such as insurance. We see such legitimization in parliamentary acts, such as the 1601 act "Concerning matters of assurances."[63] Here again, "hazard" is invoked as the justification for merchants needing "assurance," or money laid out as insurance, in order to protect the value of the goods risked. Thus we see this particular idiom of self-interest, the ethical and moral valuation of the word "hazard," arise as an inflection of a culture increasingly aware of the importance of risk-taking.

In this book I trace the growing concern with the individual's place in the larger market economy, a concern that was reflected by authors suggesting financial anxieties both in their characters and through coded use of genre. The particular cast of this anxiety at the beginning of the seventeenth century, however, was a freshly urgent self-interest, a sense that one may not only assert an individual stake in the larger economic collective, but that one had the right to do so. I chart this "right" as expressed by characters newly sympathetic, previously villainized, who staked their own economic claim, achieved credit, and contributed to a growing market economy, an economy energized by their participation in it. This shift that made self-interest acceptable in fictional characters also emboldened female authors to assert their own economic place in the world of print culture. Although these authors were mavericks in their time, their assertions were not outlandish or immoral: and the fact that the morality of the entrepreneurial risk-taker found approval even by popular priests normalized economic self-interest. The ethical approval of adventuring, necessary for larger community interests, spoke to larger notions of economic identity. As the growing market economy presented fresh financial challenges to many individuals, so too did individuals begin demanding more from the marketplace: staking one's personal claim in that public realm was no longer shameful or unspeakable. In the imaginative literature of the period authors give unique names and voices to those claims, offering them not only as mirrors, but as models for the new economic individual.

Chapter Two

Economies of Obligation in *Eastward Ho*

When the deceitful prodigals and spendthrifts of city comedy chart their scheming paths across the stage, scavenging the lives of unwitting dutiful characters, their dash and bravado often is attractive and compelling. Sometimes good and honest characters borrow behaviors from these wily prodigals. In Jonson, Chapman, and Marston's *Eastward Ho* (1605), the honest, thrifty Golding uses models of ambition and self-interest not traditionally thought to be available to characters like him. Unpacking behavior like his and what it says about early modern representations of economic self-interest is this chapter's subject.

The virtuous alderman Golding schemes at the debtors' prison at the Counter for the release of a group of cheating adventurers who have tried to swindle his father-in-law, Touchstone. Golding, certain they are repentant, wants to convince Touchstone of this so he will drop his charges against them. The means by which Golding effects this forgiveness, however, are somewhat devious and roundabout. "[B]ecause I . . . find there is no means to make my father relent so likely as to bring him to be a spectator of their miseries," he says to the prison master, "I have ventured on a device, which is to make myself your prisoner . . . and, feigning an action at suit of some third person, pray him by this token [*giving a ring*] that he will . . . come hither for my bail. . . ." (5.3.114–23).[1] Golding will make Touchstone a "spectator" of the prisoners' miseries to convince him to forgive their crimes. Golding uncharacteristically "ventures on a device" to secure the prisoners' release and to create trust between the criminals and their accuser. In bringing the two parties to this mutual solution, Golding enforces what Craig Muldrew calls an "economy of obligation." In such an economy, communal ties, interpersonal trust, and social debts lie at the root of market operations.[2] Muldrew's model holds that communal interests are as vital to market operations as are profit-oriented, "pure" market interests. What motivation would Golding have to negotiate this measure of cooperation on behalf of the criminals? And why would an otherwise conservative character risk his own personal credit to "venture on a device" and initiate the negotiation? In addressing such concerns we need to look beneath the play's theatrical stylings—the conclusion stages a burlesque of tidy morality-play reconciliations—at the ways actual economic practices are represented.

Many literary critics addressing dramatic representations of economic exchange in early modern drama have highlighted the conflict and distrust which such transactions engendered.[3] The rise of the market economy, such criticism posits, is commensurate with an individualism that is pernicious and subversive of the social order. Plays, in turn, depict that troubling force, and in the drama, social ambition is a sin to be punished.[4] Of course, city comedy is rife with such social anxiety. And unquestionably, *Eastward Ho* dramatizes some of these conflicts, depicting the conservative "disciplining" of unruly acquisitiveness—the gold-digging bride is fooled by her penniless knight, the prodigal adventurers fail and are imprisoned, and the usurer is cuckolded, for instance. Yet the play also rehearses the fulfillment of economic obligations and the strengthening of social ties. This is particularly evident in *Eastward Ho*, where market pressures serve to motivate characters to pursue, in risky and sometimes novel ways, social agreement and compromise. Within such compromise there is a place for economic self-interest, which does not emerge in the play as the social canker it seems to be at first glance. Indeed, *Eastward Ho* demonstrates self-interest as a force supportive of communal interests, a force that actually nourishes the economy. The play's characters act out the implications of that harmony, taking advantage of the commercial and social networks required by credit transactions to participate in the "economy of obligation."

To analyze this dynamic, we need to reexamine the means by which comic reconciliation is complicated in the play. The "selfless," virtuous character does not simply discipline the "self-interested" prodigal, for instance. The prodigal in fact serves a vital function as debtor: the debtor's bravado supplies a model of risk-taking economic practices helpful to more conservative characters like Golding. Thus, the positive role played by the prodigal in the credit economy reflects the more complex realities of market dynamics. An investigation into this effect entails a two-tier approach. In the first instance, it requires us to examine positive formulations of self-interest and profit in early seventeenth-century writings, charting the ways in which these concepts are harmonized in broader social notions of credit and charity. Latterly, we must explore how *Eastward Ho*'s characters act out the implications of that harmony, taking advantage of the commercial and social networks required by credit transactions to participate in the "economy of obligation."

I

Eastward Ho relies on conventional city comedy "types," usually meant to trigger specific and predictable responses, such as the admiration of thrift, and distaste at greed and opportunism. Indeed the "types" parade across the stage. Touchstone's honest, industrious apprentice, Golding, conflicts with the dissolute, idle one, Quicksilver. Touchstone's two daughters likewise represent opposite types: the humble Mildred marries Golding, while the vain, grasping Gertrude marries the ostentatious, but destitute, knight, Sir Petronel Flash. Quicksilver and Flash trick Gertrude out of her inheritance and set out on a voyage to make their fortunes in Virginia. The usurer Security joins Flash only to deceive him of his money, but is himself cuckolded and gulled. When the Virginia voyage founders in the Thames, the prodigals and Security are caught and thrown into the Counter. It is not until the play's very end, after Golding's machinations, that Touchstone drops his charges, Quicksilver is ordered to marry his mistress Sindefy, and Security must provide Sindefy's dower.

But the conflicts, ostensibly driven by the thrift/greed binary, are disturbed by the play's satire of the very conventions it employs: its prodigals are flashy, overblown spendthrifts and its prudent characters are sappy and ironic. At the conclusion, the burlesque is clear: the greedy villains' "reformation" is a parody, only to be equaled by the satire of the thrifty citizens themselves, whose wooden platitudes are echoed in grand style by the "disciplined" prodigals. The object of this satire is not so much acquisitiveness and court corruption (though clearly those representations provide much of the humor) but instead the formulaic citizen morality play. While the original London audience would have appreciated this parody, they would not have been free of the economic anxieties represented in the play.

Eastward Ho, like other city comedies in the first decade of the seventeenth century, played to packed private theatre audiences who delighted in the satirical comedy offered by the boy companies. The 1605 audience at the Blackfriars, watching the play performed by the Children of the Queen's Revels, was composed mainly of lawyers, members of the Commons, merchants, Inns of Court students, nobility and gentry.[5] The play's critique of gallants—the "railing mode"—was part of a fashion, "a mode of cynical and acerbic talking," familiar to the gallant and merchant audience to which it appealed.[6] But their enjoyment was not all the superior laughter of the complacent. Not all in the audience were "privileged," but all probably wanted to be: younger sons of gentry families apprenticed to a trade; tradesmen's wives imitating the behavior and dress of Court ladies; and artisans striving to succeed. Many in the playhouse were somewhere on the border between the smuggling tradesman and the wealthy merchant, and not all were moving upward. The desire to advance socially, in other words, was a legitimate concern for many in the Blackfriars audience.

The play itself is not a blazing satire of ambition. Admittedly it does satirize explicitly citizen values, mocking the simplicity of the claim that industrious thrift is morally superior. But it also implicitly celebrates Golding's own ambition, his scheme to broker an agreement between Touchstone and the prisoners. Likewise, it celebrates the ambitious performance of repentance the prodigals stage at the prison. Of course Golding's own formulaic platitudes parody his material ambition: "what increase in wealth and advancement the . . . industry and skill of our trade will afford in any . . . will be aspired by me" (2.1.86–89). But his underlying aspirations to join Touchstone and the prisoners—the litigant and the accused—in a common agreement to repent and forgive, reveal his larger social ambition. And his aspiration is apparent in his move up the social hierarchy from apprentice to alderman. Aspiration is the key concept here—ambition is the force which drove growth and entrepreneurship in early modern London

Before the seventeenth century, the majority of writing on the economic profit motive argued precisely the opposite. The medieval criticism of profit condemned the merchant for selling something he could not possess, for his "profit implied a mortgage on time, which was supposed to belong to God alone."[7] Man's labor was supposed to emulate God's work—creation. Thus the merchant, and especially the usurer, who created nothing but profit engaged in fraudulent work. Medievals condemned profit and social mobility by linking capital and "unnatural" sexuality in their common violation of natural teleology.[8] The official Aristotelian-Thomistic morality of precapitalist Europe condemned as aberrant the reproduction, or "breeding," of money. Money cannot breed because it is barren, the argument held; it only facilitated exchange.[9] Much of the early Renaissance humanist discourse referred to St. Augustine's denunciation of lust for money and possessions as one of the three principle sins of fallen man.

As the market economy developed in late sixteenth-century London, however, the degree to which money-making was seen as a moral peril waned. The new discourse offered an alternative way of thinking about profit, making entrepreneurship more marginal to the devil's domain.[10] The sin of avarice became less odious, with money-making viewed as an "interest" that could be used as motivation to preoccupy those who might otherwise be lured by more reprehensible "passions," such as lust or greed for power.[11]

Sir Nathaniel Bacon expressed this new attitude toward personal profit in his commentary on a usury bill in 1606. An attempt to reduce the legal rate of interest to 8 per cent from 10 per cent, the bill, entitled "An Act to Enlarge the Statute Now in Force Against Usury," was introduced by Sir Edward Grevill in the Commons on 26 March. Bacon, instead of relying on arguments from divine law, insisted that usury was "against Policy," meaning good economic policy. Bacon expressed concerns that the practice of usury would hinder more productive economic enterprise:

> The great Marchants will not venter at Sea, Winde, etc. neither will the Witt of man labor upon drayning of Marshes, or in any other good of ingenious devise, but imploy their Money to more certaine Profitt at use: And so this sluggish trade of usury taketh away all Invention, and Trade; Whereas other waies where money is, there would be devises to imploy it. Lastly it maketh Land cheape; for if money were not thus imployed to an Excessive gaine, Rich men would give good Prices for Lande, rather then Keepe Money.[12]

This is the first argument on record in the parliamentary history of usury legislation that relied on economics rather than church councils or English law.[13] Bacon was not alone in opposing the bill, and when it was put to question it was rejected.[14] The fact that Bacon objected to usury because money should be used instead for "invention and trade" differed markedly from the traditional moral argument that money should not beget money. He imagined an England full of swarming entrepreneurs, envisioning merchants venturing at sea, men draining marshes, individuals engaging in "invention" and "devises" to make money in all sorts of ways, and even generous "rich men" who, if usury did not exist to allow for excessive gain, offered land at "good prices."

Bacon, in other words, advocated the personal right to pursue profit and engage in business ventures. In his commentary, he did not suppress a moral judgment that it would be less likely for merchants to get to heaven than for a camel to pass through the eye of a needle. While the traditional scholastic arguments had not completely disappeared—they were still prevalent in many sermons, for instance—it was no longer wholly unquestionable that money was inherently a dangerous or polluting medium.

The prisoners Golding frees in *Eastward Ho* are prodigal-adventurers who, in a sense, embody the spirit of Bacon's "invention," risking money in ventures and "devises." Of course they are not his examples of rich generosity, but just the opposite: comic villains who represent dangerously unrestrained competition. Accordingly, the self-interest of their economic practices is necessarily exaggerated, and their actions are not those of the productive entrepreneur, but those of the social predator. Sir Petronel Flash, the "four-pound knight" representative of the wholesale distribution of honors by King James I, absconds with his new wife's dowry for an adventuring scheme in Virginia; the apprentice Quicksilver gulls men of their money in his master's name; and Security, the economic Vice character, exploits the others' greed to finance the plan. As "villains" of the market economy, they contrast with the responsible members of the community, Touchstone and Golding, the goldsmith and his industrious apprentice. The recognition of their villainy depends partly upon the convention that pits them against the more transparent economic agents, such as craftsmen or shopkeepers.

This seemingly clean distinction between wily market "villains" and upright, honest workers is complicated. In the theater, these stereotypes derive in part from the morality Vice tradition, rooted in a medieval worldview more conducive to such binaries. The difference between these two groups of economic agents—the rapacious schemers and the modest industrious types—relies on moral distinctions applied to economic behavior which divide risk-taking adventurism (pernicious) from conservative thrift (virtuous). In such a scheme, material ambition is tantamount to individualism, so that both are lumped into a moral junkheap of greed and social predation. What disturbs this conceptual scheme is the body of early modern literature accepting of the profit motive. The positive social model provided by the merchant-adventurer and the entrepreneur points beyond the play's stereotypes and binaries to a complex representation of ambition. Modes of action and attitudes that are satirized in the play—out-sized individualism, rapacious and greedy; wide-eyed materialism and class obsession; social grasping—survived in London streets in less dangerous forms. Pamphlets on the "art of thriving," for example, encouraged upward mobility, and traces of this acceptance of self-interest lie just beneath the veneer of the play's satire. Under the stark contrasts of the two conventional economic "types" are complicated similarities; beneath the harsh individualism lies a measure of productive economic energy.

Of course *Eastward Ho* itself is not designed, in the end, to draw all our sympathies away from the materialistic prodigals. A measure of attractiveness inheres in the adventurers' entertaining inventiveness. Their entrepreneurial skill—though obviously botched in their failed trip to Virginia—nonetheless energizes the play from the start. At the root their hijinks embody the capitalist spirit, what Werner Sombart called "Geist," a combination of a calculating faculty with the qualities of restlessness, persistence, and perseverance. Thrift and frugality, Sombart noted, were not enough to make an entrepreneur—drive and enterprise were the key attributes.[15] Among the salient qualities of the successful sixteenth-century entrepreneur, J.W. Gough identified "enterprise," the inventiveness of having an original plan, and the willingness to risk as the most important qualities.[16] Contemporary pamphleteers noted that success in business required the risk-taking spirit: Thomas Powell's *Tom of All Trades* (1631) contended that business "requireth . . . great hazard and adventure at the best" for the merchant.[17] Projectors of new processes, in the metallurgical and mining industries, for instance, had to be willing to risk losing a considerable investment.[18] Such projectors, often portrayed as villains in the drama, like Meercraft in *The Devil is an Ass* (1616), exploit participants' naivety and displace any risk onto investors. In reality, however, such projectors were not clearly demagogic, and many, in fact, assumed a considerable amount of risk which catalyzed the growth of valuable industries in early modern England. Of course not all entrepreneurs embraced risk, and many wanted to be protected by monopoly rights. But some projectors, often rich and powerful aristocrats who could afford such massive outlays, were in fact admired. Aristocrats were in the vanguard of most large-scale entrepreneurial projects.[19] Flash and Quicksilver's oceanic privateering expeditions in pursuit of Virginia's gold, then, resemble—if in ambition only—the adventuring schemes of the aristocrats George Earl of Shrewsbury and Robert Dudley Earl of Leicester in the 1570s and 1580s.

But we cannot label Quicksilver an exploitative aristocrat, because he most likely belonged to that segment of the poorer gentry who had no choice but to send children into the professions or to apprentice them.[20] His brazen plan to search for gold in Virginia is in part the bluster of the economically desperate. Since the completion of the apprenticeship, or "freedom," was not guaranteed, other means for advancement were tempting.[21] In that sense, then, the adventurers' brazen plan is not just a rapacious adventure but a plot for their own business success; it is, in a sense, a small-time entrepreneurial scheme.

In a market context, then, the adventurers model a type of positive economic energy. While Quicksilver, in his entrepreneurial economic appetite, threatens the urban world of the small artisan master like Touchstone, he nonetheless represents something substantially more. He stands for not only the insecure failing gentry, but also the vital market energy of those trying to make something from a position of disadvantage, even if those efforts are wasteful, predatory, and rash. When Quicksilver claims, "Merchants are dependent upon prodigals to thrive" (1.1.39), the statement's truth lies deeper than its surface meaning that merchants benefit from the money prodigals spend liberally. The notion that one type of economic agent depended on another recurred regularly in commercial pamphlets and often applied to the legitimate benefit shopkeepers and craftsmen enjoyed from merchants' activities. "[The shopkeeper's] welfare for the most part, depends upon the prosperity of the Merchant," argued Thomas Powell. "For if the merchant sit still, the most of them may shut up their Shop windows."[22] Literally, shopkeepers, stuck in their local shops, needed the capital and information the merchant supplied. The broader message, and a forcefully symbolic one, is that the stolid members of the market depended upon the risk-takers' example because even the most careful must sometimes take a risk. If unwilling or unable to do so, they are dependent upon others' economic activities to thrive in their own industry.

The force of this dependence pervades Golding's relationships with the play's prodigals. Their relationships turn not on Golding's need for money or goods, but the converse. Golding requires the reckless wastrels to receive his charity, and, in return, he receives a measure of social esteem. In other words, he is dependent upon their disadvantage in order to have the opportunity to supply that need. Golding's charity in this context is his good will tendered in arranging for Touchstone's empathetic response to the prisoners, resulting in their forgiveness. Their subsequent reincorporation into the community at the play's end is the fruition of his charity. This charity can be understood in terms of another moral concept occupying commercial and moral writing at the time—credit.

In his 1556 translation of Cicero's *De Officiis*, Nicholas Grimalde had translated *fides* (or "trust") as "credit." The popular tract, which reached seven editions in the next forty-five years and which saw over 9,000 copies printed for use in grammar schools, spread the notion of "credit" as the sum of trust in society. Grimalde translated Cicero's phrase *Iustis autem et fides hominibus, id est bonis viris, ita fides habetur* as "credit is given to just, and trusty men (that is) to good men."[23] Where he might have given "trust" or "confidence" for *fides*, Grimalde offered the word "credit," bringing into English the meaning of "confidence" and "trust" to the word "credit." In *Lex Mercatoria* (1622), his defense of free trade, Gerard de Malynes argued that commodities were bought and sold with "credit and reputation" and that a merchant must be "without deceit . . . and keep faith with all men."[24] During the late sixteenth and early seventeenth centuries, credit began to be seen as important in the sense that small debts aided more profitable production practices and business arrangements. Of course debt carried positive associations in medieval theology, inscribed as it was into the Christian idea of redemption. Protestant writers later developed aspects of traditional covenant theology in which man's relation with God was described with an emphasis on contract and trust. Increasingly the language used allowed for the positive valuation of credit and debt.

Having credit meant having power. To have credit in a community meant to be respected and trusted to pay back your debts. It was, after all, through face-to-face interpersonal actions of credit that agents interacted with the market. Borrowing and lending were aspects of the reciprocal obligations of neighborliness.[25] But because failed personal credit and excessive debt could be the Scylla and Charybdis of one's own fortunes, advice pamphlets stressed trust and cooperation. *The Art of Thriving* (1635) noted that lending was the "rock" and borrowing the "gulf" between which men must navigate.[26] Direct involvement with one's neighbors was necessary for individuals to succeed financially and to attain financial security.[27] And commerce itself began to be described in terms of sociability. "There is nothing in the world so ordinary and natural unto men, as to contract, truck, merchandise, and traffic one with another," wrote John Wheeler in his *Treatise of Commerce* (1601).[28] The contractual relationships of trade were often described in the pamphlet literature as mutually beneficial. In such writings, the word "interest" was not described as a harmful, predatory "self-interest," but rather indicated the mutual advantage, benefit, or profit of two or more parties, a commercial preoccupation that would come to change the very tone of the phrase "self-interest."

Richard Hooker's *Of the Laws of Ecclesiastical Polity* (1593) had, in fact, linked the development of society to economic motivations. Since men cannot furnish themselves with all their own needs and furthermore since men are "naturally induced to seek communion and fellowship," trade, and eventually credit and contractual agreements were inevitable. In Book I of *Laws*, Hooker admits the possibility of "injury" when men "seek their own commodity," thus necessitating laws to constrain conflict.[29] Hooker's notion of law, however, was "any kind of rule or canon, whereby actions are framed."[30] This did not necessarily require imposition by superior authority: vows and contracts between men, in Hooker's view, were equivalent to laws imposed on their actions. Much early modern writing on credit and contract likewise emphasized this notion of personal agreement and public reputation.

The actual dynamics of credit in the emerging market culture of early modern England, then, complicate the traditional conflation of capitalism with raw individualism.[31] Thrift and industry have often been labeled an aspect of the Protestant work ethic and understood as the foundation of individualism. In fact, much of the success of sixteenth-century commerce depended not upon individuals but on collective action in urban associations, such as local government, occupational guilds, clubs of journeymen in trades, the parish church and friendly societies.[32] Furthermore, a set of overtly collective virtues, such as sociability and fellowship, matched collective action. Urban associations were an important feature in the lives of the upper- and lower-middling sorts. The mercantile elite, such as lawyers, innkeepers, and booksellers, dominated the world of guilds, wards, and parish vestries; petty traders and artisans like Touchstone found association in ephemeral clubs based in taverns. The lesser middling orders clubbed together just to read a broadside or pamphlet, activities at a level at which the dependence upon others was the most intense. This is not to say that the profiteering motive of the individual entrepreneur did not exist; quite the contrary, the successful entrepreneur or merchant knew that in order to succeed he had to exploit the advantages of collectivism. Association provided a shared experience, and trained the middle sort in self-management, providing venues in which they could display the mastery of their art while strengthening social ties with those upon whom they relied.

The level of association, however, varied among different industries, and *Eastward Ho* exploits these differences. Guilds' communal interests are more intense than those of the entrepreneur, and indeed the associative Golding is contrasted with the more self-sufficient Quicksilver. While entrepreneurs and merchant-adventurers could flourish amidst some competition, artisans, in their constant need for credit, sought to limit competition and promote communal solidarity. The "credit" of the goldsmith Touchstone's world was generally that of the non-competitive artisan household, one appealing to traditional social ethics. In the turners' guild, for instance, masters could have only one apprentice at a time, and other ordinances were aimed at preserving the noncompetitive world of the small master. In the first act of *Eastward Ho*, Golding is the craftsman content with his meager means. In this sense he is like Nehemiah Wallington, a Puritan woodworker who kept a journal during the 1630s and 1640s that outlined the proper notion of a "calling." Wallington wrote that the purpose of one's calling was not to enrich oneself, but to be profitable and useful to oneself, one's family, church, and commonwealth. Wealth was an obligation: "We are stewards and have nothing but that we have received," Wallington believed.[33] Paul Seaver notes the economic distinction between these modest, communal practices and those of acquisitive merchants: Wallington's social ethics were, Seaver suggests, "the bourgeois values appropriate to the artisan households and small masters of [his] stripe, not to the enterprising merchant interlopers clamoring for free trade."[34] Such merchant interlopers would have identified with the Golding we see in the fourth and fifth acts. Golding's shift from one model of economic behavior to another, his motivations therein, and market behavior he represents in that shift, is the subject of the remainder of this chapter.

While at first glance, Golding seems a model of Wallington's type, of what historians call the Weberian "Protestant Work Ethic," his manipulations at the jailhouse deflate a purely moralistic reading of his character.[35] After all, it is his modeling of the adventurers' actions, not those of his church brethren, that enables his successful advancement. But his shift towards behaving like the adventurers, towards risk-taking, entrepreneurial behavior is not one which shatters social ties and alienates him from loved ones, either. The market's "depersonalizing mechanism" fails to explain adequately what occurs in *Eastward Ho*.[36] The characters never become mere cogs and do not experience alienation: their relative social mobility and independence in choosing their roles in the economy refutes a purely Marxist interpretation of market operations in the play.[37] Instead we see an economy based primarily on obligations, and where the trust that enforces those obligations breaks down, it is reinforced through social pressure.

Charity was one of the most effective and power-consolidating ways to apply social pressure. The drive to solidify one's power was not always commensurate with ruthless exploitation, of course, as the charity of London's aldermen illustrates. In London, the alderman had a long tradition of involvement in provisioning the City and controlling the markets. These traditions reflected the strength of the corporate ideal, the sense that the magistrate should rule for the benefit of all citizens, an idea voiced often in the sermons of the period. Aldermen in early seventeenth-century London also exercised immense discretionary jurisdiction as arbitrators. They administered poor relief; licensed alehouse keepers, hucksters, and fishwives; and chose suppliers. To be sure, they were sometimes guilty of coercion or corruption. Yet their formal coercive powers were weak because the alderman ultimately relied on an unpaid constabulary.[38] What the aldermen could not achieve through the formal machinery of government, they sought through what Ian Archer has called "the tyranny of vocabulary."[39] Archer finds that the London aldermen of the 1590s mobilized the support of the middling sort by generating institutional loyalties which ensured that the redress of grievances remained institutionally focused. Not only were they successful in the prosecution of offenders against market regulations, but they mobilized the benevolence of the wealthy.

The aldermen's consolidation of power highlights the social benefits of charity for both recipients and donors. For recipients it encouraged collectivism and communal association; for donors it strengthened their means and resources for assuring loyalty. The individual's power in the market culture depended, after all, on his ability to supply the needs of others. This capacity established one's place as an independent citizen. Even in the domestic realm, bourgeois men, in supporting their women and children, were exercising a charity that was both self-interested and yet altruistic. Charity increasingly became a civic duty, as evidenced by contemporary assumptions about the household's place as the foundation of civic order.[40]

Citizens often considered themselves charitable in a way that gave them moral authority. In the expanding market culture of early modern London, it proved worthwhile to include in that moral calculus an economic calculus as well. John Smyth of Nibley, an early seventeenth-century London lawyer and projector, had a number of "moral notes and sayings" written in a manuscript, intended for printing above the wainscot on the walls of his North Nibley home.[41] These sayings reflected Smyth's moral and religious attitudes towards business and society, consisting of fifteen "virtues" and seventeen "vices."[42] Under the heading "Liberality," Smyth wrote, "willingly to distribute to all men, wanting money counsel or neighborly duties: God is thy landlord and thy needy neighbor his rent-gatherer." Under "Alms," he wrote, "Whatsoever is given to the poor is lent to God: And what you lay out shall be paid you again."[43] To Smyth, God is a capitalist, with charity a type of investment. This linking of Christian and economic obligation provided a justification for liberality. But this is not necessarily commensurate with a pledge of self-sacrifice: God may judge in the end, but Smyth invokes Biblical injunctions for mostly pragmatic means. Self-interest and community-interest are Smyth's central concerns. Smyth wanted to confirm his social position through his liberality. "Liberality" is akin to "Hospitality," one of the methods that confirmed the social, and even the political, power of the mighty in medieval and early modern England.[44] Liberality assumed the laboring poor's dependency on the middling household, in fact, giving the middling sort more social power. By making the lower class dependent upon them, it also elevated the middling sort's own status. Through charity and liberality, the bourgeois domus took over or complemented the role once performed by noble, gentle, or ecclesiastical establishments. Smyth highlights the moral reward obtained from God, the great "landlord" of them all, for their charitable giving. In this sense, charity was a type of social credit. As an economic transaction, charity would have been understood by the recipients as an action stressing trust and personal bonds. Forgiveness is offered as a measure of social pressure urging conformity.

The precise nature of economic agents and attitudes in England's market culture illumines the play's social commerce. While Brian Gibbons is surely right to argue that city comedies do not necessarily reflect economic realities, we can nonetheless trace agreements in the plays which operate by the terms of negotiation familiar to the London marketplace. To some degree, the play's binaries still function in the early modern market economy: the prodigals offer a model of adventurous economic speculation, while the tradesmen more clearly represent bourgeois collectivism. But the terms of this binary are not always moral in the early modern economy, and the divide is not so absolute. Our analysis of the play is enriched when we recognize where these two models interact and depend upon one another for their mutual success. The play's economy of obligation is upheld both by Golding's emulation of the scheming adventurers and by the adventurers' agreement to reciprocate his charitable actions and measures of generosity. The role of self-interest in both sets of behaviors reinforces communal interests. In extending charity, Golding serves both the prisoners and himself by consolidating his power. The prisoners, through their agreements to repent and in their subsequent performances, establish the force of their inventive energy. Their songs function as yet another scheme that insures their survival.

II

The economic world represented in *Eastward Ho* does not draw our attention to these implicit agreements and moments of cooperation. But the play's literary texture calls for a closer reexamination of its conflicts and exaggerated binaries: its prodigals are satiric prodigals and its prudent characters are sappy and ironic. As a satire, *Eastward Ho* responded to Dekker and Webster's farcical cony-catching intrigue, *Westward Ho* (1604). The new play was designed to mock the old prodigal plays and public moralities such as Gascoigne's *Glass of Government* (1575) and the anonymously authored *The London Prodigal* (1603), which were used to demonstrate the rewards of economic prudence. In place of their didacticism, *Eastward Ho* offers a burlesque in which the virtuous mouth tired aphorisms and the repentant sing to the tune of well-known ballads such as Mannington's "Repentance." In part, the play critiques King James I: the Thames watermen's cry "Eastward Ho!" symbolized the gallants who flocked to court pursuing favor and cheap knighthoods. But it also parodied the form of Dekker and Webster's

Westward Ho, exaggerating successes and foibles to highlight their unreality. The fifth act of *Westward Ho* is a triumph for the virtuous citizen women, while *Eastward Ho* burlesques that virtue.[45]

Recent treatments of *Eastward Ho* have focused on the latent social content beneath the manifest satire, rescuing the play from timeworn moralist interpretations.[46] Theodore Leinwand, for instance, highlights market realities underlying the satire.[47] Although it is the work of the play to discipline the prodigal Quicksilver into marriage, Leinwand notes, Chapman, Marston, and Jonson equally target the dissolute apprentice and the smug, virtuous one. He finds that no one "class," no single market behavior, nor any particular social conflict is highlighted. Instead he sees the politic and calculated aggression of the "virtuous" goldsmith Touchstone. Golding exhibits a similar level of calculation and his own social trajectory is not devoid of strategy. His ability to "discipline" the prodigals at the play's conclusion arises from his own position of authority. For once he attains the office of alderman, he stretches that power by manipulating events at the prison, drawing on the risk-taking and theatrical mode exemplified in the prodigals' behavior.

Only when Golding emulates Quicksilver's double-dealing does he succeed. Though Golding trumpets the virtues of "honest industry," the "device" he ventures on is, in fact, somewhat deceitful and opportunistic. When he calls the failed voyagers to be arraigned before him, he asks the constable, "What are their names, say they?" (4.2.232), when he already knows the answer. His playacting includes the implicit threat of a harsh sentence. He reiterates this hard line with a defense of his actions: "magistrates, and men in place . . . must not wink at offenders" (4.2.290–1). And yet all this is a bluff because his subsequent actions are mild and forgiving.

Golding's hard line quickly devolves into a series of charitable actions. First, he convinces the Keeper of the Counter, Master Wolf, to pass on a sum of money to the prisoners, as a "token" of his love (5.2.89). Next, he lures Touchstone to the prison on the pretence that Golding himself has been arrested. The ruse is predicated on his friendship with Touchstone; ironically, its effectiveness in summoning Touchstone rests on the value of Golding's personal credit. He employs his symbolic capital in a trick that, if unsuccessful, would surely deplete that capital. But when Touchstone witnesses the prisoners' elaborate repentances, he is so impressed that he subsequently thanks, rather than resents, Golding for the lie: "the deceit is welcome," he gushes (5.5.112). Golding's successful scheming at the play's climax highlights his skill in policy in contrast to his former probity. To the delight of Touchstone, he appropriates the cheekiness of the prodigals. The audacity that makes Golding successful in reclaiming social ties also makes him attractive as a dramatic character. Golding is compelling only when he acts most self-interested.

Golding's scheming in the fifth act seemingly sits uneasily with his earlier career as the modest, unassuming apprentice. Many critics have noted that Golding's world had been circumscribed and dull in comparison with Quicksilver's exploits.[48] Joseph Sigalas, for instance, contrasts Golding with the adventurers: "Golding . . . possesses only the most tame sort of valor and adventurism. Knightly virtue has been supplanted by something akin to a 'work ethic,' centered on restrained ambition and accented with frugality and honesty."[49] But instead we might recognize Golding's resemblance to more daring and outlandish characters like Sir Petronel Flash. We could in fact interpret Golding's development by the words Security uses in the second act to describe Flash's behavior: "who would not sell away competent certainties, to purchase, with any danger, excellent uncertainties? Your true knight venturer ever does it" (2.2.186–88). As an audience we are meant to admire Golding not as the predictable apprentice, but upon his incarnation as the scheming and ambitious alderman, an effect recently highlighted by Helen Ostovich:

> [Golding's] puritan work ethic drops off and he bursts into imaginative flower with a scheme to rescue his brother apprentice Quicksilver from prison and redeem him in Touchstone's eyes . . . its mode of undertaking is exuberantly theatrical . . . Golding's scheme is entirely successful, only because he abandons his puritan philosophy of hard work, and leaps into enthusiastic pretence.[50]

By combining the work ethic with pretence, Golding is the model of success in London's early seventeenth-century market culture. The shrewd social climber—whose ambition is valorized, not excoriated, in the play—knows to position himself socially, which may itself have required keen levels of "enthusiastic pretense."

Golding's capacity as a type of disguised magistrate deploys the traditional adjudicating role: the masked authority figure casts off his disguise to judge and to arbitrate a conflict, as is the case with Vincentio's unmasking in *Measure for Measure*. And just as Vincentio manipulated a balance between mercy and justice, lechery and asceticism, Golding arbitrates a compromise between the adventurers and the citizens' behaviors. His is a sort of economic alchemy, mixing the characters successfully into a transformation that associates them all. Their alchemical tags suggest the characters' roles throughout, roles that are nonetheless thwarted. Touchstone attempts to change the mercurial Quicksilver into a fixed and stable element, like the virtuous Golding. With his skill at real transformation, Golding seems to be the only one in possession of the metamorphic Stone.

Golding's efforts to urge the adventurers back into an economy of obligation exemplifies "public dispute resolution." This type of resolution, which operated at both an informal and a legal level, expressed its participants' desire to live in a state of communal relations with their neighbors to the degree that reciprocal trust and mutual hospitality and civic duty could be maintained.[51] Why does Golding wait until the adventurers are imprisoned, and why does Touchstone accept their feigned performance of repentance? Part of the answer lies in the communal nature of such dispute resolution. It was centered on the concept and process of reconciliation and, as such, involved the attempted resolution of disputes *after* they had occurred, first by informal, then by legal means.

How should we then analyze the other side of the economic equation, the recipients of Golding's charity, the prodigals? In what ways do they take advantage of the growing social pressure toward communal concerns in market transactions? Before they find themselves in a position to rejoin the "community of obligation," they employ its language to their own advantage. Sir Petronel Flash, in particular, seems to pick up on the nature of "obligation" and use it to convince Security to join in his scheme. His employment of it betrays the nature of his deepest loyalties, which lie with his own profit. When he asks Security to be his confidant, for instance, he confides,

> I must now impart
> to you . . . a loving secret,
> As one on whom my life doth more rely
> In friendly trust than any man alive.
> Nor shall you be the chosen secretary
> of my affections for affection only;
> For I protest . . .
> To make you partner in my action's gain
> As deeply as if you had ventured with me
> Half my expenses . . .
>
> (3.2.232–41)

Flash here contorts the language of friendship into that of commerce, engaging Security in a sort of emotional joint-stock company that would ensure his support. But here the bond of money serves as the standard up to which the bond of friendship is held: the faith and trust between friends, Flash is saying, is as deep as if they had risked money together.

The prodigals also appropriate the language of communalism through the argot of "credit." They employ the term to apply social pressure at sensitive moments, most often as reminders of the social networks that depend upon reputation. In the world of complex webs of creditors and debtors, one could play the trump card of "credit" to impugn or threaten someone else's sense of his own social capital. It is not just the prodigals who take advantage of this jibe. When Winifred wants to shame her husband Security over his exploits from the night before, she reminds him that his money is tied up with his public reputation: "All night abroad at taverns? Rob me of my garments, and fare as one run away from me? Alas! Is this seemly for a man of your credit, of your age, and affection to your wife?" (4.1.291–294). But the prodigals use the term liberally in defense of their own dissolute behavior. When Golding chides Quicksilver for his wastefulness and drunkenness, Quicksilver replies, "Lend me some money; save my credit" (2.1.116). When his master Touchstone challenges his drunkenness and whoring, Quicksilver simply retorts, "'Tis for your credit, master" (2.1.129). On the one hand, Quicksilver parodies the equation of trust with contractual obligation newly current in the word "credit," by implying that even his whoring is in the name of his master's "credit." But he also reinforces the older, traditional usage of "credit" which associates virtue with gentle blood when he finally defends himself, in a last-ditch parry, by blurting out "My father's a gentleman" (2.1.131). Quicksilver tries to trump the newer usage with the older one, which associated the chivalric "credit" and "honor" with the aristocratic blood of gentlemen. In the new economy achieving wealth is seen as a means to a type of social, material gentility but Quicksilver wants his gentility to stand in for the virtue of creating wealth.

When questioned about his audacious behavior despite his indenture to Touchstone, Quicksilver refers to his own "gentle" blood. He defends himself by saying "my mother's a gentlewoman, and my father a justice of the peace and of quorom; and though I am a younger brother and a prentice yet I hope I am my father's son" (1.1.26–29). Refusing to accept the sting of primogeniture, Quicksilver pits swagger against birth order, and he repeats his claim of gentility to Golding: "though I am a prentice I can give arms, and my father's a justice o'peace by descent" (1.1.119–120). He even tries to lure Golding into the game of social one-upsmanship with regard to their master: "We are both gentlemen, and therefore should be no coxcombs; let's be no longer fools to this flat-cap Touchstone . . . his father was a maltman, and his mother sold gingerbread in Christ Church" (1.1.131–36). Insulting

Touchstone's "flat-cap" tradesmen's hat, Quicksilver reveals his anxiety that he not be so attired. Indeed in the second act when he doffs his apprentice's clothes after leaving Touchstone's service, he says "There lie, thou husk of my envassalled state" (2.2.39).

Quicksilver's claims to gentility are paralleled in the character of Sir Petronel Flash, a parody like Middleton's Quomodo. Flash's comic abuses begin and end with his put-on appearance—his clothes are so overblown he looks like an "elephant" (1.2.161)—which fittingly impressing the gullible Gertrude. Flash is such a prototype for pretense that Robert Burton uses him as an example in *The Anatomy of Melancholy*:

> In our gullish times, him whom you peradventure in modesty would give place to, as being deceived by his habit, and presuming him some great worshipful man, believe it, if you should examine his estate, he will likely be proved a serving man of no great note, my ladies Taylor, his Lordship's barber, or some such gull, a Fastidious Brisk, Sir Petronell Flashe, a mere outside.[52]

Burton speaks directly to the gentry's greatest fear that they will fall from their social position to become a "serving man of no great note," or worse, a masterless man. Someone such as Flash without the skills of even a "tailor" or a "barber" is left with nothing but his pretentious clothing, his "outside." Even that is stripped from him as indeed the adventurers "come dropping to town like so many masterless men, in their doublets and hose, without hat, or cloak" after the shipwreck (4.2.101–3).

Faced with situations in which they cannot rely solely on the pretence of their "outside," the prodigals fall back upon the resources of association. Quicksilver is relegated to such a turn when Master Touchstone refuses to lend him money. His retort at his exit signals that he knows the communal association integral to bourgeois success. When told that Touchstone will give him "not a penny," Quicksilver retorts, "I have friends, and I have acquaintance" (2.1.155–56). Quicksilver gestures to the collective virtues of sociability and good fellowship in this crucial moment. He is "freed" from his apprenticeship by Touchstone, and in that uncomfortable freedom from association he asserts the loyalty and unity of friendship. He embodies the tension at the heart of the experience of the middling sort between independence and dependence. Unlike the poor, the middling orders saw themselves as fundamentally free and able to act voluntarily. But they assumed that this freedom arose out of a set of legal rights and responsibilities, such as those of the freemen of incorporated towns.[53] What Quicksilver faces, and one of the factors that sends him adventuring with Security and Petronel Flash, is the need for a social network.

It is this same desire for the potential advantages of membership in a social and economic network that Gertrude expresses when she faces penury. But her expression is an about-face of her more typical rejection of social and familial networks. Gertrude has, up until this point in the play, rejected family ties, detaching herself from family association at every turn. She has anticipated their need for financial aid once she and Flash set up their aristocratic country house, and has found that need utterly distasteful. The scene—the opening scene of the fifth act—emphasizes the social fact that even the most recalcitrant can not refuse charity. Often in city comedy, charity is a shaming ritual because the beneficiaries are the most blatantly selfish characters notable for their aversion to offering charity themselves. In *Eastward Ho*, Gertrude laughs at the thought of charitable actions before realizing she herself needs charity. When she thinks she's securely wealthy, attaining the status "lady" with her husband Sir Petronel Flash, she says to him, "When [my father, mother, and sister] come a-begging to us, for God's sake, let's laugh at their good husbandry. . . ." (3.2.157–59). She refuses to recognize any obligations, telling her sister Mildred, "call me sister no more" (3.2.101).

Gertrude follows the force of this rejection to its logical conclusion when she herself falls on hard times. Forgetting family ties, when left by her false knight and destitute at the play's end, she imagines a resourceful ploy of her own. She plans to hock her worthless title, her ladyship, as if she herself could profit by selling it. Realizing near the play's end that she desperately needs the communal ties she's severed, she urges these ties upon her "lady-in-waiting," a prostitute named Sindefy. "Do I offer to mortgage my ladyship for you and for your avail, and do you turn the lip and the alas to my ladyship?" Gertrude asks her (5.1.67–69). Her appeals to "Sin" provide an apt punning commentary on the wages of sin, while devolving into a calculation of the minimum domestic needs of these two, their "needles": "I would lend it—let me see—for forty pound in hand, Sin; that would apparel us; and ten pound a year; that would keep me and you, Sin, with our needles" (5.1.80–84). They are left with little but their domestic identities.

Gertrude soon accepts the folly of her plans to sell her worthless title and, instead, imagines a mysterious charity that will rain money their way. Her musings begin with a whimsical fantasy: "A fairy may come, and bring a pearl or a diamond" (5.1.91–92). But the fantasy slowly enters the realm of the possible: "may not we rise . . . and find a jewel in the streets?" (5.1.95–96). Her dream sounds more like a plan that could live viably in the minds of many on cold London nights: "Or may not some old usurer be drunk overnight, with a bag of money, and leave it behind him on a stall?" (5.1.102–4). This fantasizing ironically brings Gertrude solidly into the world of real economics, taking the mythical and translating it into actual market realities—here the economy of obligation presided over by the alderman—to imagine herself being out of debt. "If I had as much money as an alderman, I would scatter some on't i'the streets for poor ladies to find, when their knights were laid up," she laments. "And now I remember my song o' the 'Golden Shower,' why may not I have such fortune?" (5.1.105–110). While Gertrude is no Danae—she will not be seduced by Zeus appearing as a shower of gold—she yearns for charity from the alderman, charity that she will receive before the play's end.

Gertrude's foolish idealism impulsively seeks jewels in the streets. When this fantastic vision meets with the real fact of her dependence on others, it devolves into an acceptance of charity from the alderman. But in the end charity comes from her own family, the very people she had relished scorning in their own time of need. When her mother, Mistress Touchstone, finds Gertrude bereft, she tells her "Go to thy sister's, child; she'll be proud thy ladyship will come under her roof" (5.2.177–8). Her mother takes the word "pride," a character trait Gertrude uses to disparage others, and reverses its meaning for Gertrude. She turns Gertrude's proud and haughty disdain for her sibling into the pride of grace her sister will exhibit towards Gertrude. Mistress Touchstone goes so far as to claim Gertrude's debts: "I'll take order for your debts i'the ale-house" (5.2.191–2). And even Sin the prostitute receives communal charity (by order of the alderman) in the end. Golding orders that Francis Quicksilver "make amends to Mistress Sindefy with marriage" (5.5.186–7). Golding's last words in fact make his alderman's order ring through the play's conclusion, ordering Security's charity—like Zeus's shower of gold—to overcome the selfish and cheating adventuring driving the play's central action. He says "Security give [Sindefy] a dower, which shall be all the restitution he shall make of that huge mass he hath so unlawfully gotten" (5.5.189–91).

Gertrude's object lesson compelling her to accept the charity echoes loudly throughout the fifth act. Charity resolves the plot not just in the form of money, but also through grace of action. It not only provides the single poor women with marriage matches and dowries, it frees the adventurers from prison. As the fifth act gains momentum in its progression towards the unlikely scene of repentance and forgiveness, moments of association spur that momentum. That is, the social value of associative action begins to emerge for the prisoners as their only apparent solution.

The point at which the prisoners are most compelled to accept the terms of associative action is when they find themselves at the Counter. The condition of their imprisonment which forces them to seek legal redress also forces them to admit, as Quicksilver admitted when cast out by Touchstone, that they must rely on "friends." Master Bramble speaks to the communal force of friendship when he tries to reassure Sir Petronel Flash and Quicksilver that they indeed might be freed from jail. "[T]here are none of the judges in town, else you should remove yourself, in spite of [the judge], with a *habeas corpus*," Bramble explains to them. "But if you have a friend to deliver your tale sensibly to some justice o'the town . . . you may be bailed" (5.3.77–82). Here Bramble suggests bail from a friend as an alternative to the legal method of pursuing a writ of habeas corpus. Interestingly the two methods are not that dissimilar in terms of the community involvement actually needed in either case. To use the writ, after all, a prisoner would rely on friends, family, neighbors, and professional help to file the writ—communal participation and aid was needed much as it would be needed to procure bail.[54] But habeas corpus was a prerogative writ, meaning it traditionally concerned the exercise of discretion by judicial and administrative officers and agencies; with it, subjects could assert the king's prerogative against those whose authority threatened them.[55] King's Bench had the power of superintending matters over prerogative writs. For an individual to pursue a writ of habeas corpus, was, then, symbolically, to appropriate royal power. Significantly, Bramble mentions these alternatives—either the writ or a friend delivering their tale to a judge—to the imprisoned adventurers, because it offers an example of individuals appealing to the law not out of some great respect for rule of law (clearly they didn't care about that) but out of a sense that they could appropriate power with this particular writ. Their participation in the legal system and their pursuit of communal aid both arise from self-interest, and not any altruistic communal spirit. In the end, the community that comes to their aid is Golding, the "friend" urged by Bramble, who can use his influence as an alderman to free them from jail. In order to receive this charity, however, they have to do their part in mouthing the necessary repentance. To redeem their place in the communal market culture, they must perform repentance.

Quicksilver sings his repentance to convince Touchstone to forgive him:

> I scorned my master, being drunk;
> I kept my gelding and my punk
> . . . .
> Still 'Eastward Ho!' was all my word;

> But westward I had no regard,
> Nor never thought what would come after
>
> (5.5.69–83)

Quicksilver does not explicitly ask for any reformation of his inward condition, but for a change at the hands of Touchstone. When he sings "make me current by thy skill" (5.5.88), his alchemical reference asks Touchstone to convert him from his false metal state to a true metal form, silver or gold. Doggerel repentances were popular in Jacobean drama, but Quicksilver's song is a parody of "neck verses" recited as a test by those hoping to receive benefit of clergy. In his plea to Touchstone, Quicksilver acts as if he is confident of forgiveness, not as a prisoner on the way to his death. In gesturing to imminent death, Quicksilver implies that Touchstone would be giving him the gift of life. For his part, Touchstone accepts the performance, and agrees to forgive and free the adventurers.

But Touchstone's acknowledgement of Golding's role in the scheme draws attention to a crucial dynamic. Touchstone thanks Golding and Wolf for drawing him to see the spectacle:

> [. . .] I thank you: the deceit is welcome,
> [*to Golding*] especially from thee, whose charitable
> soul in this hath shown a high point of wisdom
> and honesty. Listen. I am ravished with his
> 'Repentance,' and could stand here a whole pren-
> ticeship to hear him.
>
> 5.5.112–17

Touchstone's gratitude articulates an appreciation for "deceit" that is concomitantly a "high point of . . . honesty," pointing to Golding's shrewdness in getting Touchstone to forgive the prisoners. Touchstone's comment that he could stand and listen for "a whole prenticeship" to Quicksilver's "Repentance" might be understood as his acknowledgement that it is a feigned performance, as an apprentice learns from a master how to feign. At the very least, Touchstone appreciates the performances on both counts. He approves of the performances by virtue of the fact that he participates in them; likewise, he fulfills his obligation to respond as expected, or to "repay" the performances, by saying he is ravished by them. The deceit (by Golding) and the performance (by Quicksilver) both depend upon reciprocation for their efficacy. Touchstone responds to Golding's deceit by rushing to the Counter, and to Quicksilver's performance by forgiving his trespasses. Touchstone's speech acknowledges the crucial equation that binds this economy of obligation together. In an economy where reciprocal obligations remain intact, deceit and performance are permissible options so long as they reinforce the spirit of negotiation.

In the theater, entertainment value is part of this negotiation. Quicksilver's last song, "Farewell," only increases the satire in the conclusion's tone. He mouths Golding's earlier adages to potential prodigals, advising them instead to be conservative and thrifty, to "thrive little and little,/Scape Tyburn, Counters, and the Spital" (5.5.128–9). The songs get more ridiculous and hypocritical, with the prisoners spouting more Puritan jargon, until we get to Security's song, a crude cuckold song repeating the laughably flat phrase "My heart is full of woe" (5.5.154, 160). The songs are pure burlesque; yet in terms of the negotiation, they signal complete participation and association. As the ultimate requital of Golding's charity, the performances give Golding everything he feels he needs in order to restore the prodigals' credit.

The prodigals' reliance upon a social network does not, of course, lessen the energy with which they declare their scams and trickery. In fact, their dramatic value depends upon the naked boldness of their deceits. Flash the penniless knight admits to Quicksilver that "all the castles I have are built with air" (2.2.246–47). In most city comedies, the folly of the scheming social climber is exposed as misguided pretension. In *Eastward Ho*, however, the resourcefulness required to ascend the social ladder serves as a model. The playacting of Flash and Quicksilver is a formula for the playacting profitable in a commercial world. Of course theatrical standards persist: Flash and Quicksilver are attractive to the audience because they represent the vital energies, however outlandish, around which the other characters orbit. The adventurers' performances serve also as a kind of ritualistic or festive force. Quicksilver's cozenings, like those of Subtle in *The Alchemist*, are presented in a festive spirit. They are used, as Susan Wells writes, to "subdue the motions of trade to the misrule of the feast."[56] Sir Petronel Flash, especially, represents the rousing Lord of Misrule against which Golding's staid conservatism is measured. We are meant to cheer Flash's bluster, recognizing the Falstaffian bravado while expecting it to be punctured in the play's comic resolution. What we might not expect is Golding to model his own social rise on the scheming and outlandish spirit he will work to restrain in the resolution. To adjust Wells's observation, we might say that the motions of trade are actually energized here by the misrule of the feast.

One way in which Golding models his behavior on the prodigals is the manner in which he employs the catchword "credit." When Golding wants Master Wolf to treat the prisoners well and "let 'em want nothing" (5.2.94), he pads his cash bribe with the phrase, "as far as I have any credit with you" (5.2.93). The word "credit" bears the dual freight of its meanings as both trustworthiness and the symbolic power of capital in a community increasingly dependent upon credit. The word may be understood as: a) the promise of future specie; or, b) the fulfillment of a verbal promise. While it may signal trust, it also signals the need for cooperation in a stressful situation: marketplace competition drives this plea for cooperation, which is predicated upon the agreement to accept individual credit.

But the type of credit that both Golding and the adventurers utilize is not always, and not simply, the credit of open cooperation. Instead it is the credit of what Craig Muldrew calls a "negotiated community."[57] This is one of the central aspects of the economy of obligation which accounts for self-interest. Its social process is bargaining, in which the outcome is agreed upon by all the parties concerned. The process of bargaining necessarily entails some conflict: as Muldrew argues, "conflict exists where cooperative bonds are the most interpersonal."[58] The economic alchemy of the play's conclusion is one expression of this process of bargaining. While the characters' alchemical tags suggest their various roles, these distinct roles are thwarted. Touchstone attempts to be the Philosopher's Stone that makes a golden temper of Quicksilver—that is, to change the mercurial Quicksilver into a fixed and stable element, like the virtuous Golding. But it is Golding, with his skill at transformation, who seems to be the only one in possession of the metamorphosing Stone. In signaling that he too is somewhat mercurial, Golding urges the others to transform as well. The sincerity of the transformations is not at issue here. The disciplining of the prodigals is resolved in their staged repentance and forgiveness. The resolution obtains as much from their decision to perform their repentances as from Golding's plan and Touchstone's forgiveness.

This "negotiation" complicates our interpretation of the typical generic "reconciliation" city comedy provides. Here the formal disciplinary structure of dramatic comic resolution dovetails with the informal social pressures working in a market economy. The satire portrays the "reformation" of character as sheer performance, and it is satisfying because it is so theatrical. Since the witnesses of the prisoners' repentances believe the spectacle without any hesitation, the community that is affirmed at the conclusion is a community of performance. Both sides participate by mutually extending the credit of belief, thereby making each other credible. The "economy of obligation" is predicated upon a culture of credit that prefers cooperation and reciprocity—usually a product of conflict—to punishment. Distinct from the resolution of most city comedies, the prodigals here willingly reenter the economy of obligation; they perform their way back in as a sign that they will rejoin the community. Golding's last words fulfill their desire to do just that. He says "Security give [Sindefy] a dower, which shall be all/the restitution he shall make of that huge mass he/hath so unlawfully gotten" (5.5.189–91). His alderman's decree rings through the play's conclusion, ordering Security's charity to overcome the selfish and cheating adventurers driving the central action.

What the play offers is a model of economic negotiation that invites spectators to witness the action of negotiation. In place of a scenario in which Golding depletes the prodigals' credit with the shaming ritual of spectacle, the prodigals redeem their own credit with a performative spectacle. They are empowered to participate in this negotiation because Golding has signaled his cooperation with them by tricking Touchstone and by sending them a "token" of money at the prison. But what we observe is that Golding is not just the lender in this transaction. He has also borrowed behaviors from the adventurers. He has had to become something of a risk-taker to manipulate reconciliations and to consolidate his power. His behavior confirms both the social position that he has all along denied pursuing and his ambition. By performing their own repentance, the adventurers solidify the associative market community that such characters are usually suspected of destroying. The capital they retain that keeps them afloat keeps the drama afloat as well. The social capital of their popularity is staged in the final scene as equivalent to the social (and literal) capital bestowed upon the theater with a full house. Quicksilver, who addresses the audience in the play's last word, figuratively looks beyond the stage to peer out into the streets of London: he proclaims that the "streets and the fronts of houses" are "stuck with people" (Epil.3–4), heralding the prisoners' release from the Counter. The adventurers' contract to perform willingly their part of the "economy of obligation" is here offered as the same promise of entertainment that makes the London theater thrive.

Chapter Three

Utopias of Paternalism: *Timon of Athens* and the *New Atlantis*

To study the expression of self-interest in early modern English literature is more than simply to interrogate the justifications of individual fictional characters struggling for economic identity and position. Thus far, we have examined individual subjectivity and its expression in the turbulent market economy; we need now to pan back to survey broader formulations of economic relationships and pay particular attention to the ways in which self-interest disrupted systems of economic reciprocity between unequal members. Among shopkeepers, artisans, landlords, courtiers, and the king himself in early seventeenth-century England there existed a sense that the self-interest of their subordinates had to be addressed. But the way in which this concern was addressed depended upon an ideal of social harmony. The Lancashire landlord James Bankes of Winstanley, for instance, advised his children, "Be vere kynd and loving unto youre tenantes and so they wyll love you in good and godly sort."[1] Bankes expressed the paternalistic conception of a landlord's duty in its central formulation: care and generosity were extended with the aim of producing deference and obedience in return.[2] Paternalism was a system of governing relations by which a social superior would protect a subordinate. It developed primarily as a strategy of estate management for farmers who, as a form of social control, nurtured relations with their tenants. A reciprocity in *unequal* obligations, paternalism was based upon the ossified stability of each party's power. But the growing force of economic self-interest and the increasing number of credit transactions among tradesmen, farmers, and gentlemen alike meant an increasing awareness of the conflict and dissatisfaction such unequal obligations might produce. The social and psychological force of this awareness emerges clearly when we examine the points of strain between traditional concepts of paternalism and newer relationships of contract (and other arrangements involving equal obligations on both sides). A paternalistic system in the emergent market economy recognized the conflict and insubordination self-interest sometimes produces.

Shakespeare's *Timon of Athens* (1608) and Francis Bacon's *New Atlantis* (1627) emblematize those works of literature which registered the inadequacy of an outmoded ideological paternalism to meet this challenge. The utopian systems of paternalism represented in those texts may also be seen to have been the misguided ideologies of aristocrats like the Earl of Essex and James I himself. That these texts stage different, but equally rigid, responses to insubordination and self-interest suggests that the early modern English experience of self-interest was undergoing turmoil and adjustment. Paternalism reveals itself, in both *Timon* and *New Atlantis*, as a means to control the self-interest of subordinates, a means that is sometimes inadequate. But just as paternity can be a point of uncertainty for an anxious father, the certainty of subordination in a paternalistic system is unsure too. The control and the surveillance necessary to keep these paternalistic utopias in control of the not-so-controllable eroticism of human desires and passions underlies the anxiety driving both these literary works. Ultimately, as Shakespeare and Bacon suggest, that denial causes the eruption of the central drive in ways harmful to the society.

I

The *New Atlantis* treats an ideal of social control, meeting private desires with an overarching paternalistic program. Sir Francis Bacon advances, in his utopian society, a perfect community of scientists and discoverers who work for the glory of the state. The role of self-interest in this particular model and Bacon's theories of natural science more generally continues to be fodder for scholarly debate.[3] The central question is whether Bacon identifies an ideal political system that incorporates self-interest while being most conducive to scientific discovery and the advancement of learning.[4] One line of argument locates contradictions between Bacon's political and scientific programs: these are seen as commensurate with Bacon's own conflicting identities as a state servant and a scientist.[5] The *New Atlantis* joins those identities, however, in the figures of scientists who provide service to a state whose focus is to advance scientific understanding. In this work, individual self-interest, in terms of the pleasures of independent discovery and learning, is ostensibly joined with the general interest of the state. Apparently there is no contradiction between serving one's own interest in learning and service to the state.

When we examine the ways in which individual interests are channeled and disciplined in Bensalem, the island described in the *New Atlantis*, slight contradictions arise. Government is designed less to foster the pleasures and inducements of individual learning and scientific discovery than to curb and control self-interest. We can find justifications for Bensalem's controls if we compare its organization and modes of discipline to Bacon's other scientific writings, his letters to James I and to court advisors, and his legal arguments. Such a process runs the risk of what Markku Peltonen calls the folly of relying upon a "rhetorical similarity" between Bacon's philosophical and political thought, an approach which obscures the distinction Bacon makes between the values required for the advancement of sciences and those needed for political success.[6] But it is the very separation of these values that the structure of society in the *New Atlantis* highlights. That societal structure elucidates clearly these very distinctions which are so important to understanding Bacon's political theory. It is the work of the social order in the *New Atlantis* to maintain the distinctions between personal will and ambition, on the one hand, and the overarching structures which administer and control that self-interest, on the other.

New Atlantis's title suggests a philosophic and political program similar to Plato's Atlantis.[7] The allusion to Plato's *Critias* and *Timaeus* in the title signals an engagement with that philosopher's description of the ideal state.[8] A further reference to Sir Thomas More's *Utopia*, along with the utopian framework of the narrative likewise puts *New Atlantis* in conversation with other "ideal commonwealth" exercises, such as Andraea's *Christianopolis* (1619) and Campanella's *Civitas Solis* (1623).[9] But there is no explicit ethical or political program offered in *New Atlantis*, for natural history seems to trump political theory. Self-described on its title page as "A Worke unfinished," the *New Atlantis* was first published at the end of a volume containing the *Sylva Sylvarum*, a natural history. While More's *Utopia* offers a detailed description of Utopia's government and laws and proposes the abolition of private property, *New Atlantis* touches on neither of these subjects in its treatment of Bensalem.

The *New Atlantis* is described in the preface by Bacon's secretary and early biographer, William Rawley, as a "fable" that contains a "model." "This fable my Lord devised, to the end that he might exhibit therein a model or description of a college instituted for the interpreting of nature and the producing of great and marvellous works for the benefit of men, under the name of Salomon's House, or the College of Six Days' Works," Rawley noted.

> And even so far his Lordship hath proceeded, as to finish that part. Certainly the model is more vast and high than can possibly be imitated in all things; notwithstanding most things therein are within men's power

> to effect. His Lordship thought also in this present fable to have composed a frame of Laws, or of the best state or mould of a commonwealth; but foreseeing that it would be a long work, his desire of collecting the Natural History diverted him."[10]

This raises immediate interpretative problems. Is Bacon offering a fable that, like an allegory, requires interpretation? Or is he offering a model that is impossible in this case to imitate? Is the notion that Bacon never completed the "model," meant to include the missing "frame of Laws," significant in that it emphasizes the work's incompleteness? One line of thought highlights the text's "unfinishedness" as indicating that there is always more to know.[11] At the very least, the tension between the ideal and the possible is evident in the contradiction that the model cannot be imitated in all things, but that "most things therein are within men's power to effect."[12] In the text of *New Atlantis*, Bacon deems the collection of knowledge as the most vital pursuit within "men's power." And Rawley emphasizes Bacon's own "desire of collecting the Natural History"—his larger project—as that which supposedly "diverts" him from completing the *New Atlantis*. This meta-narrative links individual desire with collecting knowledge: that is, the text's incompleteness speaks to Bacon's pursuit of his own "desire." In this sense the text, as Rawley prefaces it, foregrounds the very notion of Bacon's own self-interest in scientific discovery. In the narrative of the *New Atlantis*, however, individual self-interest is not emphasized but instead is subsumed into the work of society's communal interests.

Scientific discovery, nonetheless, provides the *raison d'être* of society in the *New Atlantis*. We are introduced to the island of Bensalem by a Spanish sailor who, with his fellow sailors, is thrown off course and lands at the strange port. Initially forbidden to land, the sailors meet with the leaders of the island on the water and are eventually brought on land to stay at the "Strangers' House," from which they are not permitted to leave for three days. On the fourth day the sailors are visited by the Governor of the House of Strangers, a Christian priest by "vocation" (44), who informs them that the state has given them "licence to stay on land for the space of six weeks" (45). Told that they can ask any questions they like about the island, they are given a detailed account of the history and structure of society on Bensalem. The most recognizable utopian element is the description of the college called "Salomon's House," a group of learned men working together for the common end of being "the noblest foundation that ever was upon the earth; and the lanthorn of this kingdom" (58). The college exists for the sole purpose of interpreting nature and of producing great works for the benefit of man: for the "enlarging of the bounds of Human Empire, to the effecting of all things possible" (71). The systematic use of knowledge and the control of nature through science, Bacon argues, make this ideal attainable. The endowed fellows of the House experiment, devise philosophic inventions, and conduct research; some are sent abroad every twelve years to study the affairs and sciences of other countries, after which they return home with the information they have collected. On the one hand, Salomon's House seems based on institutions from contemporary London and Cambridge: the mercantilist Chancery, guilds based on an apprenticeship system, the Bar, the Inns of Court, and the society of fellows at Cambridge. But on the other, Bensalem is an idealized, fictional place, intensely focused on one goal: the perfect ordering of society to discover and interpret nature. The twelve "Merchants of Light" travel abroad to collect "books," "abstracts" and "patterns of experiments" (81); "Depredators" collect the experiments from books (81); "Mystery-men" collect the experiments of mechanical arts and liberal sciences (81); "Compilers" draw up reports of the various experiments (81); "Dowry-men or Benefactors" analyze the various findings for practical uses and applications (81); "Lamps" or consultants advise Bensalem on future experiments (82); "Inoculators" carrying out those advised experiments (82); and "Interpreters of Nature" write up the discoveries as axioms or aphorisms (82). There is a clear division of all scientific labor.

We might question the ends that are served by the collection of facts and the pursuit of knowledge in Bensalem, however. The Merchants of Light "maintain a trade, not for gold, silver or jewels, nor for silks, nor for spices, nor any other commodity of matter; but only for God's first creature, which was Light" (59). The means to a better knowledge of God's creation is, in principle, through scientific investigation of "light . . . of the growth of all parts of the world" (59). The "light" that the fellows pursue is one in the same, it seems, with "the knowledge of Causes, and secret motions of things" (71) which is the "end" or purpose of the House of Salomon. Since part of this "end" is the "enlarging of the bounds of Human Empire," it seems that the purpose of mental cultivation is also to serve human ambition to enlarge human empire.

This goal of empire places *New Atlantis* in a peculiar place among Renaissance utopias, most of which primarily emphasize the ethical and moral nature of their programs. The end of intellectual discovery, in utopias from Plato through Thomas More, is to serve God.[13] Not surprisingly, then, many of the famous utopias had been written by priests and monks. The goal of the ideal Christian commonwealth is emblematized in the title of Andreae's utopia: *Christianopolis*. Science was pursued as the means to a better knowledge of God and his works and to the creation of a truly Christian society. Likewise Campanella's *Civitas* subordinated scientific and technical interests to spiritual ends. But the nature of this subordination is less explicit in the *New Atlantis.* Although the Governor of the Strangers' House tells the travelers that Bensalem converted to Christianity through "a true Miracle" (48), Salomon's House is designed primarily for scientific, not sacred, purposes. In Bacon's utopia, scientific discovery is a glory unto itself, as if learning is a devotional practice. Bacon's literalizing of this metaphorical concept is notable for its pairing of what most preferred to keep separate: the commerce in "light" in which the Merchants engage joins the two disparate lexical fields of religious "light" and capitalist "commerce." In early seventeenth-century England, the notion of commercial "traffick" was just beginning to emerge from under a shadow of vice, with which trade and "commodity" were sometimes associated. For the figure of a merchant, often a focus of suspicion and vanity in tracts and pamphlets (and not just in sermons), to be linked with the gathering of "light," the universal symbol of grace and holiness, undoubtedly offended some.

Even more touchy might have been Bacon's depiction of these "Merchants of light" as intelligencers, or spies. As informants, the merchants spied on other countries' activities under the cover of secrecy. The merchants are state servants who, when they explore other nations, "colour themselves under the names of other nations" (59), thus working in secret to gather information for the state. Paradoxically, they are enjoined to keep some secrets from the state. The fellows all take an oath of secrecy for the "concealing of [the inventions and experiences] [they] think fit to keep secret: though some of those [they] do reveal sometimes to the state, and some not" (82). This type of secrecy, ostensibly in service of knowledge, and to the improvement of the society as a whole, is striking for the fact of the fellows' discretionary control over it.

It seems clear that, with his merchant-spies, Bacon meant to echo the system of intelligence-gathering of the Tudor and Stuart spy networks under Elizabeth and James I. But whereas in those systems, the intelligencers fall under control of the sovereign, in Bensalem the system apparently monitors itself. In fact, the sovereign falls away in the *New Atlantis*, so that, as John Archer has noted, "his sovereignty is subsumed in the sovereignty of knowledge that his explorers provide."[14] Centralized control here means not an absolutist state but the disembodied sovereignty of the remote state. Some critics have found this system of secrecy sinister, an example of ruthless political control concealed just beneath the surface of Bensalem's perfect system.[15] But in such secret-keeping arises one of many questionable inconsistencies in the information-gathering processes in Bensalem. Only some of the more privileged scientists, the Merchants of Light, are allowed to carry and deliver the secrets of learning, which become the secrets of state. Other scientists are not let in on these secrets. Jerry Weinberger believes these inconsistencies invite skepticism about the utopian nature of the text itself. "It is not that we learn nothing about modern scientific politics in the *New Atlantis*," he argues, "but rather that we are forced to wonder why the scientists remain in the dark about the full range of possibilities illuminated by the new science. . . ."[16] And yet for the Merchants who do decide which secrets shall be kept from the state, we see an example of an odd appropriation of the concept of *arcana imperii*. The *arcana*, or the notion of "mystery of state," was sometimes used to justify absolutist policies in the context of the sacredness or mystery of royal power.[17] Bacon transforms the *arcana* into a tool for the scientists gathering information.[18] If the *arcana* traditionally works as a means for rulers to forestall dissent and perpetuate the mystery of divine rule, it carries a similar function for the Merchants. The mystery of their discoveries is maintained, they retain control over the dissemination of their findings, and in turn control a veil of secrecy over their own work.

In this privileging of secrecy are glimmers of individual self-interest in Bensalem. Since the Merchants do not reveal to the state all the secrets they discover, there exists a power independent of the state. And yet the visitors' experience of Bensalem is one that discourages discovery. The ubiquity and ideological force of "secrets" is meant to emphasize the closed, authoritarian nature of government there. For instance, the only citizens of Bensalem allowed to leave the island are the chosen "merchants": as the narrator is told, "For our travelling from hence into parts abroad, our Lawgiver thought fit altogether to restrain it" (57). The island itself is in "a secret conclave of such a vast sea" (51). The Bensalemites can discover other cultures, but no one is allowed to discover theirs. The Governor explains that "by means of our solitary situation, and of the laws of secrecy . . . we know well . . . and are ourselves unknown" (46). Notions of the *arcana* are invoked when the narrator expresses his wonder at the Bensalemites' knowledge of distant cultures: "it was a thing we could not tell what to make of; for that it seemed to us a condition and propriety of divine powers and beings, to be hidden and unseen to others, and yet to have others open and as in a light to them" (51). The formula pits the powerful unknown Bensalemites as the secret hoarders of a divinity unavailable to the other cultures. The salient point about the lines of intellectual commerce in Bensalem is that the trade in information is one-way. The society's laws enforce a putative monopoly on pursuing knowledge of other cultures.

This one-way relationship is experienced by the narrator and the travelers as well. They cannot go outside the city walls, and when they arrive they are cloistered for three days. They are sworn to secrecy about Bensalem (until the end, when they are told to report well of it). When a Father of Salomon's House arrives "in state" to where the travelers are staying, they are told that "the cause of his coming is secret" (69). This general refusal of reciprocity would seem to enforce the visitors' sense of subordinate position to the Bensalemites. The narrator in fact says "[we admired] this gracious and parent-like usage" (45). And, of their guide, the narrator notes that he leaves them with the sense that they have been provided for: "his noble free offers left us nothing to ask" (45). The subordinate relationship is further implied rhetorically in the visitors' expressions of gratitude and honor: "[we were] his true servants" (46). The paternalistic situation that keeps the visitors in subordination under the Bensalemites is preserved, it seems, regardless of whether or not the visitors have questions. The Governor in fact maintains his dominance even when they do have "something" to ask, by stressing the fact that his knowledge is power: he tells the visitors, "he that knoweth least is fittest to ask questions . . . [thus] it is more reason that ye ask me questions, than I ask you" (46).

The paternalistic social commerce is not limited to information exchange but extends to financial exchange, as well. When the visitors try to express their gratitude by offering payment to the governor and their guides, they are refused: all offers of their "pistolets" are rejected with the claim that the recipients would be "twice paid" (39, 41, 43). The unequal nature of the economic relationship is reinforced most strikingly at the end of the narrative, where the Father gives the narrator a gratuity, or "largess," of ten thousand ducats despite the fact that the Bensalemites forbid tipping of any kind on the island (83). The tip is significant in its context: it is given at the end of the Father's visit to the narrator (and at the end of the text), when he grants the narrator permission to tell others about Bensalem, or "leave to publish it for the good of other nations" (83). Is this gratuity a bribe? At the very least, it imparts an expectation or social obligation on the part of the visitors to obey the Father's wishes in reporting well of Bensalem. Financial reward operates within Bensalem, as well, as an inducement for the citizens to produce inventions "of value": "For upon every invention of value, we erect a statua to the inventor, and give him a liberal and honorable reward (83)," says the Father of Salomon's House. The deployment of honors is not merely symbolic, but takes the form of material possessions. With such rewards and incentives is an implied inducement to loyalty and obedience on the part of the recipients.

Bensalem is designed to encourage its citizens to behave properly in the pursuit of knowledge; conversely it discourages improper behavior of other kinds. The Bensalemites are restrained from vice, the character Joabin (a Jewish merchant living on the island) says, by religion and "reverence of a man's self" (68). But this is not entirely accurate, because they are restrained by laws too. Joabin, introduced as "wise . . . and learned, and of great policy" (65), explains the laws surrounding marriage and the events leading up to marriage. There are laws against polygamy, brothels, and prostitution. There is no "masculine love" (67). Joabin repeatedly asserts "the chaste minds of this people" (66) but he betrays the reason for Bensalem's own strict laws in this area. He faults the Europeans' immoral and lascivious practices (as he describes them), such as availing themselves of brothels and prostitution, as a hindrance to the practice of marriage. He characterizes these vices sarcastically as "remedies": "when men have at hand a remedy more agreeable to their corrupt will, marriage is almost expulsed" (66–67). By extension of this logic, it is man's "corrupt will" that strict laws in Bensalem stanch.[19] The terms of justice are at times explicitly economic. Thus rigorous economic consequences are a means of social control. For instance, the laws of nuptial union require parental approval, so that marriage without consent is fined, or "mulct[ed] in the inheritors" (68). In "Adam and Eve's Pools," friends of the engaged couple "preview" the bride and groom for any possible "hidden" defects, in a process that revises a similar scene from More's *Utopia* (68), in which the bride and groom previewed each other's naked bodies before marriage. The issue of proving chastity before marriage highlights the danger of secrecy in marital relations. These peculiar rituals bring to light some of the hidden excesses and problems in Bensalemite culture, while also drawing attention to the ways in which desires are controlled.

Legal constraints are likewise revealed in the largest ritual on Bensalem, the Feast of the Family. This state-sponsored ritual is ostensibly designed to celebrate and reward any man who lives "to see thirty persons descended of his body alive together" (61). The Father, or "Tirsan," is given a resplendent feast, but first sits with his descendents "in consultation concerning the good estate of the family" (61). The paternalistic governing system of Bensalem bears directly upon issues of—and anxieties about—paternity and what we might call "parental control." The Father's consultation really is an ersatz trial at which the Father sits in judgment over his children, mending disputes but also settling debts. "If any . . . be distressed or decayed [behind in paying rent]," "order is taken for their relief and competent means to live" (61). But some are punished too, though the means of punishment are sufficiently vague. "If any be subject to vice, or take ill course, they are reproved and censured" (61) the visitors are assured, an assurance at variance with earlier assertions that the Bensalemites are free of vice. A paternalistic judicial system is alive and well at the Feast of the Family.

The Tirsan's role of authority in this ritual, however, is questioned. Throughout he requires assistance from the governor. "The governor assisteth, to the end to put in execution by his public authority the decrees and orders of the Tirsan, if they should be disobeyed" (61). Why would the private authority of the Father not suffice, so that a "public authority" is required? Here the state system of paternalism steps in where the patriarchal family system breaks down, where the authority of the *paterfamilias* is inadequate.[20]

Long before he wrote *New Atlantis*, Bacon had expressed concern regarding paternal control and the legal authority behind it. His argument in Chudleigh's Case (*Dillon v. Freine*, 1594) raised the concern: the loyalty assumed by a father from his son was not something to be depended upon, but instead needed to be regulated and subject to discipline.[21] While Bacon's arguments only touched briefly on patrimony as it related to devise of land (the broader argument concerned the Statute of Uses), he made the case for stronger legal mechanisms of parental discipline of disobedient children.

Chudleigh's Case contains the plea Bacon delivered in 1594 in a civil trial involving the interpretation of the Statute of Uses (1536), an act for regulating the settlement and transfer of legal estates in land. The Statute of Uses abolished the power to devise for the future, in its stead instituting a statutory fiction called "executing the use." "Uses" originally allowed evasion of feudal restrictions on the devise of land. The Statute attempted to restore the overt and public transfer of land which was avoided by the creation of a use. Prior to the Statute, if x granted land to y, "to the use of" z, y was the *feoffee*, and z was the *cestuy que use*. The Statute "executed the use" and turned z's equitable estate into a legal estate. The Statute took away common law seisin from the *feoffee*, so that the result of the legislation was that the *feoffee* became a nonentity.[22] When Bacon cited the Statute of Uses in Chudleigh's Case he defended the Statute, saying that it addressed the inconveniences and evils of the secrecy of uses in transferring land, namely the problem of secret conveyances. Furthermore, he argued that the Statute addressed the "mischiefs" of severed uses.[23]

One of the mischiefs that Bacon thought the Statute addressed was the frustration of what he termed the "discipline of families."[24] "Though I reverence the laws of my country, yet I observe one defect in them; and that is, there is no footstep there of the reverend *potestas patria* which was so commended in ancient times," Bacon contended.

> A man can sue his father; he can be a witness against his father; the father cannot intermeddle with the goods of his son; [the son] is not bound by the law to grant maintenance to his father if he does not choose: if [indeed] the father be killed by the son, which is a case rare and monstrous, he shall be drawn on a hurdle; but in no other cases the father and son are as strangers.[25]

Bacon invokes patricide, the most extreme example of family tumult, to lend gravity to his argument regarding the consequences of filial disobedience. "This only remains: if the father has any patrimony and the son be disobedient, he may disherit him; if he will not deserve his blessing he shall not have his living," he insisted.

> But this device of perpetuities has taken this power from the father likewise; and has tied and made subject (as the proverb is) the parents to their cradle, and so notwithstanding he has the curse of his father, yet he shall have the land of his grandfather. And what is more, if the son marry himself to a woman diffamed, so that she bring bastard slips and false progeny into the family, yet the issue of this woman shall inherit the land, for that the first perpetuator will have it so, who is dead a long time before. And these are the bad effects, besides those of fraud and deceit.[26]

Here Bacon linked contingent remainders and family discipline, emphasizing that a father should be able to disinherit a disobedient son. But he highlighted the danger by introducing the scenario of the son marrying a "diffamed" or defamed woman, implying that a bastard child, or "false progeny" would resultantly inherit the land. By arguing all this in the context of the Statute of Uses, he joined the device of the "secret conveyance," with the more private, personal, and alarming deceit of adultery. In this case, the secret conveyance, he suggested, implicitly raises the specter of something as disturbing as uncertain paternity. In both cases, secrecy must be frustrated and prohibited. If we collapse the simile, applying legal terminology to issues of paternity, the "bastard slips and false progeny" is as a "secret conveyance" of the family name and lands to a "false" grandchild. The solution in this case is to create a "non-entity" of the "issue of this woman" by disinheriting the son.

The significance of this argument for the *New Atlantis* concerns the subject of parental control. The "Feast of the Father" endows the father with some control, and yet the father's discipline, meant to be carried out by the patriarch, is authorized by the king, in the form of the King's Charter. While the Father apparently hands out "decrees and orders," his authority is ratified by that of the king. At the conclusion to the Feast of the Family, "the King's Charter, containing gifts of revenue, and many privileges, exemptions, and points of honor, [is] granted to the Father of the Family" (62). Owing to these "exemptions" and "points of honor," the father is obliged to the king. The subtle system of obligation enforced by paternalism trumps the father's patriarchal dominance.

This ritualistic representation of royal authority, the general narrative of secrets and mystification, and Bensalem's laws and restrictions combine to impress upon Bensalemites the importance of obedience and their willing subordination. A reciprocity of unequal obligations is maintained by the state—in some cases by the Father of the House of Salomon, and in other cases simply by the forms of government and ritual on the island. In all cases, the citizens of Bensalem feel the constraining bonds of obligations, on terms that most likely minimized their sense of independence. Why would Bacon highlight these particular mechanisms of control and hierarchy? Did he mean to imply that this paternalistic system was necessary to control self-interested individualism? Or, conversely, did he think that self-interest was unjustly hindered? Where did the individual's own ambition fit in to the health of the general commonwealth?

Bacon addresses the problem of individual ambition elsewhere. In the *Novum Organum* (1620), for example, he writes about the "kinds . . . of ambition in mankind."[27] There he contends that mankind possesses a general will to power or ambition. This will to dominate is least dangerous for the general welfare of the state, according to Bacon, when channeled towards learning. In fact the ambition of men to dominate nature, or to extend their knowledge of scientific learning, is, he insists, the most socially acceptable of the "three kinds . . . of ambition in mankind":

> The first is of those who desire to extend their own power in their native country; which kind is vulgar and degenerate. The second is of those who labour to extend the power of their country and its dominion among men. This certainly has more dignity, though not less covetousness. But if a man endeavor to establish and extend the power and dominion of the human race over the universe, his ambition (if ambition it can be called) is without doubt a more wholesome thing and more noble than the other two.[28]

This argument shines light on Bacon's argument in the *New Atlantis*, for we can see him there sketching the process of man endeavoring "to establish and extend" the power of the human race over the universe. The very purpose of Salomon's House is the discovery of "Causes and the secret motions of things," or the pursuit of knowledge. This channels ambition in ways that enhance, rather than disrupt, social harmony.

Bacon explores the advantages of intellectual pursuit in other works as well. He explicitly states "the true ends of knowledge" in a posthumous tract, *Valerius Terminus*, a plea for an active science which offers an exposition of idols and formulates his scientific method.[29] "And therefore it is not the pleasure of curiosity, nor the quiet of resolution, nor the raising of the spirit, nor victory of wit, nor faculty of speech, nor lucre of profession, nor ambition of honour or fame, nor inablement for business, that are the true ends of knowledge," he posits,

> some of these being more worthy than other, though all inferior and degenerate: but it is a restitution and reinvesting (in great part) of man to the sovereignty and power (for whensoever he shall be able to call the creatures by their true names he shall again command them) which he had in his first state of creation.[30]

Does Bacon mean that the true end of knowledge is a "restitution and reinvesting . . . of man to the sovereignty and power . . . which he had in his first state of creation"? Commentators have interpreted it in light of utopian thinking: J.C. Davis believes Bacon meant that "it was the business of learning to undo the consequences of the fall of man,"[31] while Krishan Kumar thinks that "Bacon sought to fuse orthodox Christian conceptions of original sin with decidedly unorthodox views of its overcoming."[32] Kumar uses Bacon to support of his larger point that "utopia is always Pelagian; anti-utopia is frequently Augustinian."[33] But if we look at the inconsistencies within the *New Atlantis* itself, Bacon's utopia is not one informed by the Pelagian heresy of perfectibilism. Instead it operates with an awareness of man's inherent imperfections, chiefly his desire for the power that knowledge confers. While clearly public service has a moral status because it furthers a collective good in Bensalem, the means to public service are organized to allay man's drive toward individual glory and power. Scientists are motivated to direct their energies toward discoveries for the state by awards, recognition, the lure of secret knowledge; men are motivated to be monogamous and fruitful through laws, public celebrations, rewards and honors; and travelers are bribed to report well of the island.

It is the channeling of individualism into a cooperative spirit that fuels Bensalem. One line of criticism holds that "as a cooperative public undertaking,

[Bacon's] new science has little room for the ambitious struggle for recognition that characterizes political life."[34] We should, instead, understand Bensalem as a society that makes room for that ambitious struggle. It is a society structured to channel the inherent drive for recognition. That structure is reflected in the literary landscape of the *New Atlantis*: on the surface the members of a utopian community work toward the collective good, with everyone content, fulfilled, and satisfied. Just under the surface, in minor but decipherable inconsistencies, there lies a governing system of discipline and incentives that rewards proper behavior and punishes harmful individualism. That is not to say that Bensalem is an amoral utopia, or an outright dystopia. Bacon was, after all, a Christian of the Calvinist sort. In his preface to Bacon's works, Robert Leslie Ellis writes that Bacon "declared . . . that the end of knowledge is the Glory of the creator and the relief of man's estate."[35] Virgil Whitaker finds that "the effects of Calvinist views may reasonably be found at the center of Bacon's thought."[36] Bacon's "ideal" society as represented in Bensalem is one that, in line with Calvinist thought, provides for man's central depravity and tendency toward self-interested, sometimes unethical behavior. In *Novum Organum* Bacon had emphasized that the "mind," which is "beset with the vainest *idols*" must be "subject to rule."[37] Again, Whitaker: "The essence of Bacon's method . . . is to supply the senses with such helps and so to govern the reason . . . an elaborate methodology will atone for the worthlessness of man's senses and understanding."[38] In Bensalem it is not an elaborate methodology that atones for the worthlessness of man's understanding, but instead a complex system of organization that works to channel man's ambitions. The state bureaucracy in the *New Atlantis* administers an entire society in a process that distracts them from their individual, self-interested pursuits.

This need for central administrative control and direction was a recurring theme in Bacon's work. He finds it necessary in government, in institutions of learning, and in families. In the *Valerius Terminus* he asserted that knowledge should be administered as the king of Spain administered his dominions, with men subject to central control and direction: "though he hath particular councils for several countries and affairs, yet hath one council of State or last resort, that receiveth the advertisements and certificates from all the rest. Hitherto of the diversion, succession, and conference of wits."[39] In his 1616 letter of advice to James I's favorite, George Villiers, Bacon outlined various ways of directing and controlling private interest for the greater security of the state, including the importance of: "suspecting" those who sue for appointment as Judges; refusing those sheriffs who are nominated "for money"; making "examples of justice . . . for terror to some"; preventing any "competition" for the crown; "compelling" merchants to trade in "solid" commodities and not excessive luxuries; and managing colonies "in a discreet way."[40] And in January 1620, Bacon advised James I to develop commissions to centralize control of information in the realm, proposing that the king institute a "fourth part of the square," the other three parts being the two uses of the Star Chamber (as a supreme Court of Judicature and as an open Council), and the "several jurisdictions of [the royal] courts."[41] The "commonwealth commissions" would, among other things, "invite and direct any man that finds himself to know anything concerning these commissions to bring in their informations."[42] Bacon proceeded to outline the commissions, meant to monitor agriculture and manufactures such as clothing, regulate coining, recover drowned lands, and provide for "warlike defence."[43] And in his "Advice to the King touching Sutton's Estate" he encouraged the development of "ordinances and institutions" to "preserve [men] from turning corrupt, or at least from becoming unsavoury."[44] Such ordinances and institutions shape Bensalem. Its division of labor follows a decidedly centralized form for the Fellows of Salomon's House. At any given time, there are only twelve "Merchants of Light" and three each of the other types of scientists (Depredators, Compilers, Inoculators, Lamps, etc) who are responsible for the creation and reporting of knowledge in Bensalem.

This connection between Bacon's writings and actual state bureaucracy has not gone wholly unnoticed by others.[45] Julie Robin Solomon, for instance, highlights the connection between Bacon's political philosophy and actual commercial culture: "Bacon's is the work of a Jacobean political official confronted with the problem of attending to the ways in which an increasingly commercialized society could erode, transform, or empower the monarchy . . . the mercantilist policies of the monarch sought to contain and channel the activities of merchant traders for the benefit of the royal state."[46] Further, she points out that "the Jacobean court culture that Bacon inhabited sought simultaneously . . . to both dominate and reconcile itself with commercial culture."[47] Elizabeth Hanson likewise finds that Bacon is "a pioneer of bureaucracy as much as of science."[48]

Francis Bacon recognized the power of pecuniary self-interest at work in commercial culture, too, and directs the king's awareness towards it. He effectively warns the king, in his *Advancement of Learning* (1605), about the dangers of neglecting his employees' financial self-concern. By pointing up the preoccupation for wages, Bacon attested to the existence of self-interest in the king's subjects, an interest that could at times supercede their service to James I. That the same concern motivated the privy counselors and other government officials was Bacon's assumption, but he did not encourage the culture of trust that Craig Muldrew, for instance, finds operating generally in early modern markets. In a speech to Sir John Denham upon the latter's accession to the position of Baron of the Exchequer in 1617, he warned Denham that Denham's personal credit was not enough to suggest him to the king: he said "The King takes you not upon credit but upon proof."[49] This all reveals the extent to which James I's heavily paternalistic notion of sovereignty was not just symbolic, but translated into practical methods and bureaucracies. Bacon ultimately defended the monarchy and its prerogatives against the claims of commercial subordinates and their self-interest, in his various strategies for James I to control and contain the challenges of commercial culture.[50] Bacon's sense of the social discontent arising in heavily paternalistic systems, reflected in the social fissures in the *New Atlantis*, is apparently not something he would urge upon the king himself.

Bacon admitted to James I himself that he might employ suspicion towards Bacon's own activities and commercial interests. He uses the metaphor of larceny to describe his own motivations, in his dedicatory epistle to the king at the opening in the *Great Instauration* (1620). "Your Majesty may perhaps accuse me of larceny, having stolen from your affairs so much time as was required for this work," he begins.[51] The "time" that Bacon has stolen for his own literary project is a thievery, the phrase "having stolen from your affairs" denoting not just the moments he might have used to attend to the king's business as his civil servant, but also the honor and respect due the king in attending to the king's affairs, that instead has been used to honor his own work. But the very nature of Bacon's rhetorical ploys—his admission of the crime of larceny, his heist of time owed to the king—suggests his awareness of his own recalcitrance to control and surveillance. He himself, guilty of accepting bribes as Chancellor in a system founded on virtuous behavior, corrupts state working.[52] He disturbs the efficacy of state control and systematic "helps" to curb human passions and appetites. His own behavior exemplifies the contradictions he introduces into the *New Atlantis*.

Some of these contradictions are apparent in the *New Atlantis* narrator's own observations. The visitors astutely recognize aspects of state control and surveillance to which they are subjected, and like good courtiers they adjust their behavior accordingly. When they first arrive and are shuttled to the "Strangers' House," the narrator briefly reflects on their reaction to being "cloistered":

> For they have by commandment (though in form of courtesy) cloistered us within these walls for three days: who knoweth whether it be not to take some taste of our manners and conditions? And if they find them bad, to banish us straightways; if good, to give us further time. For

> these men that they have given us for attendance may withal have an eye upon us. Therefore for God's love, and as we love the weal of our souls and bodies, let us so behave ourselves as we may be at peace with God, and may find grace in the eyes of this people (43–44).

Notably, the narrator privileges not God's providential eye, but the eyes of their captors. The idea that they behave well "for God's love" is subordinated to the fear of the guard's eyes on their activities. The narrator also distinguishes, as if to highlight the difference, between the "form of courtesy" used and the actual fact of "commandment" with which they were cloistered by the Bensalemites.

The "form of courtesy" is the underlying means of control in paternalistic systems generally. Paternalism attempts to represent the subordinates' self-interest as already provided for, in the process precluding any expression of self-interest on the part of the subordinates, or, ideally, even any recognition of it. In Bensalem, the analogies invoked by the "Feast of the Father" are those equating kingship with fatherhood. The idea of a naturally appointed hierarchy maintained by such analogies serves to enforce obedience to authority. But the Father does not enforce his decrees; the Governor does, so that the ultimate patriarch is the state. Ultimately, Bacon reveals the fissures within an institutional system that attempts to control its citizens in this way. Through moments of subtle recognition on the part of the narrator the state apparatus is revealed for its coercive manipulations. The scientific society in Bensalem is ostensibly one based on man's essential goodness; actually, it is one that operates by laws and policies that admit of man's "corrupt will" and baser nature. We also see the fissure in the attitude of the "Merchants of light" toward their own discoveries. In a land where the state is based upon secrecy and controls such secrecy fastidiously, the Merchants nonetheless decide which secrets they will "see fit to" reveal to the state. Insofar as the Merchants treat the secrets as a form of private property, we could almost read the moment as an early expression of intellectual property right. It is not that Bacon is necessarily asserting that right, however, but instead expressing the difficulty of its management for the state.

II

The web of social control that obtains in the *New Atlantis* under a paternalistic system is one that is irreparably rent in *Timon of Athens*. Shakespeare reveals, more dramatically and violently than Bacon, what happens when the self-interest of subordinates, and, for that matter, social equals, is not adequately recognized. The *New Atlantis* reveals the relatively minor and uncomfortable aspects of paternalism; in *Timon*, Timon's recalcitrant, paternalistic attachment to economic control destroys the relationships upon which that control is based. In other words, where the *New Atlantis* reveals paternalism as workable but flawed, *Timon of Athens* shows its unsustainability and implosion. With that destruction, Timon himself is dismantled psychologically, in a drama which suggests that the recognition of others' interests is essential both for social reputation and political survival and for the integrity of personal identity and mental health.

Timon of Athens depicts a man obsessed with paternalistic, overly generous giving and the outsized friendship that generosity implies.[53] Shakespeare derives his story from Plutarch's *Lives* and depicts ancient Greece as a place of corruption and greed in which usury was even more prevalent than in early modern London. Timon's great expenditures reflect those of James I whose indebtedness reached massive proportions in the first decade of the seventeenth century: Timon's resemblance to James I is one reason the play may not have been produced in a Jacobean England in which not only the king but most aristocrats painfully felt the credit crunch.[54] Timon's paternalism is of aristocratic proportions: for the first two acts he extends limitless loans, gifts, and dinners to his friends. All his offers carry with them his idealistic philosophy. "O what a precious comfort 'tis to have so many like brothers commanding one another's fortunes," he says early on in the play (1.2.101–3). Despite praising reciprocity, Timon actually prefers sole command of others' fortunes. When Ventidius tries to repay the five talents Timon spent to release him from debtors' prison, for example, Timon rejects his payment, saying "You mistake my love;/I gave it freely ever, and there's none/Can truly say he gives, if he receives" (1.2.9–11). Timon's utopia is not only that of extended one-sided giving, but also of boundless trust. When it becomes clear that his means are limited and his land is either sold or forfeited, he responds: "I account [wants] blessings; for by these/Shall I try friends" (2.2.185–6). All his "friends," however, fail that trial, as each calls in Timon's debts at the same time, in a sudden demand for payment on his loans that resembles an impersonal run on the banks.

Their heartlessness is only outweighed by Timon's apparent lack of insight. Timon's myopia draws comment from Apemantus, who compares others' ill-use of Timon to feeding: "What a number of men eats Timon, and he sees 'em not!" (1.2.39–40). It is obvious to those around him that Timon is victim to his own blindness in the face of manipulative money-lenders and -takers alike. Exploitation by moneylenders was a common fear in early modern England: the "gentleman made bankrupt by usurers" was a conventional depiction in pamphlets.[55] But the public recognition of Timon's ruin, and the acknowledgement of his prodigality, is not meant as a lesson that he turn to a life of puritan thrift. Instead the point is that he should be more vigilant. "He would embrace no counsel, take no warning by my coming./Every man has his fault, and honesty is his," says Lucullus (3.1.26–28). The second Lord uses the image of a missing guard at his front door: "No porter at his gate . . . It cannot hold; no reason/Can sound his state in safety" (2.1.10,12–13). No one could "sound" or test Timon's "state"—his economic means or his estate—and find it safe. These repeated exposures reveal the dissonance between Timon's apparently selfless generosity and a place like Athens where such naivety means self-destruction. Lucullus speaks for the crowd in a justification of his refusal to repay Timon's generosity. He tells the servant Flaminius that Athens is a city of pragmatists, that it is "no time to lend money, especially upon base friendship, without security" (3.1.41–43). The unreliability of the unsecured loan is likened to the general insecurity of friendship, reducing Timon's social trust to fiscal folly.

Lucullus' cynical aphorism that renders Timon's trust as folly is not simply an indictment of Athens' mean streets. It expresses one aspect of humanist political thought in sixteenth-century England. Toward the end of the sixteenth century, a humanism emphasizing moral skepticism and self-interest began to replace, or merge with, the Ciceronean idea of the virtuous citizen.[56] Early humanist political discourse had been dominated by Ciceronianism that in its republican form encouraged the citizen to lead a virtuous life for the good of the commonwealth. In its monarchical form it placed an emphasis on a prince exhibiting cardinal virtues in order to protect the good of his subjects. But a pragmatism based upon the principles of reason of state began to emerge in the late sixteenth century. Even earlier in the century, a pragmatic pursuit of personal profit and advantage was given a positive valence. In *The Book Named the Governor* (1531), for instance, Sir Thomas Elyot defines "providence" as, among other things, a kind of wisdom necessary in a leader, an especially pragmatic type of prudence. "Providence is, whereby a man not only foreseeth commodity and incommodity, prosperity and adversity, but also consulteth and therewith endeavoureth as well to repel annoyance, as to attain and get profit and advantage, he argued '[I]t is the part of a wise man to foresee and provide . . . he be not endamaged or impeached by his adversaries.[57] Timon clearly lacks this "providence." His inability to "repel annoyance" is, in the context of Elyot's formulation, a crucial weakness. He meets this "annoyance," the Athenians' expediency and greed, but instead of trying to gain "advantage," he embraces the fact that he has been "impeached by his adversaries," and exiles himself from Athens.

Timon's response actually serves as a negative example of such providence, its positive counterpart evident in the actions of another character who responds quite differently to "annoyance," Alcibiades.

Alcibiades, an outsider whose reputation for military valour precedes him, initially shares Timon's idealism. When Alcibiades arrives in Athens to plead before the Athenian Senate for the life of a friend, his idealism takes the form of a devotion to the codes of honor and courtesy instead of those of pragmatic civic values and laws. His language with the Senators is that of a courtier: "I am an humble suitor to your virtues" (3.5.7). His friend has killed a man in a duel, but he does not bother to specify the nature of the conflict. He justifies his friend's action, made "in hot blood" (3.5.11) as if this hot blood were normal. His defense rests on the notion that the virtue of courage—"an honor in him" (3.5.17)—somehow outweighs the vice of murder. His friend is described in terms of martial valor, or *virtù*: he behaved "with noble fury" (3.5.18) and "unnoted passion" (3.5.21), Alcibiades says, and in order to save his "reputation" (3.5.19) did "oppose his foe" (3.5.20). When the Senators reject his plea on the grounds that false valor belongs to a time of sects and factions, Alcibiades adjusts his rhetoric. "My lords then, under favor, pardon me,/If I speak like a captain," he pleads (3.5.41–42), but his rhetorical shift does not win them. For they counter Alcibiades' valorization of martial skill with a recognition of its dangers to civic order: of his friend the duelist, they say "He's a sworn rioter" (3.5.69). But Alcibiades cannot relinquish his devotion to the honor code, and he can only think to exchange the thing of greatest value to him in security for the life of his friend: "I'll pawn all my victories, all/My honour to you, upon his good returns" (3.5.82–83). At this the irritated Senators are provoked to silence Alcibiades, and they immediately reply "We are for law; he dies." (3.5.87). As A.D. Nuttall has noted, "in the case of Alcibiades it is hard to avoid the inference that the aristocratic ideology is now, so to speak, at the very limit of its tenure."[58] Alcibiades is reluctant to recognize this fact, however, and leaves the Senators with his own idealistic restatement of the thesis of *virtù*: "'Tis honour with most lands to be at odds" (3.5.117).

But at the next clash between the Senators and Alcibiades, he is not so resolute in his idealistic attachment to "honor." At the play's end, the Senators, fearful for his martial might against the city, dissuade him from personal revenge. The besieged Senators decry the code of *lex talionis*: the city of Athens, they say, is separable from personal crimes against Alcibiades and Timon. Of those who have wronged the two, they plead, "These walls . . . were not erected by their hands . . . nor are they such/That these great tow'rs . . . and schools should fall/For private faults in them" (5.4.22–26). When they finally appeal to Alcibiades in words he will understand—"Throw thy glove,/Or any token of thine honour else" (5.4.49–50)—he responds in kind, offering his glove and his cooperation. Tellingly, he also adjusts his rhetoric. Though poised to "cull th'infected forth" in Athens, he agrees with Athenian communal values, assuring the Senators that he will reestablish "regular justice" where criminals "shall be rendered to [Athens'] public laws/At heaviest answer" (5.4.61–63). There he promises to "use the olive" with the "sword" (5.4.81).[59] Alcibiades' shift is apparent in his new approval of the civic, communal "regular justice" of the polis. When feeling "emdamaged" by his adversaries, Alcibiades is able to employ a bit of Elyot's "providence" whereas Timon cannot.

This central difference between Timon and Alcibiades accounts for Alcibiades' very presence in the play, a presence that has long been questioned by some critics. E. K. Chambers, for instance, is unsure whether Alcibiades is Timon's foil or is, instead, "Timon over again, in a weaker and less clearly motivated version of the disillusioned child of fortune."[60] This is to misread Alcibiades's dramatic purpose. Instead of being weaker, Alcibiades exhibits a certain type of strength, attaining the advantage, through providence, that Elyot advises for his "Governor."

The distinction between codes of honor and behavior founded on pure pragmatism also points to a growing difference in aristocratic languages of "honor" in Shakespeare's England. The demise of the honor-driven, "aristocratic" philosophy has been the subject of scholars of the Tudor court. Mervyn James traces a shift in language and thought at the court in 1601, where the putative heirs of Essex, Arundel, and Southampton learn from Essex's ill-advised dependence upon the language of honor in its definition as bold and heroic action. They participate in a larger shift in political language at court, one which privileges law over the cult of honor and its code, a shift which eventually spread to the Parliament.[61] Pauline Croft notes that "honor" loses its definition as a virtue with an aristocratic tinge, and with a military prerogative, and becomes something more pragmatic, associated with, among other things, money concerns. For example, Sir Robert Cecil uses the word "proper" to denote not a code of behavior, but instead a kind of "practical," fiscally responsible behavior.[62] Alcibiades' shift can be seen in the context of this larger shift in the language of self-interest. We could interpret it as a shift from the behavior and language of an Essex to that of a Cecil, who learned to work through Commons and lesser nobility, rather than only through high nobility at court, whom Essex, for example, considered the only true bearers of aristocratic "honor."[63] This discursive shift has also been the study of Anna Bryson, who notices a shift from "honor" to "civility" among seventeenth-century aristocrats.[64] Alcibiades' actions embody such shifts in political language, serving as one example of a paradigmatic shift in languages and idioms at the time. This shift, described by J.G.A. Pocock as a move from the validating discourses of grace and custom (honor) to those of rights and commerce,[65] is dramatized in the play through the respective success and failure of Alcibiades and Timon.

The actual contrast between Timon and Alcibiades becomes keener when we look again to Elyot's *Governor*, where Elyot uses the historical character of Alcibiades himself as an example of the "prudence" we see missing in Timon. Elyot discusses Alcibiades in his section on "industry." "Alcibiades . . . by the sharpness of his wit, the doctrine of Socrates, and by his own experience in sundry affairs in the common weal of the Athenians, became so industrious," Elyot suggests, "that were it good or evil that he enterprised, nothing almost escaped that he achieved not, were the thing never so difficult (or as who saith) impenetrable, and that many sundry things, as well for his country as also against it. . . ."[66] Alcibiades' "industry" belongs to that application of wit, Elyot says, "by the which a man perceiveth quickly, inventeth freshly, and counselleth speedily."[67] Industrious men "do most craftily and deeply understand in all affairs what is expedient, and by what means and ways they may soonest exploit them. And those things in whom other men travail, a person industrious lightly and with facility speedeth, and findeth new ways and means to bring to effect that he desireth."[68] Of course here Elyot sketches Alcibiades' self-interest as harmful to the state—his achievements "as well for his country as also against it." And indeed Alcibiades poses a danger to Athens, but, in Shakespeare's version, his agreement to comply with Athens' "public laws" redeems him. Whether Shakespeare ever read Elyot's characterization is unclear, but he certainly knew Alcibiades from Plutarch's account, where Alcibiades is presented as a man of great adaptability.[69] Both Plutarch and Shakespeare depict Alcibiades as making this shift to incorporate some civil values; each offers, in the characterization, an example of Elyot's providence. Whether or not Alcibiades is ultimately self-serving is less crucial than his public agreement to act upon "civil" values with the Athenians.[70] We never see this shift towards providence in Timon.

Timon's lack of providence is not solely rooted in his refusal to utilize Alcibiades' rhetoric of communal values. His carelessness extends to many aspects of his behavior. It could be described as an enthusiastic improvidence, in terms of his literal giving: a drive to produce gifts in unlimited quantities. He brings a supernatural notion of production to a natural world: that this sort of idealism cannot be reconciled to the real world is the subject of comment and conjecture in Athens. Those who report on his gift-giving, or "production," describe it in terms usually reserved for usurers, highlighting its unnatural quality as artificial "reproduction." Throughout the play, his bounty is seen as "breeding." The 2nd Lord says, "No meed but he repays/ Seven-fold above itself: no gift to him/But breeds the giver a return exceeding/All use of quittance" (1.1.276–79). A Senator says "If I want gold, steal but a beggar's dog/And give it Timon—why, the dog coins gold" (2.1.5–6) and "give my horse to Timon;/Ask nothing, give it him; it foals me straight/ And able horses" (2.1.8–10). Here Timon is maligned in the familiar Aristotelian formulation condemning the use of money to gain interest as sexual reproduction.[71] In trying to remove himself from the grimy business of moneylending by acting as if he gives it freely, Timon only becomes (in the mouths of Athenians) a more sullied version of the base usurer. Of course these characterizations stem from the Athenians' own vision, which sees all behavior from behind envious, carping, green-colored glasses. But the contrast between their depictions and Timon's exalted view of himself betrays his own misprision as well. Timon does not believe himself equal to their grubbing: he is above and separate. It is exactly this perception of superiority that causes Timon his greatest trouble.

That Timon cannot separate himself from the mire of rapaciousness in Athens is highlighted in imagery of cannibalism and feeding upon his body: others do not just accept his generosity, they feast. And to accept his generosity is to betray that generosity. When Apemantus says "the fellow that sits next him, now parts bread with him, pledges the breath of him in a divided draught, is the readiest man to kill him" (1.2.46–49) we hear echoes of the Last Supper or of Judas. At the very least we join traditional images of greed and usury as scavenging or gorging. Lucian, in his "Dialogue of Timon," subjects Timon to "having his liver eaten by so many vultures" who "had . . . eaten him down to the bone, and sucked the marrow."[72] Shakespeare draws upon those images but also confronts them in the milder commentary of strangers who comment upon the scene after Lucullus has denied Timon. One of the strangers says to the other: "I never tasted Timon in my life" (3.2.79). These more moderate evocations of feeding liken Timon to a nurturing mother, or may, as some psychoanalytic critics say, enact Timon's anxiety of dependency through an identification with the mother.[73] The point is that Timon's identity—in his own eyes and in the eyes of the Athenians—is embedded in his ability to provide for needy recipients. This notion is supported by Timon's parent-like (and Lear-like) railing against those who forget their "gratitude" to him (2.2.119). In the end, however, it is the repeated imagery of a solitary Timon without familial or community bonds with which we are left. He exists apart, as godlike and as solitary as, in the words of one Senator, the "phoenix" (2.1.32).

But instead of stopping at the ingratitude of his debtors qua creditors, Timon extends his outrage to all Athenians, as if the world has been turned upside down by this failure in personal loyalty. The trajectory of misrule in Timon's vision is bleak. Bleaker still is the progression of his bitterness. First, at his last feast for the ingrates, he offers only warm water to the "detested parasites" (3.6.90). Then he rails "Sink, Athens" (3.6.100). By the opening of Act IV, Timon's description of the natural world is rapturously maligning all, not just his economic adversaries. All order is upset: he cries "Matrons, turn incontinent" (4.1.3); "Obedience fail in children!" (4.1.4); and "Slaves and fools,/ Pluck the grave wrinkled senate from the bench,/and minister in their steads!" (4.1.4–6). Timon narrates the upsetting of all hierarchy.

In these characterizations, Timon draws upon a common early modern analogy: social disruption as natural disorder. More specifically, such disruptions were treated as imbalances in the body politic.[74] Timon expresses such imbalances when he says "Consumptions sow/In hollow bones of man" (4.3.153–4) and tells the earth to "Teem with new monsters" (4.3.193). He draws upon a normative idea of harmony that accommodated disagreements and dissent in the state to ideals of unity and wholeness. Of course Timon takes it further and treats the imbalances as permanent, cosmic, and irredeemable, but the import of his rhetoric is the same: the subject and the sovereign—imagined as the Athenians and himself, respectively—are analogous to the body and soul, meant to exist in the same balance.[75] For Timon, this natural order was predicated upon his continued ability to give but also upon the continued willingness of his subordinates to receive. This formula conflates Timon and the sovereign.

To his very end, Timon hints at his sense of sovereignty. Even exiled and powerless, he betrays a willingness to describe his own condition using the metaphorical language of the "sun," typically reserved for the sovereign. Near his end, he laments, "Sun, hide they beams, Timon hath done his reign" (5.1.222). The fact that his "reign," such as it was, depended upon his ability to provide for others, is not completely lost on him. When Alcibiades asks him how he had changed so much, Timon replies, "As the moon does, by wanting light to give./But then renew I could not like the moon;/There were no suns to borrow of" (4.3.68–70). In painting himself in imagery commonly associated with feminine changeability, he is saying he feels emasculated. He wants money to lend to restore his credit and power in Athenian society, but he also suggests that he envies the sun. He wants the sovereign power of the sun in nature and of a king on earth. When he later meets a group of bandits on the road and employs metaphors of thievery to rant against mankind, his curses extend to nature. In those curses he uses the same object he has used to describe himself, the moon, but this time in a metaphor of theft: "the moon's an arrant thief/And her pale fire she snatches from the sun" (4.3.440–41). Since he still "wants" the sun's light, he approves of the moon's ability to steal. Conversely, he would like to be the sun himself, or at least the "phoenix" as he was once described. When Timon, in his misanthropic ranting, condemns the bandits for "wanting," we hear his self-condemnation as Timon the moon, who "wanted" light to give.

Timon's sense of personal sovereignty is premised on a stable natural order the harmony of which is dependent upon his continued provision for others. His ostensibly utopian communalism is actually a stringent monarchism, with himself as economic sovereign. There is little place in Timon's ideology for cooperation or reciprocity between equal members. In fact he rails against any sort of communal justice, conflating human laws which operate according to objective, common standards with theft. He articulates these attitudes in a long tirade—arguably his most lyric passage—against the bandits' expression of "want." The passage requires a bit of unpacking. In his first few lines he advises them to steal, punning that they are "thieves profess'd," or thieves by trade: he says "there is boundless theft/In limited professions" (4.3.430–31). Timon is saying that, like city guilds that limit the number of apprentices at any one time, such professions that claim to be exclusive or to control their membership engage in "boundless theft." Of course he is not singling out guilds—he probably means to indict all professions. But he attacks a practice that was meant to protect the working community from dangerously individualistic economic entrepreneurship. The rules imposed on artisans and tradesmen by their own craft guilds may have been medieval in origin, but they were particularly relevant to the early modern household shop in an increasingly competitive urban market.[76] Timon speaks against not only these helpful communal rules of incorporation, but also against laws. Before he does so, he explains the thievery in nature:

> The sun's a thief, and with his great attraction
> Robs the vast sea; the moon's an arrant thief,
> And her pale fire she snatches from the sun;
> The sea's a thief, whose liquid surge resolves
> The moon into salt tears; the earth's a thief,
> That feeds and breeds by a composture stol'n
> From gen'ral excrement; each thing's a thief.
> The laws, your curb and whip, in their rough power
> Has uncheck'd theft.
>
> (4.3.439–447)

Instead of describing nature in traditional terms—as operating according to a hierarchical order in which the great chain of being keeps each of nature's elements in its place—Timon sees nature's workings as a series of heists. When his description abruptly shifts to the human world, he seizes on human laws as the source of all this natural thievery. It is as if Timon, in his resentment over not being able to reign as the sun over his own world, is left only with fury at the "laws" that allow for, or even encourage, this theft. But economic laws, in his case the laws of debt and repayment, simply operate according to civic rules of reciprocity, the legitimacy of credit, and public accountability. The "public laws" that Alcibiades has come to uphold are mere symbols of corruption to Timon, who prefers private, unaccountable trust to any objective contract.

Timon had hoped his bounty would give him god-like status. His steward had voiced this hope, while admitting its dangerous allure for mortals: "For bounty, that makes gods, do still mar men" (4.2.41). One point of these references, oft-mention by critics and perhaps accounting for the fact that *Timon of Athens* was not performed in Shakespeare's lifetime, is the parallel to King James I himself. Many have commented on the rather clear parallels between Timon's debt and the debt crisis at the end of the first decade of the seventeenth century. By 1611 the King's Exchequer was £300,000 in debt.[77] Not just the King, but many aristocrats found themselves in a similar position: Robert Cecil, the chancellor of the Exchequer owed £53,000 on a landed income of £6200.[78]

Timon's figuring himself as a kind of economic god that reigns through endless giving without receiving has been likened, by some critics, to status relationships in gift-giving cultures.[79] Marcel Mauss describes tribal potlatchers who unilaterally provide food and dispense valuables to exhibit high social status.[80] But we do not have to go as far back as the potlatch to find a model for Timon's actions. His behavior is consistent with the strategy of authoritarian paternalism, through which early modern employers maintained their claims to authority by remaining sensible of their own traditional social obligations.

The paternalistic relationship followed a number of patterns in England: a landlord might extend certain tenants preferential terms, such as long leases; aid them in times of emergency; find their children places of service; stand surety for a recognizance; or intervene in a court case. And not only landlords, of course, exhibited paternalistic generosity. The rich, the parish notable, clergymen, even the yeoman farmer recognized their social obligations in this way.[81] The advantage for the paternalistic gentleman was the stability the relationship secured for his position: it served his self-interest because its latent function was to give stability to a society which embraced the gross inequalities defining the unequal obligations. Someone like Timon could justify his position by his own actions, generous actions that implicitly legitimized his social sovereignty.

The paternalistic relationships in early modern England that involved the middling and lower sort were sometimes founded on the employer's great attachment to the claims of authority that went with his social obligations, to the point at which he thought of himself as "master" and his worker as "servant." The terms implied not only the existence of constraining bonds of reciprocal obligation, but within parameters defined from above, and on terms which quashed the independence of the subordinate in a demand for deference and obedience. Timon operates according to these "master-servant" conditions. Timon so internalizes the model of superior-subordinate relations that when they break down, he articulates this refusal of subordination as the eruption of a topsy-turvy world. In this new world, nature operates only by, he says "contempt of nature" (4.3.8). Subordinates unnaturally attain good fortune, while aristocrats fall: "Raise me this beggar, and deny't that lord" (4.3.9). In opposition to the workings of proper social order, "honor" comes to beggars as their birthright: "The senators shall bear contempt hereditary,/ The beggar native honour" (4.3.11). The thievery against which he's been railing obtains even in the senate: "place thieves,/And give them title, knee and approbation/With senators on the bench" (4.3.36–38).

Of course if Timon's railing were not so radically misanthropic, many of his barbs would fall in line with early seventeenth-century English articulations of concern over social change as a result of the new science, of "all coherence" being gone.[82] Hierarchy was symbolic of order generally, and social subordination was one of the most important links in that chain. It was a relationship between superior and inferior the ideological underpinning of which had assumed particular importance in the late sixteenth century by moralistic preachers and pamphleteers. The rich were reminded of their duties, while great stress was laid upon the duty of inferiors to obey those in authority, placed there by God. Not just the 1562 *Book of Homilies* with its six discourses "Against Disobedience and wilful Rebellion," but the catechism, too, in which the young were told by their parish ministers to "submit" themselves to all their "governors, teachers, pastors and masters" and to order themselves "lowly and reverently to all" their "betters."[83] Such a social order was meant to preserve the effective hegemony by the lack of any practical alternative. But of course the durability of the relationships which made up what Mervyn James calls "a graduated ladder of dominance and subordination" from the lower sort of servants up through the gentry and their own social "betters," was governed by the relative dependence of the subordinate partner.[84]

It is this dependence that Timon hoped to maintain with his generosity. To Timon, that dependence would insure a social order in which all Athenians, like the painter in whose work he showed interest, would "wait attendance" on him (1.1.164). Like the gentry's belief in their inherent superiority and natural right to regulate the "lower order," Timon believed it was his obligation and his right to "help the feeble up" (1.1.110).[85] Timon's paternalism is reminiscent of a figure such as the Earl of Arundel, for instance, who had used it in 1549 to quash a peasants' revolt in Sussex, one of many in that year of the general "Peasants' Revolts."[86] The Earl summoned both the peasants and the gentry of the shire to his hall in Arundel Castle, offered them open hospitality, and listened to the complaints of both sides day after day. He issued summary judgments: gentlemen who had evicted their tenants were ordered to reinstate them and destroy the enclosures, and peasants who persisted in talk of rebellion were thrown into the stocks. Procedures of common law, property rights, and individual rights all were subsumed to this general arbitrary and personal system of natural justice. Lawrence Stone notes that the efficacy of paternalism was unusual by this time in England: "[the Earl] relied upon the traditional bonds of medieval society—the bonds of paternalism on the one side and of deference on the other—which in this unique case were still strong enough to withstand the disruptive effects of violent social and economic change and the rise of possessive market individualism."[87] While Stone may overstate the uniqueness of these types of bonds (paternalism would be at work in seventeenth-century household shops and with journeymen, among others), it is true that the "disruptive" social and economic changes of the subsequent century would challenge paternalistic modes of social control. What we find applicable from Arundel for Timon's case is the feeling of primacy of a personal system of justice over that involving legal bonds and official judicial procedures.

But for Timon, as in early modern England, paternalism breaks down when the subordinates' feeling of dependence breaks down. While such a model of dependence worked well in some situations in the seventeenth-century English economy, it did not work well in larger manufactories, such as shipyards. Even in certain rural leasing situations, it began to be frayed. Sometimes both parties to a lease were aware of the potential conflict of their interests, and the deference of the tenants was conditional. The fair exchange depended upon the client feeling he or she had tangible benefits in return for loyalty. The notion was expressed in a remark by a fifteenth-century landlord: "The people will go with him that may best sustain and reward them."[88] The relevance of Timon's underlying faith in paternalism is put into question as those around him do not only not consider themselves his "subordinates," but see little value in remaining loyal to him. His misanthropic rants and self-imposed exile expose his refusal to admit that paternalism is no longer a workable model for the real-world workings of Athenian economics. Instead his reactions are proof of his steadfast reliance on this model which has, he believes, been sinfully ignored. He is outraged that the hierarchy insured by the economic mechanism of paternalism has been unseated.

Because he holds to a model of static hierarchy, Timon is unable to countenance the challenges to that hierarchy. Further, he is unequipped to enter into any sort of conflict in order to refit or reorder his imagined hierarchy in Athens. In early modern England, the survival of certain aspects of paternalism was contingent upon the ability of the interested parties to engage in a measure of conflict, allowing for self-interest on both sides. Any equilibrium of social relations in England's towns in the early seventeenth century was the product of a constant dynamism the impetus of which came from conflict. As Wrightson explains, "conflict between individual neighbors was an essential feature of the constant process of readjustment of social relationships at the local level."[89] By not rising to the challenge of meeting his own personal and pecuniary conflicts, Timon becomes a sort of poster child for Lawrence Stone's "crisis of the aristocracy," assuming that he could still operate by rules of hierarchy that did not fully or universally obtain in his community.

Timon believed in an ideal paternalistic world without contract, consequence, or legal bond. His paternalistic order operates along the lines of Gonzalo's utopian Commonwealth in *The Tempest*, with no laws except Timon be "king on't." In this context, Timon's recalcitrance could be interpreted as resistance to the transformation of a society based on paternalism to one based on law and contract.[90] Timon's utopia could not admit of the expression of self-interest on the part of its economic agents: all must be subsumed under cover of the paternalistic generosity through which the needs of subordinates are always already provided for. We have seen where this model began to break down and modify in early modern society. Shakespeare expresses this breakdown in the crisis met by a character who refuses to recognize the place for self-interest on the part of all agents, including the subordinates, in his society.

Chapter Four

The Genre of Self-Interest in the Poetry of Isabella Whitney and Aemilia Lanyer

Timon of Athens and the *New Atlantis* explore the deleterious social consequences of the suppression of self-interest, either in the individual himself or by a paternalistic system. Other authors during the late sixteenth and early seventeenth centuries also portrayed inadequate responses to their own authorial self-interest, though often by necessity in coded ways. Early modern women writers with an interest in their own literary success, for example, faced proscriptions against writing for profit, either personal or economic. Isabella Whitney and Aemilia Lanyer are particularly illustrative of the subtle ways female poets addressed the financial pressures of the early modern female writer. Each manipulates genre conventions to assert a private and emotional obligation upon those in positions to aid them in the public marketplace.

Both meditate on exile from economic opportunity in a particular poem, but each uses a distinctive literary genre to express her sense of exclusion. Whitney's "Wyll and Testament" (1573) employs the mock-testament, bequeathing the teeming commerce of London to the city of London, while Lanyer's "The Description of Cooke-ham" (1611) deploys the complaint in her farewell to Cookeham. Both Whitney and Lanyer skew the conventions of these genres—the mock-testament, and the complaint—to critique their economic exclusion. Issues of genre are often at question in considering early modern women's writing,[1] and recent scholarship has analyzed how writers' appropriations of poetic forms skew traditional generic conventions. This chapter examines the ways in which Whitney and Lanyer manipulate poetic conventions to articulate both economic self-interest *and* poetic aspiration. By using "public" genres to express private concerns both poets offer a public and communal authority for their private financial distress.

I

> And Bedlam must not be forgot,
> for that was oft my walk:
> I people there too many leave,
> that out of tune do talk.[2]

The speaker in Isabella Whitney's "Wyll and Testament" (1573) leaves to the Hospital of St. Mary of Bethlehem "many" people who talk "out of tune": her mock-testament provides London's asylum with the insane who are already patients there.[3] The paradox is double: her bequest fills, with a bounty of sickness and insanity, a hospital already full; yet the lunatics are not hers to give. Thus she bestows an impossible, impractical gift to a recipient—Bedlam—that in turn is implicated through her satiric offering. This formula, intrinsic to the mock-testament, highlights the testator's oppositional relationship to the recipient or, as in this case, to the cultural formations responsible for the recipient's continued "success": a fully occupied and thus "successful" hospital reflects upon the society that produces its mad inhabitants. But whether Bedlam was "oft" the speaker's "walk" because she was one of the Londoners who visited it to watch the ravings of the mad for amusement or because she skirted the fringes of insanity herself, the condition of madness is nonetheless highlighted. And the bequest, offering hoards of mentally ill, provides not just for a more crowded hospital, but also for instability and noise, an "out of tune" cacophony to jangle London's already noisy streets. These lines attest to Whitney's own antic mode—and to her deliberate employment of the mock- testament genre—in a poem that has often been placed in the female legacy tradition.[4] But legacy poems authorize mothers' dying bequests to their children, offering advice in the guise of last wills. Whitney's poem is itself "out of tune" with that genre, and instead, in the speaker's rollicking and outlandish bequests of the indebted, the insane, the indigent and the widowed, needs to be placed firmly within its proper genre, the mock-testament. A satiric literary will that exposed vices and burlesqued legal authority, the mock-testament, whose origins lay in the twelfth century, was a well-known genre by Whitney's time. Certain mock -testament conventions, including the "outsider" status of the dead or dying and often impoverished speaker, and the shattering of social stratification, further Whitney's primary goals: she is both dramatizing the ambitious female writer's plight as an "outsider," and calling for the opening of credit networks to the city's marginalized figures.

This chapter examines the ways in which Whitney manipulates mock-testament conventions to narrate one female writer's economic disadvantage in London. The poem itself follows a female speaker who is forced to leave the city: denied credit, room or board and spurned by her lover, the city "London," she offers a fantasy that all of London is hers to bequeath. First she offers him the city's luxuries, but the poem quickly devolves into a bequest of poor laborers, tenements, and prisons. The will implicates a "London" refusing credit to those in need, but at the same time the speaker envies those in debt, members of the lending community from which she is barred. This ambiguity (and Whitney's use of the mock-testament to express not only the relationship of debtors to creditors, but also the consequences of exclusive credit channels) illumines conflicting attitudes toward debt in London's growing credit economy. The ways in which Whitney employs and then shifts centuries-old mock-testament conventions also highlights her strategy in reaching readers attuned to such conventions, specifically her strategy of exposing economic iniquity.

We can assume Whitney faced the frustrations exhibited by her speaker without necessarily equating author with speaker. Whitney's origins and life and shrouded in obscurity. Probably born to a gentry family in Cheshire near the middle of the sixteenth century, she is thought to be the sister of Geoffrey Whitney, author of the well-known *A Choice of Emblemes* (1586).[5] After some education Isabella may have become a domestic servant in London, serving as a companion in the household of a noblewoman, though admittedly we have no real evidence.[6] What is known is that she was among the very first women to print a complete volume of secular poetry—the miscellany *The Copy of a Letter* (1566–67)—under her name. Her second miscellany, *A Sweet Nosgay* (1573), revises the adages in Sir Hugh Plat's *Floures of Philosophie* (1572), adds a section of epistles, and ends with her "Wyll and Testament." In the latter collection, Whitney makes explicit her professional literary aspirations: the book is presented to her hoped-for patron George Mainwaring, an affluent neighbor of the Whitney family in Cheshire, and to her addressees as payment for past debts and in hopes for future patronage. It includes the section of "Certain familiar Epistles and friendly Letters by the Author: with Replies" to brothers, sisters, a cousin, and two friends. The epistles create an illusion of closeness to a social context which is absent. Her goal seems to be to create a store of personal credit to offset future insecurity. But ultimately hers is a sense of *exclusion*, not inclusion. Her letters to her sisters express her exile from domesticity, for one. And though she had used the epistles as a means to establish a sense of social credit, the concluding poem in *Nosgay*, her "Wyll," figuratively erases that credit. Saying that she is "weary of writing," she expresses her departure in terms of the mock will and testament.[7]

The bequest itself is to the city of London, the ruthless lover who has spurned the speaker. The mockery lies in the poem's central irony: the things she wills to London are the things she is without, things London has already. Indeed she recites an extended catalogue of London's abundance: "Brave buildings, "Churches," "Pauls," and "fair streets" (28–29). When she leaves "people goodly store" (30), the list becomes a bountiful Homeric catalogue of provisions, with "Butchers" (33), "Brewers" (35), "Bakers" (36), "two Streets" full of fish (39), "Woollen" cloth (42), "Linen" (43), "Mercers" offering "silk" (47), "Goldsmiths" with their "Jewels" (51), and "Plate to furnish Cupboards with" (53). Such supply suggests demand: London's citizens are her next offering, whose "keeping craveth cost" (31). The "goodly store" of people includes the fashionable who indulge their extravagant tastes for "French Ruffs, high Pearls, Gorgets and Sleeves" (63), and those relegated to serving such indulgent buyers. Emphasizing what we call the class divide, the speaker supplies boys who sell the buyers trinkets: "For Purse or Knives, for Comb or Glass,/or any needful knack/I by the Stocks have left a Boy,/will ask you what you lack" (65–68). The street hawkers' cry "what ye lack" signifies the all-pervasive supply that the city market, or "Stocks," provides. Yet in that word we also hear "stocks," the wooden device to which miscreants were chained, suggesting the presence of crime, poverty, and punishment corrupting and monitoring the market system. Within this supply, she hints, are the less comfortable consequences of demands which exceed, and potentially disturb, the marketplace.

Such consequences begin to crowd the poem, as market demands include the stresses of a competitive environment. City ills—from sickness to social unrest—require provisions such as "Apothecaries" (93), "Physicians . . . for the sick" (95), and "cunning Surgeons" (101) to apply poultices to the wounds of those injured in duels. And the abundance of London's streets is undercut in the very way Whitney describes them. When she writes "In many places, Shops are full,/I left you nothing scant" (107–8), the end-stopped word "scant" hints at the shops' potential for lack. Her description of the Royal Mint, "At Mint, there is such store, it is/impossible to tell it" (111–12), suggests the great wealth in the Mint and also its ultimate material impenetrability for the speaker—unlike upper gentry or aristocrats, she would never be in a position to "tell" how much money the Mint holds. And even the wine she will leave only "glads" "dulled minds" (114). The disconnect between the city's material abundance and its inability to provide fully for all its inhabitants backdrop the poem's second, darker section.

The speaker scathingly bridges the poem's remaining two thirds—a satiric critique of points of failure in London's mercantile society—with a brief discussion of single male apprentices: "handsome" apprentices who "must not wed/except they leave their trade" (115–16). Referring to the formal indenture of apprenticeship to a master, she touches on one of the promises apprentices made in return for instruction, room, and board. The indenture agreement included refraining from fornication, gambling, and the haunting of alehouses,[8] promises the apprentices broke. "They oft shall seek for proper Girls,/and some perhaps shall find:/(That need compels, or lucre lures/to satisfy their mind)" (117–20), she grouses. For once the speaker will not supply a social need: for this rather unseemly demand, the apprentices are on their own. She instead provides for the "girls'" needs. Their compulsion to sell their bodies to the eager tradesmen draws the speaker's sympathy. She leaves "houses" for the girls and others in the neighborhood to "repair" and to bathe themselves "to prevent/infection of the air" (123–24).

The prostitutes' fortunes seem to spur the speaker to reflect on her own compelling financial needs, and subsequently she pauses to comment explicitly on her difficulties in the market economy. Of her own economic fate in London, she laments, "I little brought/but nothing from thee took" (131–32), itself a reprise of the poem's opening thrust blaming London for not extending her credit: "Thou never yet, would credit give/to board me for a year" ("communication," 21–22). London did not fulfill its end of their market relationship. The speaker registers her disappointment in an extended pathetic fallacy, as the poem turns from Golden Age abundance to Silver Age competition.[9] Here Whitney attributes her own sense of competition and penury to London—or in this case, to its prisons, depicted as gaining advantage through her offerings. Golden Age "provision" becomes an abundance of indigence, where London's prisons are "supplied" through her gift of prisoners:

> I wyll to prisons portions leave,
> what though but very small:
> . . . .
> And first the Counter they shall have,
> least they should go to wrack:
> Some Coggers, and some honest men
> that Sergantes draw aback.
> (137–44)

This pathetic fallacy carries some material truth, however: the speaker's freshly motivated focus on debt and debtors' prisons, while perhaps pathetic, is not entirely fallacious.[10] The poor and indebted certainly existed in London—it is just that they become, in a brilliant turn, a synecdoche for her generosity. They are the "bequest" she offers to the prisons. While to debtors' prisons she leaves people to fill them, to the Newgate prison for felons she leaves "a sessions" (150), or court hearing, to empty it out. The narrative here—the workings of justice, relayed in matter-of-fact description of the sessions' results—becomes more cynically carnivalesque. Some prisoners emerge from court with "burning near the Thumb" (154), the branding received by petty offenders as punishment; others are allowed to beg discharge fees; and finally there are "such whose deeds deserveth death" (157). All punishments are provided for: even to those on their way to execution she leaves "a Nag" (161) to carry them up Holborn Hill.

The speaker's own relationship to debt colors her descriptions of the Counter, Fleet, and Ludgate. To the debtors' prison, the Counter, she leaves cheats or "Coggers" (143), unlucky souls like herself without credit, either economic or social: "such as Friends will not them bail,/whose coyne is very thin" (145–46). From the Fleet, the prison for those found guilty in Star Chamber or Chancery, she fears a "curse" if she doesn't leave the prison—"him"—a portion (167, 166), so she bequeaths a recusant, "some papist old" and a money box for the poor. If her adversarial tone is not clear from her reluctant bequest of a dying papist, it becomes so in her subsequent provision to Ludgate, where we might interpret her bitterness at being denied credit as carrying a religious *gravitas*. We could understand her socio-economic anxieties in terminology of the covenant, and see her using Ludgate as a metaphor for heaven welcoming abject sinners, where she envisions herself in the role of the abject. She "did reserve" Ludgate for her debtor days: for when she "ever came in credit so/a debtor for to be" (181–82). Sinners admit their indebtedness to Christ as creditor, who insures atonement; and so she anticipates her indebted state.

Reading Whitney's "Wyll" through this interpretative lens is neither speculative nor entirely outlandish. In a culture in which the boundaries separating the religious and the secular were nonexistent, many late sixteenth-century readers would have read the poem in the same way. Indeed, Whitney escalates the religious tone with the intensely evocative image of shrouding, suggestive of Christ's shroud: "When days of payment did approach,/I thither meant to flee./To shroud myself amongst the rest,/that chose to dye in debt" (183–86). While indebtedness at first glace may seem to impart a weakness, in London's early market economy, exactly the opposite is true. Indebtedness is not only a desired social condition, connoting community ties, but is the yearned-for spiritual condition, related in the New Testament embrace of debt, dependence, and obligation. The voluntary recognition of obligation, familiar from Matthew 6:12, is explicitly termed "debt" in the Geneva Bible, "forgive us our debts, as we also forgive our debtors."[11] The repentant sinner, according to doctrine, confesses that she is a bankrupt, unable to discharge the least of her sins, and thus dependent upon Christ to do so. This state nonetheless remains elusive for the speaker: "Yet cause I feel myself so weak/ that none me credit dare:/I here revoke: and do it leave,/some Bankrupts to his share" (189–93). Since she cannot attain the indebted state, she cannot be imprisoned for debt; instead, she will leave her prison spot to "some bankrupt." To use the poem's operating logic, she actually will leave to Ludgate some bankrupts in her "wyll," since she herself cannot occupy a cell there. On the one hand these lines reinforce the central complaint of the poem, anger that the speaker has been denied access to London's credit networks, and is forced to leave the city. But there is also something radically aggressive in "revoking" her place in the debtors' prison. Why, after all, would she refuse the "bankrupt" state of the repentant sinner, if that is the expectation for all Christians?

Acceptance of Christian grace necessarily implies a wholesale acceptance of indebtedness, a sign of humility in the sinner. But there is no easy one-to-one correlation of this concept in secular, socio-economic reckoning. Whitney suggests that indebtedness in the secular world cannot carry the same degree of faith and acceptance as it does in Christian doctrine. Some signal of reciprocity is requested by the debtor from the creditor, for instance. Writers in the period take up business ethics in economic pamphlets and religious tracts, including casuistry manuals which allow for some measure of self-interest in economic practices.[12] But Whitney is among the first to suggest that a woman's right to London's credit networks is a secular right, distinct from accepted social proscriptions for women's public behavior. And she is the only woman, so far as we know, to do so by invoking the genre of the mock-testament.

From this point forward in the poem, the speaker claims a more active economic agency. Denied credit, she in turn refuses culpability. Like Coriolanus's radical and stoic "I banish you!" to the citizens of Rome, the testator's "I here revoke" asserts an identity separate from the economic community that at the same time hints at a wish to be accepted.[13] Like Coriolanus, who rejects the Roman populace upon whom he depends, the speaker reveals a hostility to the social norms excluding her. This gesture, however, admits to a desire for incorporation into the community's means of economic membership. She hints more explicitly at that desire in the poem's subsequent section on the book trade in London, where the tone of her bequest moves from bitterness to something more like generosity.

Thus far the sympathy informing the spirit of bequest has been undercut by the nature of the items: poultices, prisons, an old papist. It is only in envisioning the "Bookbinders by Paul's" (194) that the speaker sounds sincere—she leaves them "money" "when they from Books depart" (195–96), staging a perfect market economy. Of course her books (or those sold by her printer) get note as well: "Amongst them all, my Printer must,/have somewhat to his share:/I will my Friends there Books to buy/of him, and other ware" (197–200). When the speaker leaves money to bookbinders and leaves customers to buy her printer's books, she is subverting—or at least sidestepping—a traditional call for patronage. The poem becomes a marketing tool, a successful print advertisement for marketing her printer's books to an expanding clientele. Of course by using print in the first place, Whitney was making a radical, opportunistic move. Like Tottel, Whitney, by publishing her miscellany in print and not circulating it in manuscript, took advantage of print technology's ability to open the closed communications of an elite to a wider audience.[14] Wendy Wall has noted the significance for *Nosgay* of the miscellany, a form traditionally circulated in private exchange, among a group of elites. Wall contends that "Whitney counters the anxieties of print publication by presenting a book that replicates private textual circulation."[15] But while Whitney may reproduce private circulation in the book's form, she stages a public scenario in her poem's content, where we find a printer's marketplace full of buyers for Whitney's product. Among the advantages print offered were rapid dissemination, preservation, and amplification of a writer's output.[16] In writing a female "author's" bequest providing friends to buy her books from her printer, Whitney stages a *mise-en-abyme* in a poem she hopes will sell well and make her a popular writer.

Of course Whitney had no direct financial interest in the sale of her printed work. This would only have come by way of something like a royal grant of patent.[17] Typically, an author would receive a number of free copies of the book, including one to present to the dedicatee in hope of reward. The bookseller or stationer was the one who stood to profit: Whitney's pursuit was instead the cultural and social profit resulting from access to credit networks, if we for a moment find a parallel between the speaker's and Whitney's situations.[18] She inscribes her speaker into the sphere from which she herself has been in effect barred, giving that speaker the power to provide "friends" to buy her printer's books. The speaker substitutes the booksellers' trade as a circuit of literary transmission for the client-patron relationship. She stages a scenario of professional success that serves as a "counterfactual" to the poem's central complaint.[19] If, instead of being denied credit, she had been given the means to succeed and possibly to market more of her work to printers, she could have remained in the city. Like John Taylor, whose published pamphlets stage a "subscription scenario" in which he is cheated of his authorial profits by the Stationers' Company, Whitney recognizes discourse as a commodity.[20] She likely would have felt the pressure from recently penned vagrancy laws prohibiting within city bounds those "able to labor, having not Land or Master, nor using any lawful Merchandise Craft or Mystery whereby he or she might get his or her Living."[21] To avoid punishment for being what the law identified as a "Rouge," "Vagabond," or "Sturdy Beggar," the speaker needs the credit necessary to escape not just penury but also identification as one of these miscreant types.[22] The speaker's fantasy of perfect supply and demand in the center of the poem reflects her desire to be safe from the laws' proscriptions. Her exile and departure at the end of the poem, however, simply reinforces the laws' consequences. Here the dictates of genre and law meet, in that both the mock-testament and the vagrancy laws require the same result: the speaker's or vagrant's departure, respectively. This is one of the reasons the mock-testament is so suitable for Whitney's purposes in narrating effects of the credit crunch.

And yet many critics pass over the mock-testament entirely in their discussions of Whitney's poem. Some link Whitney's "Wyll and Testament" to the genre of the "mother's legacy," as part of a broader critical conversation about the testamentary powers of women in the Renaissance.[23] Mothers' legacies—dying mothers' bequests and last words to their children, often in the form of "advice books"—were hugely popular works, and one of the few acceptable outlets for women who wanted to publish their writing. While a few women were involved with bookselling and printing, writing was a suspect activity which carried, for women, the "social and sexual stigma of print."[24] Women's writing threatened to subvert the injunction to be chaste, silent, and obedient.[25] The most well-known "mothers' legacies," Elizabeth Grymeston's *Miscelanea, Meditations, Memoratives* (1604), Dorothy Leigh's *The Mother's Blessing* (1616), and Elizabeth Joscelin's *The Mother's Legacy to her Unborne Childe* (1624) actually became bestsellers.[26] While the later legacies were more influential, a number predate them, such as Lady Frances Abergavennny's prayers, a deathbed gift to her daughter, printed in Thomas Bentley's *Monument of Matrones* (1582). It is appropriate to link Whitney's text to these women's works, in the context of the will as a rhetorical strategy for women's published thoughts. Mostly relegated to providing translations of humanist works or the psalms, women risked public opprobrium for their literary endeavors.[27] As Wendy Wall has pointed out, "the legacy's enabling vantage point . . . became a more general cultural script for empowerment."[28] Private farewell scenes could serve as apologies for presenting final legacies that were more public in nature. The genre also allowed women to offer prophetic utterances to a reading public.

But many of the defining characteristics of the female legacy—its address to intimate family members, its advice to children, its private farewell scenes—are not found in Whitney's poem. Of course her epistles throughout *Nosgay* are addressed to family members, but "Wyll" takes quite a different tone. The underlying justification of most legacies differs significantly from Whitney's. Many focus on sacrifice for the younger generation, whereas Whitney's speaker is primarily concerned with her own gain. Grymeston's *Memoratives* for example preserves her "last speeches" to her son, and she describes herself as a "dead woman among the living," so that the will becomes a "portable *veni mecum*," a counseling voice for the child in the parent's absence.[29] The emphasis lies on the child's needs after the parent's death. Dorothy Leigh writes, "the first cause of writing, is a Motherly affection," and "[parents], some sparing from their own bellies, and . . . not caring if the whole Common-wealth be impoverished, so their children be enriched; for themselves they can bee content with meat, drink, and cloth, so that their children by their means be made rich. . . ."[30] This articulation of self-sacrifice is entirely missing from Whitney's poem, where the whole point is not sacrifice of the self, but assertive self-interest. In fact Whitney's self-interest in "Wyll" seems connected to her very lack of family ties, in direct opposition to the familial connections asserted throughout the rest of *Nosgay*.

To contextualize properly Whitney's poem, we must leave the female legacy behind and look to the mock-testament, a very different genre rooted in economic concerns of a more biting and public nature. Her title itself, "Wyll and Testament," virtually identifies it as a mock-testament, one in a genre the members of which most often were titled "[x's] Wyll and Testament," or "Last Testament."[31] Satirical, admonitory, and often vituperative, mock-testaments employ the topsy-turvy festive logic of the dead or powerless willing grotesque or extravagantly impossible legacies (parts of their own body, for instance) to those they wish to implicate in their death.

The critics recognizing Whitney's poem as a mock-testament fail to contextualize its significance for the genre's development. Lorna Hutson, who goes furthest in this direction, identifies the poem as a mock-testament, a genre, she says, "in which unreliable travellers or dying festival fools expose the madness and hypocrisy of 'things as they are' in the real world."[32] Hutson does not take this analysis much further, however.[33] Betty Travitsky does squarely place "Wyll" in the mock-testament tradition, noting that "[Whitney] can be viewed as a trend-setter for her composition of . . . a mock-testament," and concluding that as a female writer in this genre she is unique, but Travitsky does not elaborate.[34] More typical of Whitney scholars in her relative neglect of the mock-testament is Danielle Clarke who focuses attention on the conventional legacy at the expense of the mock-testament genre. "[T]he will is a legal document that substitutes for the processes of exchange engaged in by a living person, a form of writing which organizes the disposal of material goods," she argues.[35] But while admitting that the form employs the catalogue or list, Clarke sees Whitney's technique as disordered: "Her listing of places, persons, professions and commodities reinforces a sense of chaos and disorder, and she swings from area to area, and trade to trade, without any apparent sense of connection."[36] The only thread, Clarke finds, is Whitney's exclusion from the abundance. The "disorder" and absence of "connection" Clarke finds is belied by the fact that, upon closer inspection, Whitney's description of London is actually quite ordered and deliberate, employing conventions peculiar to the mock-testament. By examining these conventions we can uncover the nature of Whitney's deployment of the genre. Further, we can retrieve aspects of the mock-testament itself that suit Whitney's concerns over economic stresses of the marketplace.

As a mock-testament, Whitney's "Wyll" belongs to the genre known as the "worthless bequest," a form with its origins in the Menippean confession. Also heavily influenced by Lucianic dialogues of the dead, the Renaissance genre figured in English festive pageantry. During the Reformation, Catholic institutions would stage their own festive funerals, but the genre mostly targeted the Catholic Church, as in ballads of "Jack a Lents Testament," where uneaten herring and stockfish were "bequeathed" in a political satire against Lent.[37] And "The Wyll of the Deuyll, and Last Testament" (c. 1550) was an early Reformation attack upon the Roman Catholics in which "Beelseebub" gives his chastity to the clergy, the Church's "millions of gold" to the usurers, and relics to dead popes in Hell.[38] In other versions the fool confesses through his last will and testament, and figuratively takes himself to pieces by narrating his own dismemberment, bequeathing merriment in the revelation of his impotent, dispersed body. Whitney's "dismemberment" of London becomes more trenchant when placed squarely in this tradition. In festive mockery the victim cheerfully offers himself or herself up for consumption, with satirical disinterestedness. In *Wyl Bucke His Testament* (1560), Wyl bequeaths his throat to the hounds, his blood and guts to the woman of the house for puddings, and his muzzle to the king. The testament concludes with various recipes for cooking buck and other dishes.[39] This type of testament can be traced to a fourteenth-century Latin genre, a type known collectively as *Testamentum Asini*, or more generally the animal testament. Satirical attacks primarily on things ecclesiastical, these testaments often were composed by Goliardic clerics. When this type of literary will became fully popular in France in the fifteenth century, the genre was used both to entertain and as subtle social criticism, as in *Le Testament de la mule Barbeau*, by Henri Baude (1465) and *Le grand testament de Taste-vin* by Roy des Pions (1488).[40] In the former, an overworked, underfed mule has suffered from cold weather; death is upon him, and he wills his voice to a lawyer and his song to a curate. In the latter, "Taste-vin" leaves his walking stick to men with nagging wives and his dice and cards and other gambling implements to the town's *pipeurs*.

The genre reveals the impotence of the lower orders, the poor, and the drunken; such parody hinges on the notion of the inherent social power vested in a legal document such as the last will. The most remarkable example of the genre is Francois Villon's *Testament* (1489), in which the narrator-testator assumes a series of identities, such as the prisoner, the Christian penitent, the Job-like sufferer, the musician, the joker, and the student, among others. Villon employs the motif of growing weakness as the occasion of the will, but it is the nature of this weakness that provides a link to Whitney's work. He admits that his weakness is "more in wealth than in health" ("Trop plus de biens que de sancte").[41] The legal formula is given a specifically materialist interpretation: his bank balance is suffering. In place of the conventional praise of a patron or benefactor, Villon substitutes malediction of a Bishop, the "patron" of all the testator's woes and misfortune.[42] We hear echoes of Villon's prefatory *anti-dedicace* in Whitney's opening complaint to London.

The primary echo one hears in Whitney, however, is the genre's defining aesthetic: the list. In its enumeration of inaccessible material goods and luxuries that highlight the speaker's poverty, the mock-testament emphasizes not the testator's disposal of wealth, but his or her lapse into poverty. In the contrast between the generosity of the multiple offerings and the seemingly irreversible dwindling of the testator's vital powers lies the genre's aggressive agon. Mock-testaments also employ the extensive list to implicate, within a festive sheer abundance, a moral barrenness. Often their purpose is to foreground the reduction of life to the resources of economic survival. Whitney's version of this reduction is of course her description of multiple debtors' prisons, to which she leaves "portions" of prisoners as a type of sustenance to feed the Counter, Newgate, and the Fleet. With each piece of evidence for credit failures, she transforms the city's abundance to a *copia* of punishment. Exposing the city's landscape of prisons and punishment through rhetorical amplification, the speaker foregrounds market failure. The satire excoriates not only the prodigality that sends debtors to prison, but also the exclusivity of parts of the London economy that offer such abundance, an exclusive club she nonetheless craves.

This ambivalence—scoffing at upper-class wealth while implicitly desiring riches to bestow—is characteristic of the mock-testament. But what makes the genre most suitable for Whitney's purposes is its more basic identification with "economy"—the exchange of material goods and the attendant social complications. Others after Whitney would use the genre to update centuries-old traditions of economic satire and complaint. Thomas Nashe, for example, in *Summers' Last Will and Testament* (1600), depicts the economic anxiety of Will Summers. Summers wishes that he had "some issue," imagining the economic security of an inheritance transferred from him through generations after his death. But there is no chance of such a future for Will, and Nashe's work combines the grave implications of material loss with the reckless gaiety of self-consuming festivity. Summers alludes to a much earlier mock-testament, one (among others) which may have influenced Whitney, "Gyllian of Braynfords will, where she bequeathed a score of farts amongst her friends."[43] The reference is to *Jyl of Braintfords Testament* by Robert Copland, written in 1535.[44] Copland's poem was influenced by the medieval fool-catalogues or fool-lists such as those incorporated in Robert de Balsac's *Le Chemin de L'hospital* (1502), which provides a listing of types who are likely, through improvidence, generosity, or laziness, to end in the poorhouse.[45] Those excoriated in the French lists include time-wasters, dreamers, the disagreeable, the negligent, and the overgenerous. Economic success and a hard-headed realism is valued in the figure of Jyl, stingy and judgmental. Firmly in the tradition of the "worthless bequest," Jyl bequeaths farts to both the lazy and the prodigal, such as "He that suffereth all maner of offence/and loseth his good through negligence/Shall have a fart for a recompence."[46] Like Jyl's trenchant, ironic generosity with her farts, Whitney's speaker's lavish heaping of prisons, papists, and hospitals upon the city of London adds insult to injury, willing to London nothing London needs.

Whitney's "worthless bequest" is not as purely admonitory as many of its models, however. In her critique of the hazards of London's marketplace are notes of self-incrimination. Her dystopia of perfect market supply (providing for imprisonment and even death) reflect the speaker's fraught, conflicted perception of debt relations. She desires the extension of credit but not its ramifications. One way that Whitney registers this paradox is to posit the conflicting claims of law and credit. The speaker sees the economic system in London through the lens of risk, a risk that drives many into debt. These debts are desirable on the one hand because they represent economic and social connections, but dangerous on the other when unpayable. It is this double bind, this economic paradox to which she addresses her poem. Thus she's harnessing a familiar satiric genre to represent the conflicting claims of the credit crunch upon the female author. As one of many attempting to navigate her way through the terms of credit in the marketplace, Whitney registers the urgency of achieving these terms in one's favor, a factor newly pervasive for many of London's workers.[47] She simultaneously implicates London's competitive market workings and her own individual dilemma. In doing so, however, she asserts the social capital of indebtedness across the strata of London's classes.

The value of indebtedness does not necessarily apply to marriage transactions, however, where the speaker deliberately separates economics from affect.[48] There she willfully represses a model of social relations based on emotional commitment, in favor of economic rational disinterestedness. Her use of the term "portion" is a case in point, through which she foregrounds the economic contingencies of marriage, if we read "portion" in the sense of "marriage portion" or dowry and not just a "share," the original meaning of "portion." When she says "I wyll to prisons portions leave" (137) she yokes two very different notions of "provision" in an eerie metaphor: 1) the "portion" of an estate that a bride's father provides as a dowry and 2) the fulfillment of prisons' material needs. In her weird equation, the estate "portion," a stand-in for the bride's value to the groom and a means for the couple's economic security, is imagined as a hoard of people served up as an offering for the prisons' legacy, for the ability of the prison as an institution to thrive. The marriage portion, then, is relegated to a carceral tool.

By placing her work within a genre that would implicitly join her poem with the likes of "Jyl's" carnivalesque festivity, Whitney could avoid being labeled an "unruly" woman or a scold, which brought formidable sanctions.[49] But she also could rail against an economic system while at the same time participating in it, thus inviting reading according to the norms of Carnival, which allowed for a revisionary impulse while admitting an ultimate return to "authority."[50] In wanting access to the very channels she targets, Whitney is not necessarily calling for their dismantling; instead she asserts a parallel channel of cultural capital, by way of her poem and its "treasurye."

And yet the seriousness of the speaker's ultimate conundrum—penury, exile from London—may belie an entirely "festive" reading of the testament. This leads to the question of whether mock-testaments in general were meant to be read in a festive light. The formula by which festive misrule *temporarily* usurps legitimate authority is generally not in play in mock-testaments. Lorna Hutson's reading of "The Testament of the Buck" and "The Testament of the Crab-Tree" as "festive disintegration[s] of the fool-king" misinterprets such festive conventions, according to Edward Wilson. He finds that Hutson's analysis distorts the poems: Wilson says that neither "the utterly miserable, and far from festive, crab-tree" *nor* the buck are associated with regal authority or kingship at all.[51] In mock-testaments generally, the testator is not represented as a temporary ruler, and his or her authority is based on absence. For Whitney, the testator is excluded from provision, from London's credit channels, and perhaps (we are led to imagine) even life itself. The occasion of the poem, after all, is irrevocable exclusion. The outsider status of one refused credit in the credit-oriented economy persists through the end of the poem, as does the harsh critique of the status quo and of the exclusionary "authority" of those refusing to extend credit. This outsider identity of most testators in the mock-testament genre may have been one of its most attractive features for Whitney. The origins of the genre can be traced, as mentioned above, to the poems of an outsider group, the Goliardic clerics. A vagrant, vagabond class of hedge-priests, they were monks out of the cloister, who had taken to nomadic life.[52] Their early versions of the mock-testament, twelfth-century lyrics, were outspoken satires directed against a distrusted authority, the corrupt clergy. That outsider status was, through the years, transmitted in the fact that the speaker was often a marginalized figure. But too the speaker's dramatic point of view—as dead or dying—makes him or her a *de facto* outsider. The testator's only authority—the power vested in the document of the testament itself—is located in the certainty that he/she has no possibility of return: only the testator's death authorizes the will's provision. Whitney, in choosing the mock-testament and this formula, suggests that the speaker cannot return to London's marketplace. It is only from such a perspective that she passes judgment on it. With the very absurdity of this position—the absent presence of the omniscient observer—Whitney highlights a crux for ambitious female writers. Since their ambition is frowned upon, it is not in their interest to be vocal about their ambitions. Given this situation, Whitney's strategy in voicing her ambition is to do so as a writer who has failed, and then to reflect upon the cultural conditions surrounding that failure. So here Whitney's speaker is not merely the onlooker, commenting on the city's dangers as John Donne does in his *Satire I*, but ultimately she is a departing outsider.[53] She voices her ambition as such an outsider, as one who has not been able to achieve her professional goals, because that is the most acceptable way to appear ambitious—as one who has failed.

One might expect such an admission of failure to come from a woman returned to a domestic household, exiled from the London marketplace. Instead of reflecting from the realm of private domesticity, however, the speaker is positioned as a departing outsider: first as an exile according to the poem's dramatic narrative; and secondly as a dying or dead speaker, in line with generic requirements of the mock-testament. Owing to her ultimate exile from domesticity, her familiarity with London's street life, and her public disposal of her "goods," her voice can be interpreted as more public than private. Indeed it may have been so understood at the time Whitney was writing. With an eye to contemporary definitions of "public" and "private," we may see how the speaker's identity as a public figure supports her "outsider" status. While some scholars claim that the distinction between public and private did not fully exist at the time, there is evidence that contemporaries framed the distinction with some clarity.[54] Public business, transacted for the benefit of the community, was differentiated from private household work. James Cleland outlined the notion of "public" office as opposed to private, domestic occupations: "a private person is bound to honour those who are publike, and in office."[55] John Ferne categorized "publique person[s]" or officials, naming military, church, and civil office holders, e.g. judges, magistrates, mayors, soldiers, bailiffs, bishops, and clerics.[56] And in 1630, Richard Brathwaite explained the categories as types of vocation that a gentleman may assume: "Publike, when imployed in affaires of State. . . . Private, when in domesticke businesse he is detained."[57] While women were generally advised to remain at home, prohibited from holding public office, meant to remain loyal to their "domesticall duties" outlined by William Gouge among others, London was of course full of the enterprising activity of wives and daughters of shopkeepers, assistants, prostitutes, and servants.[58] And certainly women crowded the streets for the public activity of hearing sermons, visiting churches, attending fairs, and buying goods at the Royal Exchange.[59]

Early modern women, including Whitney herself, articulated their sense of social roles according to this public-private distinction, scholars have found. Some place Whitney on the private side of this divide. For instance, Ann Rosalind Jones stresses Whitney's poetry as having a private rather than a public significance.[60] Retha Warnicke traces a certain self-imposed retiredness in the writings of women's private diaries (though her examples are mainly taken from the Stuart period), but other critics are not so ready to generalize in such a way.[61] Patricia Phillippy argues that Whitney remains between the public and private spheres.[62] And Elaine Beilin has distinctly identified Whitney as one of a few who "reposition" their work "in the domain of public poetry."[63] The public sphere Beilin claims for Whitney is one, she says, that Whitney created: the poet made "a public place for women's intellectual work," where we can see in her collection of epistles and poems a larger message whereby she replaces her sister's occupation of "huswyfery" with her own job as a writer.[64] For Beilin, the value of Whitney's work is that it serves as metaphorical commerce. But the poem can be viewed not just as symbolic commerce, but as actual commerce too. It works as an actual unit of exchange for the credit she's been denied. In other words, if her poem is read by readers who buy the miscellany in which it appears, and demand rises for her work, the poem is a commodity that in its popularity creates more demand for her work. This is not to deny the poem's value as symbolic commerce, but its function as a commodity should not be discounted.

But the role of Whitney's "Wyll" as a commodity, as a material act of exchange, coupled with its importance as a document in London's growing credit economy, should not overshadow its significance for late sixteenth-century satire. Whitney identifies herself as a satirist by the very fact that she employs the mock-testament genre. Like early fifteenth-century English satirists, Whitney offers a Piers Plowman type, symbolizing the new ethical ideas of the period. In fact some early mock-testament testators, such as Colin Blowbol, have been identified with Piers Plowman.[65] And though we find her base comparisons of a sordid London world firmly ensconced in later writers, often we see references to the originality of such approaches, as with Thomas Nashe's *The Unfortunate Traveller* (1594) or Thomas Dekker's *The Gulls Hornbook* (1609). But here is Whitney, as early as 1573, appealing to a contemporary interest in the criminal underworld that includes the laboring poor, the vagrant, and the imprisoned.

On the one hand, Whitney's poem belongs to the tradition of "rogue literature" first made popular in the 1550s and 1560s by such writers as John Awdeley, Thomas Harman, and Robert Greene, but we don't often find "Wyll" included in that genre. In another sense, Whitney's place in early modern satire might best be defined as part of the "female jest" tradition, recently explored by Pamela Allen Brown. Brown analyzes the strategies whereby "jesting links the drama of neighborhood with theatre itself," describing ways in which local conflicts get expressed in dramatic and literary forms.[66] Whitney imagines the dramas of London's byways of credit and penury through the literary "theatre" of the mock-testament, with its attendant generic imperatives. Thus Whitney suggests a double role for herself as author: as a monitor or reporter of credit networks, and as a satirist carrying on the mock-testament tradition, changing the terms of the genre as given.[67] The shift in genre that Whitney implicitly urges is one that moves the mock-testament into a credit age. Poems in the genre traditionally critiqued the economic, political, religious, or legal authority that benefited from the death of the testator, thus implicitly calling for a return to a society free of such greed or corruption. Her voice, however, goes beyond that of a "Piers" and is not just that of the country simpleton calling for a return to a debt-free golden age; she calls instead for the risks and rewards attending credit relationships—and she demands a new kind of social accountability. Just as the mock-testament often emphasizes elements of physical deterioration in terms of dispersed items or goods, Whitney highlights the aspects of a deteriorating London marketplace in terms of failed actors when crucial credit relationships are neglected. In the end she asserts a normative ideal: she presents her speaker as an actor in a neighborly, moral community where loans and debts are necessary tools for healthy participation in the marketplace.

The mock-testament is perfectly suited for this message. As a medium, it works through shattering social stratification, and anatomizing society and its seemingly stable types and professions.[68] In fact mirroring new social configurations was one function of the Menippean genre, and the mock-testament joined in the Renaissance Menippean tradition by illustrating the plight of newly emerging social groups.[69] In order to portray the condition of the lower sort most forcefully, Whitney chose to position her speaker as an outsider to their conundrum: they experienced debt and imprisonment. These are dubious goals she nonetheless regrets failing to achieve, since indebtedness is a condition the lack of which forces her speaker from London. But hers is not a London only bleared with trade and smeared with toil: in her vision of a supply of buyers for her printers' books, for example, she paints a marketplace that works. That notion of a workable capitalist society, however, necessitates open credit channels. Whitney is original in her specific treatment of credit. Her critique, less than assailing a failed system, more urgently asks of London's citizens a certain civic responsibility.

Her "Wyll" attempts to meet that responsibility. As a work of literature, it proposes the ethical consideration of those in need. As a commodity, it is a material offering ostensibly designed to gain credit. In the end, however, it seals the loss of that credit, exposing one result of failure in the marketplace. Nonetheless, it not only represents, but it *is* an economic transaction. She represents in the poem a testamentary complaint, but also transacts a poetic testament. In other words, the poem as a testament is an economic transaction through which she nearly obtains, then loses credit. We can read Whitney's poetry of economic exchange as an act of economic exchange. It rehearses and advertises economic and social loss, but does so in a way that proclaims her status as a writer who not only belongs, but who pursues her self-interest, in the public realm.

III

Aemilia Lanyer's "The Description of Cooke-ham" (1611) likewise uses the misfortune of economic disadvantage as an occasion for critique, in this case for poetic plaint. Cookeham, the estate leased by Lanyer's patron Margaret

Clifford, countess of Cumberland, symbolized loss to Lanyer because the Countess and her extended female community had to leave the estate in an apparent property dispute with the Countess's estranged husband.[70] And in the opening dedication of her verse collection *Salve Deus Rex Judaeorum* in which "Cooke-ham" appears, Lanyer contrasts her present inability to secure patronage at James's court to her earlier favor under Elizabeth.[71] Lanyer's poem is often cited as the first published "Country House poem," which may or may not have been influenced by Ben Jonson's "To Penshurst."[72] But unlike Jonson's poem, where the lady's virtues endow the estate with a grace of hospitality that opens it to the community, Lanyer's poem highlights the contingent nature of the women's relationship to the estate.[73] The reader should follow the lead of Alastair Fowler, who renames the genre "Estate" poetry, because it is primarily concerned, with the pastoral, property, and the implications of ownership and stewardship, rather than being focused on a family "house."[74] In fact we can conceive Lanyer's Estate poem as a distinctively female-voiced complaint over disrupted property rights, a response to an increasingly hostile legal environment in England concerning inheritance practices for "heiresses at law."[75]

At first glance Lanyer might seem odd to pair with Whitney. Possessed of the social advantages from which Whitney did not have, Aemilia (Bassano) Lanyer was known at court, and received favors from Elizabeth I as well as money and gifts as mistress to Henry Carey, Lord Hunsdon, the Queen's Lord Chamberlain. Lanyer however was solidly of the middling sort, born the daughter of Baptist Bassano, a Jewish lute player from Venice and court musician to Elizabeth.[76] Her father and mother died in 1576 and 1587, respectively, leaving Aemilia £100 and a few sundry goods from her mother. When she became pregnant by Henry Carey she married Alphonso Lanyer, another of Elizabeth's court musicians, for appearance's sake. While both Aemilia and Alphonso proved ambitious for social advancement and patronage—Alphonso joined the Earl of Essex's expedition to the Azores in 1597 and campaign in Ireland in 1599 in hoped of financial reward—neither were truly successful. After Alphonso's death in 1613, Aemilia was pressed financially to pursue in court the income from her husband's hay- and straw-weighing patent.[77]

Sharing with Whitney the anxieties of the poet struggling for inclusion in a network (Whitney, credit; Lanyer, patronage), Lanyer too wrote about those pressures. While both pursued patronage, each used her poetry to point in explicit terms to the very lack of patronage that kept her in pursuit of it. And they used strikingly similar formulations to do so. Indeed Lanyer's "Cooke-ham" opens, like Whitney's "Wyll," with a gesture to exile and abandonment. Leaving a potentially profitable environment, Lanyer laments, "Farewell, (sweet *Cooke-ham)*"—a keynote for any elegiac valediction.[78] She immediately foregrounds the economic favor she found there—"where I first obtain'd/Grace" (1–2)—and from which she now feels exiled. The tone of her farewell, made plaintful with the phrase "never shall my sad eyes again behold" (9), cues readers to reflect on the causes of this loss. The loss is, of course, given a local habitation and name, as she says farewell not only to Cookeham Estate but also to the source and occasion of her patronage. "Farewell (sweet *Cooke-ham*) . . . Where princely Palace will'd me to indite" (1, 5). "Princely Palace" is not a residence itself but instead refers to the Countess who "will'd" her to write the poem. In other words, this work was commissioned. While it is likely that Lanyer was at pains to acknowledge explicitly her patron here, she simultaneously uses the poem's opening to rhetorically yoke patronage with loss.

Lanyer foregrounds abundance to emphasize concomitant paucity and lack, giving her poem much the same argumentative structure as Whitney's "Wyll." Cookeham is first described in Golden Age idealization, in Virgilian Georgic mode, to make its loss more poignant. One can in fact trace the Georgic models, both specific and general: Virgil's *sponte sua* motif, in "Trees that of free will lift themselves" (*Georgics* ii.47) are Lanyer's "Trees . . . with fruits, with flowers" that "shade the bright sun" from her patron's eyes (23, 26).[79] The estate's plenitude of self-sufficient resources are amplified, like the "unbought dainties" in *Georgics* iv.132–33.[80] The spontaneous oblations of tributary fish where "the swelling Banks deliver'd all their pride" (43) and the land's natural furniture, where," each Arbor, Bank, each Seat, each stately Tree,/Thought themselves honor'd" (45–46), paint the Countess's leased estate as a hortulan Eden, emphasizing the poet's impulse to recover Paradise. The fertility implied in "swelling Banks" makes the typical Georgic gesture, joining fecundity and generosity with the Lady of the Estate, who has brought with her the new Golden Age.[81]

In Lanyer's hands, however, fertility is troubled and disrupted. The possibility of fulfillment does initially present itself: Anne Clifford, the countess' progeny, does reside on the estate. And the family tree, like Jonson's Lady Oak at Penshurst, here "that stately Tree" (53), stands at a high point on the estate, offering the Countess "goodly Prospects," and protection and fame, suggested by its comparisons to a "comely Cedar" (57), and a "Palm" (61). The tree emblematizes the poet's connection to her patron, in an odd economy involving a kiss deposited there by the Countess and withdrawn by Lanyer: " [you] with a chaste, yet loving kisse tooke leave,/Of which sweet kiss I did it soon bereave" (165–66). Yet a number of the myths used to describe the Countess undercut any sense of familial unity and fecundity. The Countess is compared to the Phoenix (44), suggesting solitary self-propagation, and on a few occasions to Philomela (31, 189), in the latter instance naming a bird singing a sorrowful ditty after the Countess has left the estate. The mournful song carries the association of the Petrarchan Spring Poem, relating sorrow in Spring to love-sorrow, but allusion to Philomela also necessarily brings with it associations of rape, muteness, and silence. Philomela wove when she could not speak, perhaps associating Lanyer's text—as a coded complaint—with Philomela's tapestry of sorrow.

Lanyer vexes the vision of happy service at the estate, as well. Disturbances to the estate poem's *beatus-ille* tradition, where the pastoral community of social equals exists in harmony, nag insistently throughout the poem.[82] Like Whitney's implication of London with its debtors' prisons and struggling fruitwives and whores, Lanyer hints at a disquiet on the estate that implicates the Countess. Animals' fears are anthropomorphized into the fears of nervous courtiers: "The pretty Birds would oft come to attend thee,/Yet fly away for fear they should offend thee" (47–48); "little creatures . . . fearful of the Bowe in your faire Hand,/Would run away" (49, 51–52). Even the "Hill, vales, and woods" appear "your honor to salute,/Or to preferred some strange unlook'd for sute" (68–70). These and other examples temper the general epideictic. And the demise of life on the estate is blamed on the Countess's departure: "these sad creatures, powerless to receive/Your favor when with grief you did depart" (152–53). Here Lanyer hearkens to the Ovidean mode of complaint, detailing the effects of unrequited love on shepherd and nature—a model she might have found in the poems collected in *England's Helicon* (1600). But "Cooke-ham" does not conclude with a tone that might honor the Countess as Astrea, Spenser's goddess who leaves the earth, making it barren. In fact when Lanyer blames "Unconstant Fortune" (103) for her inability to still be near the Countess's daughter Anne, "To honorable Dorset now espows'd" (95), she begins to point to social inequity—the heart, it seems, of her complaint.

"Unconstant Fortune" is blamed as she who, Lanyer says, "casts us down in so low a frame:/Where our great friends we cannot daily see,/So great a difference is there in degree" (104–106). Lamenting that "the lowest always are above" (110) the higher-born in the love they show their counterparts, Lanyer then abruptly leaves off, invoking the humility topos: "My Wit too weak to conster of the great" (112). The poem strikes a tense note here, registering the disharmony of a tension between orders, even as it celebrates the paradisal state where "We may behold the Heavens . . . And loving heaven that is so far above,/May in the end vouchsafe us entire love"

(114–116). Like Whitney who emphasized her own bad luck in contrast to her beloved London—to whom she wills "good Fortune" (283)—Lanyer contrasts her station with her patron's.

Emphasis upon division between estates is not an unusual element in estate poetry. But while such poems often celebrate the "natural order" of hierarchy, they do so in a way that lauds the generosity of the higher-born. For Lanyer, the departure from the estate of the Countess and her community of women disrupts any emblem of generosity the estate might once have symbolized. Generally Estate Poems celebrate a fruitful inheritance, represented in the land's abundance that institutionally is a result of the virtuous efforts of many. This historical awareness is gathered in images of enduring fruit and trees with family or genealogical associations. Often such poems culminate in an explicit eulogy of the family's virtues. But in "Cookeham" the landscape turns cold and unproductive, so that nothing lives on. "Each thing did unto sorrow frame" (132) when the women left. When she describes that "The trees/Forsooke both flowers and fruit" (133–34), she see them as martyrs attempting to prevent the Countess's departure: "they cast their leaves away,/Hoping that pity would have made you stay" (141–42) and then almost as grotesque lepers begging for alms: "Show[ing] their disasters, languishing in fears:/A swarthy riveld ryne all over spread,/Their dying body half alive, half dead" (144–46). Some read this as a critique of male owners who have caused the women to leave the estate, and the flora to languish, and indeed this was the case. But the poem's turn does not hinge on blaming men. Instead the emphasis is on the poet's grief.

The valedictory and elegiac mode of grief is Lanyer's defining mode here. "And yet it grieves me that I cannot be/Near unto her" (99–100), she laments. The grief is repeated—"Whereof depriv'd, I evermore must grieve" (125)-—in a way that merges it with complaint as the poet identifies with the trees that "yet can procure no pity" (190). With "pity" Lanyer reaches more directly to the Petrarchan pang of loss that drives the poet to lament, describe, and pursue at length the beloved's elusive "pittie." But the basis for the insistence on articulating and recounting grief is made clear in her third assertion, "I now must tell the grief you did conceive/At their departure" (128–29). Here Lanyer speaks for the land, for the estate, in a formulation suggestive of epic "telling" or "singing" the history of a place and its events. Alluding to the estate's grief as something it did "conceive" and that the poet "tells," she treats grief as progeny, perhaps the only progeny left of the Cookeham estate. Interestingly her complaint has been transferred to a third party: the property that grieves Clifford's loss. We recall the source of that loss has been named, in line 147 where Lanyer addresses the Countess directly to say "But your occasions call'd you so away," suggesting resentment that she heeded the business that called her away. As in Whitney's poem, the "effects" described in the poem express "causes," in this case the Countess's "occasions."

Her final poetic claim at the poem's conclusion illumines the logic of her displacement of the complaint onto the estate itself. "This last farewell to Cooke-ham here I give,/When I am dead thy name in this may live" (205–06). Lanyer employs Nichols Grimalde's model of complaint, itself imitated from de Bellay in *Tottel*, where time's ravages are redeemed in the descriptions of Rome. But by predicating the immortality of Cookeham on the poem's existence after her death, she foregrounds her vocation. Only through her timeless poem will Cookeham live. The poem has been produced at the "hest" (207) of Clifford, whose virtues, Lanyer claims, lodge in the poet's "unworthy breast" (208). It's an odd line, if primarily for the fact that the Countess's virtues are not said to lie in the poem. They lodge instead in the breast of the poet, and, Lanyer continues, "ever shall, so long as life remains,/ Tying my heart to her by those rich chains" (209–210). Clifford's virtues live only as long as Lanyer lives, and Lanyer ends with a reference to her own agency in yoking her heart to the Countess's by "rich chains." Two points emerge from this statement. Immediately we feel the stark contrast between the eternized Cookeham, which lives on in the poem after the poet dies, and the contracted life of Clifford's "virtues," the vitality of which is limited by the duration of the poet's life. Then there is the difficulty of the referent of "those rich chains." They could be, simply, the lines of poetry. Some read the lines as referring to the chains of platonic virtue.[83] We may be meant to read Clifford's virtues as the "rich chains" which tie the poet's heart to Clifford. But the line can also be read more darkly as a sort of bribe, if we read the phrase "rich chains" in its most corruptly material way, as the money from Clifford figuratively keeping the poet alive. Thus Lanyer will write well of Clifford, "tying [her] heart" to her, as long as she keeps paying or supporting her. Read even more bleakly, the line's literal message is that Clifford's patronage keeps the poet alive, period.

Lanyer's assertion for Cookeham's poetic immortality applies both to the estate and to its exiled inhabitants. Clifford was forced from the estate and Lanyer was left without patronage and community. The poem adumbrates Clifford's lost access to Cookeham, but also Lanyer's lost access to Clifford. The poem recalls the moment of departure that probably occurred when Margaret Russell, countess of Cumberland, and her daughter Anne Clifford moved to a Russell estate before beginning the lengthy litigation by which she and her daughter would pursue property rights to family lands.[84]

The removal of the Clifford women from Cookeham underlies the conditions of the poem's creation. In this context the poem attests to the historical fact of the fraught relationship of women and property.[85] Lady Anne Clifford, for one, would in future years become engaged in an extended legal battle to claim property denied her by her father's will. If we take Alastair Fowler's definition of the Estate genre as primarily concerned with property and ownership, we can read this poem as one example of that genre, inflected to depict, in part, the struggles of early modern women for estate ownership.

Lanyer's economic complaint over "dead" or lost property might be read as one text in the history of lost property rights. While some historians claim that women gained property rights from the fourteenth to seventeenth centuries, others see the period as one of the decline of women's rights over land.[86] The latter view holds that the early modern period saw developments in landed inheritance that increasingly edged out the rightful female owner in favor of the male. Both sets of historians agree that descent of land to female heirs was disrupted by a variety of methods, such as the development of jointure and wills, which could determine heirs other than common law heirs.[87]

The history of aristocratic inheritance is one of male elites circumventing common law rules that favored women. Since in the absence of sons, daughters inherited according to intestate rules of succession, daughters were eligible to inherit in about 25 percent of cases. Yet records show that in the seventeenth century, daughters of elite families inherited estates in only 5 percent of cases. Lady Anne Clifford exemplifies the postponement of heiresses. Whereas many historians have pointed to Clifford and her £17,000 inheritance as proof of the rise in levels of inheritance in seventeenth-century England, her case actually provides evidence for the opposite condition, the decline of female inheritance. According to the Statute of Wills, she ought to have received approximately £33,000 of her family's £100,000 estate.[88] She was an heir, or what Eileen Spring has termed an "heiress-at-law." Despite what should have been her clear legal right to her property, Clifford had to contend for her rights against her uncle. Her claim to ancestral lands as her father's only living heir was fraught with conflict. The lands were willed by her father George Clifford, 3rd Earl of Cumberland, collaterally, to his brother Francis Clifford, the next Earl of Cumberland, to revert to Anne if Francis' line produced no male heirs.[89] Since the lands had been entailed during the reign of Edward II (meaning they were to pass directly to the descendant, not collaterally), Anne's mother argued that George did not have the right to will them to his brother. Anne carried on a lifelong struggle to maintain her rights as a landowner: we have her diary entries detailing her arguments not only with the archbishop of Canterbury but with James I himself, insisting that she will not part with Westmoreland. Eventually she received rights to her land only when all other claimants had died. Her experience gives one example of how women were often barred from the general common law precept of entitlement.

To highlight women's troubles concerning property rights is not to assert their general economic disenfranchisement across the board: we should not overstate the case. Single women did occasionally hold parochial office where it rotated among local property owners.[90] And roughly 20 percent of all households were in fact headed by women. Women were not without power and Lanyer was of course not one meek voice in a storm of economic disaster for female writers.

She did, however, see the need to code and temper her criticisms of the economic and legal impediments to women inheriting and owning property. Instead of identifying Lanyer's work as an example of a radical "defiance" of patriarchal strictures, we have observed the ways in which it accommodates itself to current notions and to familiar literary models. Lanyer poses no explicit challenge in "Cooke-ham," after all, regarding women's property rights. But she implicitly "negotiates."[91] Of course the poem speaks more centrally to her own private financial concerns in securing patronage, and she would be no stranger herself to legal battles over women's rights to business profits.[92] But the focus on the loss of Cookeham more broadly suggests the legal and financial strains aristocratic women faced under ever-increasing disenfranchisement. "The Description of Cooke-ham" details the symptoms of that disenfranchisement: the weakening of patronage through the loss of ownership in the sure foundation of its power, its economic and social base, property.

Because these poets focus on the place or property from which they are exiled—Whitney's speaker from London and Lanyer from Cookeham—we must interpret their loss primarily as mediated through property. The speakers declare their loss of credit, loss of patronage, and lack of community. Readers are encouraged to search for the causes of these wrongs, and the complaint genre further signals readers to recall the private, emotional pain of the spurned lover. Whitney's speaker's exile derives from her lack of credit (and its attendant social connections); Lanyer's solitude is rooted in her loss of patronage (and its attendant social connections). Like good complainants, they seize on the solitude and exploit it for the purposes of their economic grievances. They implicate their environments for their failures, as a way to express the "causes" for their painful "effects."

But at the end of both poems, the speakers betray their own social needs and their own complicity in difficult economic relationships by returning to the world of social demands. Each does not merely rely on the poem to serve as her transport to immortality by embracing fully her solitude and privation. Lanyer is tied to Clifford by those "rich chaines" and Whitney's speaker battles greedy relatives who, she suggests, will attempt to change her will. So both poets cite the horizon of exile—a vista of independence—that could indeed release them from the burden of public pursuits. But each in the end returns to the troubling human connections that exist in any market community. The interjections at the end of both poems assert not only the social, public demands upon these poets' creative endeavors, but also the public nature of their work. The moments also attest to the heart of their enterprise: the necessity of their own economic self-interest. Lanyer must pursue the patronage that perpetuates—indeed depends upon—the social inequities she resists, and Whitney's speaker, by asserting her will in her "Wyll," must wrangle with relatives over that legacy. Both poets' endeavors are implicated in the economies that they, at times, deride. They negotiate this precarious position most skillfully, I have been suggesting, by way of genre.

By joining private concerns with more "public" genres, both poets offer a public authority for their private economic distress. But they do so primarily through the latent properties of each genre, rather than solely in manifest articulations. Both writers stake a rather public and commercial claim: a claim for financial reward and a claim for necessary risks taken in endeavors both authorial and economic. Their arguments, broadly understood, participate in a larger discourse concerning not only female assertions of poetic power in the public realm, but also of economic self-interest itself. The poetic aesthetic at work in these poems—one that joins public and private economic discourse—serves as a counter-example to a culture described by one critic as a place where "the rise of the wealthy merchant class created a separation between the public world of the men and the private one of women."[93] The pervasiveness of that separation is called into question when we examine the writings of women like Lanyer and Whitney. Understanding their efforts as representative of female writers in the marketplace, be it those seeking access to credit networks or those desiring stable patronage relationships, may lead us to link more closely, if not to span, those two worlds.

Chapter Five

"My Bloody Creditor": *The Merchant of Venice* and the Lexicon of Credit

In Shakespeare's *The Merchant of Venice,* Antonio and Shylock ostensibly use credit differently. Portia's question, "Which is the Merchant, and which the Jew?" rephrased "Which is the creditor, and which the usurer?" begs the question: we are to assume that creditors are different from usurers, not only different in practice but different in type.[1] More stereotype than type, the usurer/Jew figure, however, has no real equivalent "creditor" character in early modern drama.[2] How are "bad" creditors—or debtors, for that matter—distinguished from "good" ones? Antonio, while displaying Christian generosity, is nonetheless prodigal in his ventures. Bassanio is only saved from being an immoral debtor—from causing the death of his creditor—by Portia's legal maneuverings. And Portia, while not typically dubbed a creditor, shifts the balance of obligation in her favor. In controlling, to her advantage, the credit of all economic agents by the play's end, Portia is not assumed to be greedy or self-interested, but instead generous and merciful.

Critics are divided on the morality involved in Portia's righting the credit balances, including her own, at the plays' conclusion.[3] One line of argument holds that morally attractive credit behavior accords with social estate: that aristocrats like Portia, entitled to economic virtues such as hospitality and generosity, are inclined to them by temperament.[4] In some plays, though, economic "types" are defined less by status than by behavior. If we look at the lexicon of credit—ways in which credit terminology is deployed—we see characters using credit to position themselves socially in ways that often upset preordained hierarchies. As characters both complain about and compliment lending practices, their judgments hone the definition of "credit" as it develops in this period. Such judgments find their parallel in Theophrastian characters that satirize economic "types," but that pay more attention to specific behaviors than to social order or to general, inherent traits.[5] Thus the character, originally a genre favored by courtiers and rooted in class distinctions, begins by the 1620s to define economic types such as the irresponsible creditor or the exploitative debtor as much by their credit practices as by their degree, or "sort." In the early seventeenth century, the intermingling of these two genres—plays and characters—shaped the credit lexicon. This is evident, for example, in the ways "creditor" is alternately a synonym and an antonym for "usurer" and in the way a character such as Portia uses this lexicon to her advantage. This language of credit becomes increasingly important to the growing "culture of credit" in early modern England, a culture identified by Craig Muldrew as reordering notions of community.[6] In the early modern community, where the social ethic of credit—defined as trust—became increasingly important, fictional characters expressed social pressure towards the responsible use of credit, emphasizing community-oriented behaviors. This early seventeenth-century shift in the credit lexicon is apparent not only in actual uses and variants of the word "credit," but in plot configuration and in character relationships. Thus I use "lexicon" broadly, encompassing vocabulary, a repertoire of behaviors, and a body of stories used to distinguish types of creditors and debtors.

I

The Merchant of Venice explores the two predominant definitions of credit during the late sixteenth century: first, general communal faith or trust in an individual; and second, a loan symbolizing trust in a buyer's ability to pay at a future time.[7] Bassanio both needs Antonio's "credit," or a loan, to woo Portia; he also wants to be trusted, or "credited," by Portia when he swears his love to her after the ring trick. Both, of course, involve reputation. Credit was, in fact, primarily defined as "trust" in the late sixteenth century. In his 1556 translation of Cicero's *De Officiis*, Nicholas Grimalde translated *fides*, or "trust" as "credit": "credit is given to just, and trustie men (that is) to good men," Grimalde wrote.[8] The sort of trust signified by the word credit was a communal, neighborly trust: one maintained respect to the extent that one fulfilled one's promises and debts. At stake was one's reputation. Though many advice pamphlets stressed this sort of trust, one common criticism of merchants was that their materialism blinded them to any ethic of cooperation or generosity. In an attempt to defend merchants against this popular criticism, Daniel Price, chaplain to James I's sons, stressed that merchants venture their personal credit at great personal risk. In his 1607 sermon "The Merchant," Price compares his own sermon writing to treacherous sea travel: he is a holy merchant who has "ventured [his] credit to the wide sea of common opinion."[9] The parallel is one that associates a minister's reputation to a merchant's material credit, but the comparison nonetheless implicitly approves of the merchant's activities, mentioned in the same breath as the minister's. The emphasis, however, is on danger—placing one's reputation at risk can be as treacherous as putting one's goods in harm's way.

It is just this danger associated with credit that drives the plot in *The Merchant of Venice*. At the play's outset, Shylock's motivation to lend Antonio 3,000 ducats is itself predicated upon the sense that Antonio's credit may fail. Indeed Antonio's credit is tenuous, his "means are in supposition" (1.3.13–14), as Shylock says, as his merchant vessels or argosies sail for Tripoli, Mexico, India, and England. Here credit is presented materially, as wooden merchant ships that can founder: for the first two acts of the play, we anticipate their destruction. The ship tossed on treacherous seas is probably the most common metaphor in Renaissance literature for uncertainty, from Sir Thomas Wyatt's Petrarchan lover as a "galley" moving from "rock to rock" to the ship of state traversing social conflict.[10] Shakespeare's version of the Renaissance trope is literal. When news arrives that Antonio's ships indeed are lost at sea and his credit gone, Shylock can demand what he calls his "merry bond" (1.3.165), a deadly serious one when the pound of flesh as forfeit comes due. In anticipation of that event, Antonio applies this lexicon of danger to his own body: when he first offers to lend Bassanio money, he illustrates his devotion by saying his "credit" "shall be racked" (1.1.79–80) in order to help his friend. His physical metaphor of credit stretching on the torture rack emphasizes his willing sacrifices for Bassanio's future. Antonio in fact seems even to prefer martyrdom to life, as long as Bassanio can watch him die as he gives his pound of flesh: "Pray God Bassanio come/To see me pay his debt, and then I care not" (3.3.35–36). Antonio's return for such payment is, he hopes, Bassanio's witnessing and thus endorsement of his sacrifice. Antonio implies that his sacrifice is worth it if Bassanio will cherish him gratefully.

Discharging the debts of a loving and grateful recipient presents a credit balance opposite to that of the Petrarchan lover who remains painfully in debt to the beloved. The desire to be the creditor in the emotional balance sheet is one that creates a beloved debtor. Antonio is a subtler version of what, in many other plays of the period, is a more blatant staging of such economic redemption. There, a figure resembling the rich widow redeems a dissolute debtor by marrying him. We are familiar with the bride's power to assimilate her husband into society; what we might also notice is the bride's power to redeem her husband the debtor. In the new credit lexicon she is not always a widow, but a monied woman who marries a man primarily to discharge his debts. Thomas Heywood was particularly fond of this scenario: it occurs to varying degrees in *If You Know Not Me, You Know Nobody* (1606), *The Fair Maid of the Exchange* (1607), and *A Woman Killed with Kindness* (1607). In *The Fair Maid*, for instance, Moll the fair maid transfers her love from the solvent Bowdler to the indebted Barnard, swearing to her father that she will be "his bail," saving him from debtors' prison.[11] In the other two plays, women who act willingly to discharge the debts of others hazard their honor in order to do so. In *If You Know Not Me*, Lady Ramsey pays off her future husband's debts, saying to him and his creditors "I'll pay you both . . . and sir to do you good,/To all your Creditors I'll do the like."[12] In *A Woman Killed*, Susan Mountford sleeps with her brother's creditor to discharge his debts. Her brother acknowledges that "to soothe them in my suit/Her honor she will hazard. . . ."[13] Heywood's central point implicates Mountford's aristocratic family members and friends who refused to help him out of debt, thus relegating Susan to such a desperate and dishonorable act. But in such scenes Heywood is also commenting on the morally dubious advantage these women gain by being creditors through such means. One recent critic has suggested that Heywood, in *A Woman Killed*, emphasizes economic self-sufficiency in the face of unreliable kin.[14] Yet Susan offers her own honor—her "credit"—so that her brother may stay out of debtors' prison. Susan might be compared with Sebastian in *Twelfth Night*, as he marries Olivia and frees Antonio who was imprisoned for debt. This redemption, however, makes the recipient indebted to the creditor, giving the creditor—if just emotionally—an advantage over the debtor. Antonio in *The Merchant of Venice* relies on such logic to retain a crucial tie to Bassanio despite his friend's impending marriage to Portia. And Portia, of course, trumps this tie by creating a situation in which Bassanio is no longer indebted to Antonio, but to her.

This impulse to redeem others economically was part of the fabric of the actual theatre community as well. So often were players, sharers, and playwrights standing surety, lending money or clothes, and giving bail for their fellows in prison, that their familiarity with loans and bonds presumably influenced the prevalence of such scenes in the plays. At the very least, many players were sensitive to the obligation to come to the legal and economic aid of their fellow players. Enough records exist documenting the practice that we can assume it was common. Sometimes money was lent simply for materials needed to launch a production, as when Philip Henslowe gave players money for carpentry items for *The Jew of Malta*.[15] Of course Henslowe's comparative wealth meant that such exchanges were commonplace for him, but lending and particularly giving bail was also common among players. For instance, in 1605 Robert Beeston gave bail for Robert Lee of Queen

Anne's Men,[16] and in 1612 Thomas Downton of Prince Henry's Men at the Fortune gave bail for Richard Gunnell of the Admiral's Men.[17] Much credit was extended within families, as when Henslowe laid out the expenses for his nephew's clothing in 1596.[18] But often credit was extended between players in more dubious circumstances, as when Charles Massey of the Palsgrave's Men gave bail for fellow actor John Shanks on charges that he had bought stolen goods.[19] As guarantors of their friends' debts, players took the risks in life which they similarly assumed on stage, such as Antonio's *de facto* guarantee of Bassanio's debt in *The Merchant of Venice*, or Barnard the guarantor of the debt to Berry in Heywood's *Fair Maid of the Exchange*.[20] These debts and risks seem to have been incurred voluntarily, as a measure of communal trust: when debts or legal obligations were incurred under pressure, individuals felt free to object. In one example, T.W. sued A. Savery for confederating fraudulently in 1611 to entangle him in bonds made through "panic and causeless terrors."[21] In addition, Philip Henslowe, Francis Langley, Richard Gunnell, and others subjected players to intense pressure, at times, to sign bonds insuring they would remain at specific theatres, a pressure that didn't always succeed.[22]

Playwrights reflected such tensions by expanding the range of economic activity considered evil or unethical. Claiming ownership of one's own debts—and acknowledging proper responsibility for one's credit—assumes a new importance in plays beginning in the late sixteenth century. Commercial villains are not just usurers like Shylock and Christopher Marlowe's Barabas, or greedy monopolists and projectors, like Thomas Middleton's Dampit or Philip Massinger's Overreach, but characters who allow others to languish in debtors' prison for their own debts. This was one form of cultural pressure towards the socially responsible extension of credit. In the anonymous *A Yorkshire Tragedy* (1608), the archvillain "Husband" refuses to pursue credit, and he enjoys watching his brother suffer for his own debts. Husband's wife laments his behavior in which he "calls it slavery to be preferred./A place of credit, a base servitude."[23] His villainy is confirmed in the tragic, overdrawn ending in which a pun joins the legal "execution" of a bond and the literal execution of his brother in prison for the husband's debts: "Two brothers: one in bond lies overthrown/This, on a deadlier execution" (p. 30).

We see a milder form of this social pressure in Jonson's *The Alchemist*, where Subtle and Face engage in back-and-forth jibes concerning credit ties. Face tells Subtle that his credit gave Subtle the means to live: "I ga' you countenance, credit for your coals. . . ."[24] Subtle owes Face for the credit Face extended him: for Subtle to ignore this social debt is a form of credit abuse. Subtle replies with a judgment on the dubious nature of Face's credit: Face not only owes it to his master's household, but without his master living in the house, the credit it represents is failing. Subtle says to Face: "[the things you sold & kept in your master's house] . . . gave you credit to converse with the cobwebs . . . [since your master's house is broken up]" (1.1.57). By attacking the worth of Face's credit, Subtle assaults his social standing. The point is that these two know how to attack a vulnerability: credit standing, so vital to social success, is an elastic characteristic.

Because credit standing can shift, the economic "type" is rarely a static being. The familiar stock prodigal, for example, is socially redeemable in some instances. Prodigal indebtedness is one of the chief complaints Shylock carries against Antonio: Antonio has "squandered" his ventures, he is a "bankrupt, a prodigal" (1.3.16; 3.1.33).[25] And yet Antonio does not end the play with this tag. For the conventional prodigal, the assumption is that he pushes communal trust so far as to make borrowing dishonest, like stealing. In Chapman's *Byron's Conspiracy* (1608), for instance, Henry IV of France childes La Fin, the failing French nobleman: "Thou art in law, in quarrels, and in debt/Which thou woulds't quit with countenance; Borrowing/With thee is purchase. . . ."[26] Here the prodigal impulse is characterized as antisocial, in that the intention to repay a debt only with "countenance" or mere bearing means that borrowing is "purchase" (meaning "booty, as by an act of pillage").[27] The prodigal not only wastes money, he wastes himself; in the process, he threatens not just his family name and position, but their very existence. Thomas Dekker's *The Shoemaker's Holiday* (1600) characterizes the prodigal Lacy in this way. His uncle, the Earl of Lincoln, complains that his nephew has "burnt up himself, consumed his credit/ . . . Only to get a wanton to his wife."[28] And yet it is Lacy's loan to Simon Eyre which makes Eyre's transaction possible and which leads to his becoming mayor.[29] So while Lacy's wastefulness is frowned upon, it is ultimately his resourcefulness—his usefulness as a financial resource—that raises the social standing of other community members. Behavior that could be understood as thoroughly irresponsible might easily be redemptive, if only one's credit is ultimately put to good use. In *The Merchant of Venice*, Antonio relies on this possibility, in the hope that he can redeem himself and Bassanio too.

But while Antonio's notion of redemption—through his references to credit—emphasizes his sacrifice and potential fall into the "gulf" of debt, and ultimately, the gulf of death, Bassanio's credit talk is more hopeful. While touching on risk, Bassanio remains more optimistic. He needs Antonio to lend him *more* money, even though he has wasted previous loans, so he likens the new loan to a second arrow shot after an original arrow, now lost. Assuring Antonio that this second arrow will find the first, magically retrieving it, he says it will "bring [the] latter hazard back again" (1.1.150). With the word "hazard" (here a noun, signifying the thing that was risked), Bassanio recognizes his friend's risk, and links credit with speculation. Likewise, he likens his pursuit of Portia to the hazardous journey of Jason and the Argonauts in pursuit of the Golden Fleece (1.1.168–71). Here the play's credit lexicon supports a general cultural vocabulary that values the condition of risk in lending. Conversely, loans that entailed no chance were reviled. The notion that the goal in risk-taking is worth the hazard is encapsulated in the sixteenth-century proverb, "Nothing venture, nothing win."[30] One common complaint against usury was that the usurer took no risk but instead lent out money for certain and assured gain. Miles Mosse wrote, in his 1595 tract *Arraignment and Conviction of Usurie*, that "the usurer never adventureth or hazardeth the losse of his principall. . . ."[31]. This criticism becomes vital for our understanding of this lexical field surrounding the word "hazard" in *The Merchant of Venice,* which is of significant moment in the casket plot. Devised by Portia's father, the test involves suitors choosing one of three caskets or chests—of gold, silver, and lead—the correct choice of which determines who will receive Portia's hand in marriage. The inscription on the correct, (lead) casket containing Portia's image is "Who chooseth me, must give and hazard all he hath" (2.7.16). To bear a measure of risk—to "hazard all"—is admired, while the refusal to risk is unrewarded. Portia herself tells Bassanio, as he stands in front of the caskets, to "[pause] before you hazard" (3.2.2.). The element of chance in human venturing for love links Bassanio's risk with Portia's own conversion of personal fidelity and wealth to Bassanio, whose trustworthiness is in question. Hazard inheres, as well, in Jessica's elopement and religious conversion through marriage; the emphasis on the elopement's secrecy highlights the risks of being caught.

One way in which playwrights advanced this approval for venturing or risk-taking was by tempering characterizations of the wasteful prodigal. Bassanio himself is a self-described "prodigal" with whom audiences generally sympathize. In other plays rogue figures reinvent themselves with borrowed cash, and often there is a festive renewing aspect tied to adventurous borrowing. In *If You Know Not Me*, Gresham's witty but prodigal nephew Jack abuses familial credit when he leaves the country with £100 that Gresham lends him. When Gresham finds out, he is not upset but rather proud of Jack's boldness. "The knave had wit to do so mad a trick,/Than if he had posited me twice so much," he gushes, and "Ha ha, mad Jack, Gramercie for this flight/This hundred pounds makes me thy Uncle right" (6.957–58; 6.966–67). This implies that that a savvy attaches to those who have the ability to borrow extensively. Of course this emphasis on extensive borrowing is a point of critique, too. In *Every Man Out of His Humour*, Jonson satirizes the social truism that foolish social climbers amass too many debts when the character Carlo comments that debt is "more for [one's] credit," since it is an "excellent policy to owe much in these days."[32] But while Jonson here laments the ubiquity of debt, especially among court gallants, indebtedness did not always signify waste or foppery. Dekker's heroic upstarts, the Hieronimos like Simon Eyre in *The Shoemaker's Holiday*, are held up as positive examples of those who attain credit for bourgeois success. And prospering commercially (and socially) means having the credit necessary for any future undertaking. All of these examples cast Portia's approval of Bassanios credit manipulations in the play in a different light than most critics would have us believe.

The point is that writers in the late sixteenth and early seventeenth centuries began to depict characters as clever and resourceful who, when the odds are against them, nonetheless attain credit in the marketplace. Credit achievement becomes a new marker of status, which itself provides the cultural backdrop for a significant lexical development. Two discrete usages of credit begin to merge, invoked as if they were one meaning: 1) notions of collective trust or belief combine with 2) the ability to borrow. Firk the shoemaker in *The Shoemaker's Holiday* employs both senses when he says "O Eternal credit to us of the Gentle Craft" (18.215): he means both the monetary credit necessary for business and the trust extended by the community. The joining in Firk's mind of "o eternal trust in us" and "o eternal loans extended to us" links community faith and community coffers. George Chapman joins the two meanings in a pun in *A Humorous Day's Mirth* (1599). Verone, the host of the ordinary, says to his waiters: "accomplish the court Cupboard, wait diligently today for my credit and your own."[33] While he means that their exemplary service should be rewarded with payment or credit, he also means that it should forgive raw or tough meat, so that they will be entrusted with service in the future. Thomas Nashe likewise joins the two discrete meanings of credit in his characterization of the dishonest Astronomer in *Pierce Penilesse* (1592).[34] The Astronomer protests that if his forecasts don't come true, "let me . . . lose the credit of my Astronomy," meaning belief in his words.[35] Pierce points out at the end of that anecdote, "his Astonomie broke his day with his creditors," "creditors" referring not only to the people who might have believed him but to those extending him money.[36] And in *Every Man Out*, when Cordatus wryly refers to Fungoso's oaths to the Tailor, he says "He were an iron-hearted fellow, in my judgement, that would not credit him upon these monstrous oaths" (4.4.52–54). Credit here means both to believe and to extend loans for purchases.

Playwrights and actors may have been particularly attuned to this bifold meaning of credit because of market conditions for their activity. They needed readers and listeners to "buy" or to believe their product, receiving the credit needed to stage another work. Plays, after all, were commodities marketed for public consumption.[37] Sir Philip Sidney's defensive formulation that "the poet . . . nothing affirms, and therefore never lieth" addresses the fear that writers were not credited with writing believable things.[38] But with the belief the market extends comes the pence and pounds a ticket-buyer's hand extends. Those who railed against the theater used this dual notion of credit in their diatribes against players. William Rankins, in *A Mirror of Monstors* (1587) describes actors' work as creditless: "they shall never be able to profit their country or themselves . . . or by venturing . . . increase their credit. . . ."[39] Others lampoon bad writers as being "creditless": John Stephens, in his *Essays* (1615), writes, "all their toil/Is like the gleaning of a barren style;/Both void of gain and credit."[40] Here, credit, a synonym for "gain," primarily means profit but also belief. Stephens's simile describes a style devoid of credit and gain as "barren," an adjective we might associate with the Aristotelian critique of usury, that it makes money "breed" unnaturally. Still, Stephens implies that gleaning a productive style would result in credit, so that underlying this critique is the encouragement to good writers to pursue their credit in the marketplace of common opinion.

The specific target of Stephens's critique—the author whose "toil/is like the gleaning of a barren style"—is Sir Thomas Overbury, whose "Characters" provided critical sketches of social types, reviewing society from the experienced courtier's point of view.[41] Stephens' *Essays* were written in the Overburian fashion, itself modelled on those first printed in English, by Joseph Hall.[42] Hall's didactic sketches critiqued behavior associated with courtiers and were based upon those by the ancient Greek writer Theophrastus.[43] In Theophrastus's work, action is the essence of character, so that the study of character becomes a close attention to details of conduct. It is in the early modern version of the Theophrastian character sketch that we see explicit articulation of the actions that define the drama's economic "types." A popular early seventeenth-century form, the character sketch describes, among many other actions, specific lending behaviors. Like eighteenth-century Hogarth sketches, prose characters both satirize social corruptions and suggest alternate behaviors. The spendthrift aristocrat should avoid greater debt, the upstart servant wrangles for a loan—on the face of it, these pieces depict specific status orientations that determine credit behavior. But upon closer inspection, the opposite is often true: credit behavior affects status. Read in conjunction with plays, the prose "character" offers insights into the drama's economic types. It also helps to articulate and define behaviors that help to upset "roles" and social status.

The character recasts in epigrammatic terms the plays' social pressure towards proper handling of credit. For instance, Overbury's widely read character of "An Ordinary Widow" portrays the evil widow as one who takes advantage of her dead husband's credit: "If she live to be thrice married, she seldom fails to cozen her second husband's creditors."[44] Other Theophrastian characters offer similar warnings that at first glance stage the familiar status-based argument, contrasting aristocratic virtue and *nouveau riche* grasping. Stephens warns the gentry against falling into debt in "Of High Birth":

> Then a contempt to be a slavish debtor (if means can avoid it) especially to base-minded Tradesmen; who upon single debts enforce a double engagement: both of credit and restitution: For if you remain in their books for a commodity, you must remain likewise in their favour to avoid scandal, reiterations, and commemorations among all societies (79).

Stephens cautions that excessive debt exposes one to social scandal and debases one's name. But this very argument envisions a slippery slope requiring the higher sort to behave differently towards their inferiors: aristocrats and gentry, if forced to be "slavish debtor[s]," not only owed money to "tradesmen" but had to stay in "their favour." They not only owed them something, they had to act as if they did. We can find a similar social leveling effect regarding debt relations in Henry Fitzgeffrey's *Certain Elegies* (1618).[45] Fitzgeffrey describes the prodigal as a certain type of "gentleman" who,

> Will in the payment of the Debt be bound
> And escape free by Breaking
> . . . .
> To Borrow is a Virtue, when to Lend,
> Is to beget an everlasting Friend:
> And may a man have more said in his grace,
> Than to be Credited in every place?
> He's not a Gentleman I dare maintain,
> Whose Word runnes not as Current as his Coin.[46]

This poem might be read in one of two ways. Certainly it satirizes the gentleman who is credited in every place, whose coin runs current because he is always lent money. But to read the last two lines literally is to understand a different criticism. The social standing—the condition of being a gentleman—depends upon the behavior. One cannot be a gentleman, Fitzgeffrey argues, if your word cannot be believed, even if you have ready money, or "current" "coin." Thus to "be credited" is a function of behavior, not birth.

If the inability to be "credited," or believed, could slip one down the social scale, then the ability to inspire belief—and to gain monetary credit—could raise one in social standing. If the loss of credit debases, then credit achievement elevates. Of course, tricking the lower born still garnered criticism, as when Stephens chides court proctors who "win new credit, to deceive the poor" (14). But the talent of willfully misusing credit became a frequent topic for the character sketch. Thomas Dekker wrote of the character "Politicke Bankruptisme" in his satire *Seven Deadly Sins* (1606): "whether he be a tradesman . . . or a merchant . . . winds himself . . . into rich men's favor, till he grow rich himself, and sees that they build upon his credit. . . . and he useth his credit like a Ship freighted with all sorts of Merchandize by ventrous Pilots . . . ."[47] The abuse of credit was a favorite topic of Thomas Nashe, who, in *Pierce Penniless*, warns court favorites to beware servile peasants who would use them to crawl "into credit with [their] Lords."[48] In both these examples, though, the lower-born—a "tradesman" and a peasant—employ credit as tool for social climbing.

The resourcefulness of the successful social climber, wrangling after credit wherever he goes, is a trait celebrated in the travel play. Travel plays not only capitalized on popular New World discovery tales, but in so doing emphasized the difference between English customs and those in other lands. John Day, William Rowley, and George Wilkins, in the travel play *The Travels of the Three English Brothers* (1607), employ Will Kemp as one authentic English voice in Persia. When he is approached and asked how his fellows in England are, he replies that they are "like all good fellows," in that "when they have no money live upon credit."[49] To "live" upon credit—that is, to make one's living—or at least to get by on credit, suggests a certain resourcefulness. Kemp, characterizing Englishmen back home while he is in Persia, may be nostalgic for the English type of scrappiness. Or it may be a joke at Englishmen's expense, pointing to the folly of his countrymen in their debt-ridden dependencies. But the characteristics are not mutually exclusive. Here the idea is that the "self-made," resourceful man without many means can join a credit network and, through communal aid, live in the manner to which he has become accustomed. Social ties are necessary for this.

The Englishman who lives upon credit is the clever individual who gets by on his wits; in drama this general trait is made specific in the character of the Plautine clever slave. In both plays and jest books the clever slave gulls others with his wit when he is "credited."[50] When others fall for his tricks and deceits, he wins and exposes their relative naivety. For this clever character, "credit" is a synonym for trust, but trust in the sense that one can take advantage of others if they credit you with believability. As a result, "credit" means the money others are willing to lend you—thus the usage essentially is a stand—in for "wit." By the same logic, social climbers pursued credit not only for the pragmatic advantages of capital; they also desire debt because a social élan attached to indebtedness. Court gallants wanted to be known to be in debt, so that the condition became another type of display, an economic *sprezzatura* that spoke of a sophistication and ease with debt. The gallant practice of keeping a debt balance with tailors, for example, became the subject of a common jibe in the drama. In Edward Sharpham's *The Fleire* (1607), the title character jokes with his friend about the trust that this debt required: "If I were [a Tailor], thou wouldst intreat me to trust thee."[51] Sharpham tries the joke again in *Cupid's Whirligig* (1607), where Nuecome, the Welsh courtier, explains the general "terror" the gentility have for their "creditors" (4.4.13); but he himself boasts that he will abuse his tailor's credit. He says he is a "second Sampson," saying "I can break my bonds boy, I can" (4.4.20), meaning that he will not recognize the bond, refusing to pay when the tailor calls in the debt. The particular typology that makes Nuecome a new, or second, Sampson, recalls the Biblical tale of Sampson breaking the bands the Samaritans use to try to restrain and capture him. Nuecome's comparison of himself to the Biblical Sampson is laughable because his petty glee in breaking his pledge to pay his tailor bears little relation to Sampson struggling for his life and freedom against tyrannical enemies. And yet the joke works, because it gets to the heart of the self-importance that gallants attached to their indebted condition.

The boast that one "could" break one's promise was an antisocial marker, however, a sign of breaking social convention. Bonds were generally expected to be respected in the growing market culture. The maintenance of the social ethic of trust became increasingly important during this period, in fact, as Craig Muldrew has pointed out.[52] In order for the economy to work most efficiently, trust had to be communicated beyond local face to face dealing. The emphasis upon credit as a currency of reputation thus developed. Breaking bonds was generally not tolerated, but the nature of this intolerance was multivalent. In some cases, the legal system was employed, while in other cases, social reputation was called into question when individuals defaulted on loans or broke their promises. The border between clever economic resourcefulness and recklessness, or between harmless extravagance and dangerous indebtedness was not always clearly defined. The drama explores this line—helping to define its contours—with satirical characterizations of characters who wax enthusiastic about debt. While indebtedness is a condition to be sought after, its abuse is ridiculed and, when extreme, excoriated.

The lower-born aspired to indebtedness as an indicator, or mark, of gentility; the lower sort could signal ambition in their willingness to amass debt. In Jonson's *Every Man Out*, Carlo comments on the "excellent policy" of indebtedness (1.2.108). Cordatus also notes that Fungoso "saucily imitates some great man" by having a tailor "follow him" (4.4.30–43). But the cheeky play-acting of the court *homo economicus* becomes dangerous when it verges on criminal behavior. Jonson, in the words of Carlo, ascribes such crafty practices to the poor whose more desperate endeavors lead them to debtors' prison: he warns Sogliardo, "always beware you commerce not with bankrupts, or poor needy Ludgathians. They are impudent creatures, turbulent spirits. They care not what violent tragedies they stir, nor how they play fast and loose with a poor gentleman's fortunes to get their own" (1.2.123–27). Bankrupts, or those committed to the debtors' prison at Ludgate, are thought not merely dangerous in their need, but skillfully so. The reference is to the con-game of "fast and loose," a sort of shell game in which observers gamble on whether or not a looped belt is fixed to the table.

The line between respect for a witty, scrappy character who can play "fast and loose" with someone else's fortunes, and social antagonism for such a person was a fine one. In Bassanio's actions we see the crossing of that line: his excessive borrowing nearly destroys Antonio, his lender. But in his very daring, he draws the attentions of Portia, who admires his witty liberality. He is liberal both in his actions and with his promises to her, so while Portia is drawn to the daring of such a character, she is forced to reestablish the concrete value of his words. The value of Bassanio's word is concomitant with his value to her in marriage, since the marriage contract is sealed with a verbal bond. That is, Bassanio's promise to Portia must be believed: thus his "credit" is essential to her. Portia works to reestablish Bassanio's credit at the end of the courtroom scene and again at the end of the play, using his own promises and then a legal document to redeem his "word," or his credit. Because she does so not only for Bassanio but for all present at the end of the play, Portia exemplifies an early modern economic agent who resorts to the legal system to maintain the stability of credit in her community.

It is important that Portia renew the legitimacy of promises and "bonds" at the end of the play because throughout the play commercialism degrades the bonds of love. That the commercial and pragmatic world of Venice intrudes upon the romantic world of Belmont is, at one level, one of the play's structuring principles, and a common focus of critical attention.[53] Of course both Venice and Belmont are pragmatic and commercial, as "value" drives motivation in both locales, and the first thing we learn about Belmont is that it contains "a lady richly left" (1.1.160). Critics have often commented upon the fusing of Venice's commercial language with Belmont's language of love, especially when "bonds" and "debts" are mentioned, as when Bassanio tells Antonio, "To you . . . /I owe the most, in money and in love" (1.1.129–30).[54] Portia fuses the two most productively when she transforms the potentially tragic consequences of the bond's law into a series of contracts and bonds sealed by the marriage vow. Tragedy becomes comedy as the bonds' implications change. Yet it is not Portia's softening of attitudes towards bonds, but instead an insistence upon the law as absolutely binding that brings the comic conclusion. The exact nature of Portia's attitude toward bonds as they reflect upon Bassanio's credit, and her manipulation of Bassanio's credit, reveal the new "lexicon of credit" at work in the play. The plays emphasis on promises and oaths highlights the shifting valuation of Bassanio's credit—at first that of a spendthrift, then adjusted to that of a reliable husband as a result of Portia's scheme.

The play is rife with oaths, but they are light oaths. In Act 3, Portia swears an oath that she will not teach Bassanio "how to choose right," and yet the song sung while he peruses the caskets begins with three words that rhyme with "lead" (3.2.63–65). In the other couples' subplots throughout the play, lovers' oaths are presented as debased currency. Gratiano offers "oaths of love" to Nerissa, contingent not only on the half-life of a promise—as Gratiano indicates with his own parenthetical phrase, "if promise last"—but also contingent on Bassanio's fortune "achiev[ing] her mistress," Portia (3.2.205, 208). Nerissa tells Portia that she made Gratiano "swear" to keep her ring forever (4.2.14), a fact about which Portia immediately makes fun by replying "We shall have old swearing/That they did give the rings away to men;/But we'll outface them, and outswear them too" (4.2.15–17). In Belmont when Lorenzo and Jessica share Petrarchan lovers' quips, Jessica inserts some pragmatic realism into Lorenzo's idealized lines by pointing out that Lorenzo "steal[s] her soul with many vows of faith,/And ne'er a true one" (5.1.18–19). And when the two pairs of lovers begin to quarrel about the ring tricks, Nerissa points out that Gratiano should have kept the ring she gave him, not for her sake, but for his "vehement oaths" he swore that he would keep it until he died (5.1.153). Portia blames Gratiano for parting with the ring, a thing, she says "stuck on with oaths" (5.1.166). The play's emphasis on broken oaths participates in larger cultural debates concerning the legitimacy and seriousness of oaths. Sir Edward Coke wrote that "an oath is . . . sacred and . . . deeply concerneth the consciences of Christian men. . . ."[55] Oaths played an important role in identifying allegiance and defining belief and loyalty in early modern England.[56] It is tempting to conclude that Shakespeare is merely highlighting a general social truism—the abuse of oaths in the play represents moral laxity in Shakespeare's society. But so prevalent is the breaking of oaths in this play that we must look more carefully at its effect upon the literary texture, upon character development. Where, for instance, is an oath *not* broken? Portia, for example, wants the ring signifying her marriage bond to Bassanio to stand for an oath that will not be broken. She wants to establish Bassanio's trustworthiness, in order to "credit" him with honor in their marriage.

By finagling the ring from Bassanio as Balthazar, a ring that signified Bassanio's oath to her, Portia herself discredits Bassanio. Before she discredits him, knowing he has given up the ring, she rehearses a different scenario, telling Graziano of Bassanio: "here he stands:/I dare be sworn for him he would not leave it/Nor pluck it from his finger for the wealth/That the world masters" (5.1.185–7). She counterposes his marriage vow with the world's wealth, valuing (for Bassanio) their bond over and against material wealth, furthermore swearing "for him" that this is the case. When Bassanio admits he did indeed give the ring away, she compares his ringless finger to his truthless heart: "Even so void is your false heart of truth" (5.1.203). That compelling statement—that Bassanio's heart contains no truth, and is "false"—not only gives the lie to Bassanio, but discredits him specifically in the realm of love. Here is not a mere pledge over money or property, but a pledge of love and fidelity that has been broken. But just as quickly as she claims he is faithless, Portia offers Bassanio redemption. If he can reproduce the ring, she will honor their marriage bond: "By heaven, I will ne'er come in your bed/Until I see the ring!" (5.1.204–5). Under the negative conditional ("I will never . . . until I see the ring") is the future condition ("I will come in your bed . . . when I see the ring"). Since she had originally "give[n] [herself] with this ring" (3.2.174) the argument is circular, and is a mere reminder to Bassanio that the synechodocic relationship of the ring for the marriage bond and for herself is quite literal in this case.

Portia's synechdocic relationship to the ring can be compared to Bassanio's metaphor of the ring on his finger as life. Bassanio had sworn that "when this ring/Parts from this finger, then parts life from hence!" (3.2.186–7), a vow the dire seriousness of which Bassanio's actions belie. Of course Bassanio gives the ring to the lawyer Balthazar, the disguised Portia, in recognition of her services in the courtroom, but the act nonetheless symbolizes a breaking of faith. When Portia berates him about it, Bassanio responds by asking forgiveness, and tries to reestablish his fidelity. He says "I swear to thee, even by thine own fair eyes/Wherein I see myself—" (5.1.241–2). Here she interrupts him, with "Mark you but that?/In both my eyes he doubly sees himself:/In each eye, one. Swear by your double self,/And there's an oath of credit!" (5.1.242–44). The primary meaning of credit here is a sarcastic or ironic one—the oath is not worthy to be believed. Bassanio is swearing by his "double" or duplicitous self. Portia reminds him that his worth depends on the extent to which she decides to believe him. Her sarcastic jab at Bassanio's "oath of credit," signals his oath is worthless—she discredits him. Knowing at times that they both push the truth, Portia nonetheless wants the ring signifying her marriage bond to Bassanio to stand for an oath that will not be broken. We must look to Portia's final words, where she reestablishes the credit not just of Bassanio but of the entire community.

In the play's last lines, in an ostensibly conventional comic ending; Portia delivers a host of good news: she has the missing ring, admits she was disguised as Balthazar, and declares that Antonio's argosies "are richly come to harbour suddenly." To satisfy her hearers of the validity of this news, Portia invites the others inside her home in Belmont, saying, "Let us go in,/And charge us there upon inter'gatories,/And we will answer all things faithfully" (5.1.319–321). But it is not just her own news that requires answers, it is Bassanio's questionable behavior too.

The process of answering "interrogatories," or specific questions, upon oath as a witness in a lawsuit, was a legal procedure used to examine individual parties as part of a pre-trial, fact-finding process. It was used in the Chancery Court, where lawyers ensured that testimony was taken from written statements on a secrecy-oriented bases.[57] Rather than Chancery Court, however, this scene—featuring a lawyer from Rome, recommended from Padua, to judge a case brought by a 'alien' Jew in a Venetian play—more closely resembles the court of the Law Merchant. Set up by markets, fairs, ports, and boroughs, the (often temporary) Law Merchant court was an English tribunal that judged mercantile cases, administered in Shakespeare's age by a body of rules apart from the common law, international in nature.[58] Why would Portia take recourse to such a legal mechanism *after* the other trial had reached its conclusion? After all, she is not playing Balthazar any more at this point in the play.

Most critics have misread Portia's behavior here. The Cambridge edition, for instance, suggests that "this is Portia's last bit of legal jargon, perhaps spoken with a momentary return to her courtroom manner." In considering why Portia might return to her "courtroom manner," we need also to consider what Portia is doing as an *economic* agent at this moment. I think it is crucial to appreciate what sort of community is formed at the play's conclusion and what that formation says about communal notions of credit. Portia affects here what Craig Muldrew identifies as a "negotiated" community. In the early modern economy of obligation, one crucial feature was public dispute resolution, a practice that expressed its members' desire to live in a state of communal relations with their neighbors to the degree that reciprocal trust, mutual hospitality, and civic duty could be maintained. This type of resolution centered on the concept and process of reconciliation and, as such, involved the settling of disputes *after* they had occurred, first by informal and then by legal means, to effect the "negotiated community." Portia, by setting up the ring trick to begin with, creates the conditions for this type of public reconciliation. Rather than testing Bassanio privately, she tests and challenges him publicly, creating a dispute that finally is settled in the public arena. By making this settlement legally binding—and reestablishing the veracity of oaths—she creates a reinvigorated measure of trust in the community. Where any doubts or suspicion have the *potential* of unsettling the conclusion, she institutes anew the "economy of obligation" with the sworn interrogatories. Ultimately, the steadfast notion of "bonds" Shylock insists upon is not discounted—Portia does not soften her attitude towards bonds, but instead insists upon the law as absolutely binding, and this brings the comic conclusion. In this dramatic comedy, the conclusion incorporates real economic concerns that affect what we might previously have interpreted as the comic ending of medieval romance, or as Portia's providential intervention as the Virgin Mary from the continental miracle play tradition. Most critics interrogating that ending look to Shylock's exclusion, ignoring the significance of Portia's legalism at the very end. Reevaluating the ending for Portia's role in reestablishing trust leads us, in turn, to reevaluate the shape of romantic comedy in general in this period. In other words, real economic concerns, revealed through language and plot, affect characterization and genre imperatives themselves.[59]

Just as we can read *The Merchant of Venice* in terms of the dictates of genre, too we can read it in terms of its credit vocabulary. That is, just as it is meant to be understood as a potential tragedy that resolves into a comedy, we see how, in the expression of credit relationships, warnings against the tragic consequences of excessive greed and dishonesty give way to rewards for resourcefulness and probity. The credit lexicon in the play, as it does in literature throughout the period, raises questions of trust, but does so in the interest of strengthening notions of communal obligation. The credit lexicon in *The Merchant* celebrates resourceful social climbers like Bassanio, while holding him to standards of honesty through Portia's watchful eye.

Chapter Six

Conclusion

In his 1606 commentary on the usury bill, Nicholas Bacon praised the "invention" of trade.[1] Likewise Francis Bacon condemned usury as dampening the "inventions" of industry.[2] The Bacons were thoroughly typical of those early seventeenth-century writers who legitimized industry and individual profit within the context of attacks on usury. Contrasted with merchants whose "inventions" and ventures are ennobling by virtue of their hazardous nature were usurous moneylenders who took no risk—Shylock is the exemplar of the latter type. In early modern English literature, to "hazard" one's goods or one's self is a positive trait. In *The Merchant of Venice*, for instance, the person who chooses the correct casket for Portia's hand in marriage must "give and hazard all he hath."[3] Thus Bassanio's choice is the virtuous one, aptly rewarded. In *The Merchant*, then, to "hazard all" implies a risk-taking that ostensibly subordinates self-interest to a sense of charity or selflessness in a willingness to give up "all" possessions in an act of faith.

This connection of the willingness to "hazard" with an act of faith seems an unlikely intersection. How is it that to "hazard," or to venture, became associated with a selflessness and a trust in providence? Put another way, how was the type of risk-taking behavior that was associated with groups like the Merchant Adventurer's Company connected at all with religious faith? The moral evaluation of such activity in sermons and religious tracts, sources that we assume would excoriate profit-seeking and individual gain, actually tell us quite a lot abut the changing idioms of self-interest that are this book's subject. Lancelot Andrewes' Cambridge lectures and sermons from the 1580s are particularly revelatory. Andrewes (1555–1626) first made a national name for himself during the 1590s when he preached as a prebend of St. Paul's Cathedral. He would later be named first dean, then bishop, of Westminster; would oversee the production of the Authorized Version of the Bible; and would be one of the leading anti-Calvinist churchmen of the Jacobean Church. It is in his Cambridge lectures that we find his first reference to "hazard," used as a term to justify acquisition and profit: while the first printed edition of his manuscript notes to those lectures did not appear until 1630 in the unattributed *A Patterne of Catechisticall Doctrine*, the notes circulated widely from the 1580s to the 1650s, were cited in theological controversies, and were extremely popular with laymen and divinity students alike.[4]

In his "Exposition of the First Commandment," Andrewes offers examples of virtues corresponding with the first precept (commanding the belief in God), one of these being faith. He compares faith in matters of religion to those in civil affairs, and as examples of the latter he offers the husbandman who tills and sows his ground, uncertain of any profit. "This it appears in all civil affairs wherein men go upon a civil faith, without certain knowledge of the things, and therefore much more in matters of religion, which are supernatural, may we live by faith," Andrewes argued. "Thus we see the husbandman, who though he sees the weather unkindly etc. yet fits himself to till and sow his ground, and bestows his cost, though he have no demonstrative knowledge, whether he shall reape any profit or no."[5] He then offers the example of merchants, *following* his mention of husbandman, connecting the often more diligent and deliberate work of husbandry with that of the adventuring seafarer. Of the merchant he says, "And so the merchants, though their goods and ships are subject to storms, pirates etc., yet they run the hazard, and adventure upon this civil faith."[6] In a striking formulation, Andrewes directly correlates hazarding, adventuring, and faith, in the process making the object of the commercial activity of "adventuring" a "civil faith." He suggests a moral and civil understanding of the word "adventure."

Andrewes draws on a tradition in which the word "adventure"—going back as far as the fourteenth century—is defined as risk-taking in money matters. In the medieval period, though, "aventure" was something wholly unsavory. In Chaucer's *Canterbury Tales*, for instance, the Canon's Yeoman tells a tale that exposes fraudulent alchemists, who defend their risk-taking actions by comparing them to merchants who put their good "in aventure":

> Us moste putte oure good in aventure.
> A marchaunt, truly, may not ay endure,
> Truste me wel, in his prosperitye,
> Some tyme his good is drowned in the see,
> And some tyme cometh it sauf unto the londe.[7]

For Chaucher, to put goods "in aventure," means to put them in jeopardy, or to imperil them.[8] Adventure, aptly associated with merchants' uncertain "prosperitye," was used in this prepositional phrase to mean the state of uncertainty. Derived from the Old French *aventure*, and the Latin *adventura* ("a thing about to happen to anyone"), adventure meant fortune or contingency, and during the fourteenth century, those who took advantage of that uncertainty for personal gain were seen as unscrupulous.

Two centuries later, Lancelot Andrewes does not excoriate profit's dependence upon chance. He cites contingency as a rationale for merchants' enterprises and uses it to support profit-taking. In his "Exposition of the Eighth Commandment," he examines ways of "unjust getting," as well as the "lawful ways of acquiring."[9] Among the lawful, or just, ways of acquiring are those that come "by industry and pains."[10] Here Andrewes categorizes the sorts of labor or effort that justify acquisition: "a man may have a right to those things which he hath neither by gift, nor inheritance, and that in a threefold consideration, viz. in respect of his 1. Labour. 2. Peril or hazard. 3. Cost or charges, which he may lawfully value, in any contract, as in buying. . . ."[11] He likewise offers biblical examples of those who acquires "in respect of . . . peril and hazard. . . ."[12] Among the examples are Saul, who challenged anyone to "venture upon . . . that Philisti[ne]," meaning Goliath the Philistine whom David slew; David, as a reward, earned Saul's daughter's hand in marriage.[13] Andrewes uses David to make the broader point that greater rewards are given to those who willingly take the greater risk and who withstand the uncertainty that attends true risk. Thus the merchant's gain ought to be greater because he ventures his "estate and life," whereas the husbandman only ventures his "seed."[14]

In this same exposition on the eighth commandment, Andrewes also examines the degrees of the "just price" for goods.[15] Here he offers biblical law, examining the rules that God gave "for sale of cattel, of lands, houses, etc.," and he considers "point[s] of equity."[16] Andrewes explains that since "length of time [until the land is to be sold] is to be considered in the price [of land] . . . according as a thing is more or less durable. . . ." then too, "as for merchants, because of the danger and hazard they run, in venturing their goods, and sometimes their lives too . . . a greater proportion of increase by way trade, is to be allowed them, then unto others."[17] Merchants deserve a profit, in other words, that at first seems excessive but that is justified ultimately because they have placed their goods and lives "in aventure" or in danger. Although Andrewes approves of this type of material gain, he reiterates common theological warnings about the moral requirements for those who benefit from worldly gain and riches. "Whomsoever would have *divitias sine verme*, riches without cares and sorrows, as Saint Augustine sayeth, must be persuaded, that riches are the gift of God; and that whomsoever

God would have to be rich, he would have them use only lawful and direct means for the attaining of them. . . ."[18] Andrewes is typical of theologians and moralists of the time in reminding merchants that their success lay in God's hands.

What connection are we to make between Andrewes' defenses of personal profit and those sketched out in works like as *Eastward Ho* and *The Merchant of Venice*? This book argues that critics who stress the period's negative definitions of self-interest have got it all wrong. Early moderns were not nearly as hostile to or suspicious of self-interest as modern critics have asserted. To understand depictions of self-interest in early modern literature, then, we need to pay closer attention to the points at which both moralists and playwrights find communal health served by the pursuit of individual gain. And it is this emphasis on risk-taking or "hazard" that we find a common argument for that gain. Even merchants' defenses of profit-seeking employed moralistic defenses that assert risk as virtuous.[19] A public acceptance arose for those willing to take chances: in Chapter Four, we viewed the depiction of risk-taking debtors through the lens of prose "characters" that highlighted public expectation of such ambitious personalities. Risk-takers were also celebrated in 1616 by Nicholas Breton who published a series of characters titled *The Good and the Bad, or Descriptions of the Worthies and Unworthies of this Age, Where the best may see their graces, and the worst discern their baseness.*[20] He compares the "Worthy Merchant" to the "Unworthy Merchant," where the latter is one who remains on land and does not venture out to sea, who "fears to be too busy with the water."[21] The worthy merchant, on the other hand, courts danger: "A Worthy Merchant is the heir of adventure, whose hopes hang much upon the wind . . . in a merry gale, [he] makes a path through the seas: he is a discoverer of Countries, and a finder out of commodities, resolute in his attempts, and royal in his expenses."[22] This description gives the hopeful seafarer a Moses-like power to part the seas, a traveler who by virtue of his resolution and fortitude "find[s]" out commodities. Breton continues the description by connecting merchants and soldiers: "[the merchant] is the life of Traffic, and the maintainer of trade, the sailor's master, and soldier's friend."[23] The emphasis here is on his adventuring spirit and characteristic courage: "he fears not Scylla, and sails close by Charybdis, and having beaten out a storm, rides at rest in a harbor."[24] Just as in Andrewes' expositions, here risk-taking behavior is characteristically rewarded: "By his sea gain, he makes his land-purchase, and by the knowledge of trade, finds the key of treasure."[25] Breton draws a comparison between these two paired sets of deserts: dangerous sea travel begets the just reward of purchased land, and the knowledge gained by that travel begets the "key of treasure," which suggests not just treasure itself, but the "key" or source of treasure (meaning perhaps in some cases the map to the land that produced that treasure). In this comparison Breton elides adventuring sea travel, material gain, and knowledge. Authors such as Andrewes, Breton, Shakespeare, and Jonson provided models for courageous entrepreneurial activity; they suggested that the rewards for such action were not merely commercial but intellectual and social too.

These writers reflected a shifting attitude towards risk and chance, notions that in the later sixteenth and early seventeenth centuries were used to legitimate mercantile trade and traffic. Earlier, in the middle ages, and up through the early sixteenth century, the taking of chances was more narrowly connected with gambling. As the word "venture" or "aventure" was connected with sharp practices, as exemplified in Chaucer's Canon's Yeoman's quote above, "hazard" too was connected with disrepute. Most often it carried a negative association with "hazardrye," dice, or gambling in general. The Pardoner uses it in a negative reference to gambling in Chaucer's *Canterbury Tales*, when he describes the vices of a group of rioters: "O glotonye, luxurie, and hasardrye!"[26] While here it probably referred to the rioters drawing lots to see which one should separate from the others, "hazard" typically described a type of dice game, where players would bet on a certain number thrown in dice, throwing until an original number came up again.[27] The term originated from the Arabic "al zahr," meaning the die, and in fact the "hazard" type of dice game was of Arabic origin and came to Europe around the time of the Crusades.[28]

Early references to gambling with dice in England include those of Ordericus Vitalis (1075–1143), who wrote "the clergymen and bishops are fond of dice-playing," and John of Salisbury (1110–1182), who referred to "the damnable art of dice-playing."[29] Although very popular and widely practiced, dice gambling was generally morally condemned and was the subject of numerous laws and edicts, including a twelfth-century edict prohibiting any person in the army beneath the degree of knight playing any sort of game for money.[30] Up through the sixteenth century, dice-playing was often associated with cheating, especially when described as an "art." A *Manifest Detection of Dice-play* (1552) provides a historical account of cheating at dice, where speaker "M" describes cheaters learning their trade in criminal schools and tells how skill in cheating requires "four or five years practice."[31]

How did "hazard" move from its negative definition as a type of gambling to a more positive, general risk-taking action? When and why was chance-taking removed of its moral taint? The tracts detailing types of cheating at dice that were popular, such as Thomas Dekker's *Jests* (1607), highlighted certain aspects of dice-playing and gambling admired as skills.[32] At the same time, and developing on the continent for the previous century, was a new "knowledge of numbers" or probability. In late fifteenth-century Italy, mathematicians like Fra Luca Pacioli and Geronimo Cardano wrote treatises on the calculation of chances.[33] Cardano himself was a gambler who used his experience of gaming in the calculation of dice throws, and who wrote his *Liber de Ludo Alea* (1550), or *Book on Games of Chance* (printed in England in 1663) to explain probability theory in various games.[34] Here is where the "illegitimate" world of gambling and the "legitimate" realm of commercial activity intersect and influence one another, through this science of numbers. The thrust behind the development of probability theory was, after all, connected with mercantile activity. As Gerda Reith writes, "[merchants] . . . were interested in matters of commerce: problems such as the distribution of goods in trade, the insurance of those goods and the likelihood of a journey being completed successfully. There were essentially numerical issues dealing with proportions, divisions and relative amounts: all problems intrinsic to probabilistic reasoning."[35] Double-entry bookkeeping was a result of this commercial impetus as well, and was employed by merchants to keep track of profits and record transactions.

But insofar as commercial activity advanced the development of probability theory, moral concerns still troubled this discussion. Questions were raised about the social byproducts of excessive speculation as recreation. Cardano himself elaborated on the role of gambling in life, warning readers of the dangers. In *De Utilitate*, he describes the acts which are liable to bring a man to bankruptcy: "Among these are five: gambling, alchemy, architecture, lawsuits, and luxury. Gambling brings loss in two ways, first because a man loses money, secondly because he is led to neglect his business, arts, and studies."[36] But it was in the human activity of calculating chances—whether in dice, a card game or in a business venture—that the greatest concern lay. Excessive gambling was condemned in ancient Jewish law because, among other reasons, of contrasting notions of chance and divine will. That is, man should not attempt to calculate his chances in any venture, because only God determined outcomes. In *The Art of Giving* (1615) Thomas Cooper wrote that dicing was unlawful because "It consists in hazard and casting of a Lot, which being a religious ordinance, appointed of the Lord . . . to determine the doubtfulness [of a matter], ought not to be transferred to matter of recreation."[37] God's will could be determined, it was believed, through lottery or the casting of lots. One biblical explanation in Proverbs 16:33 reads: "The lot is cast into the lap; but the whole disposing thereof is of the Lord." The outcome of lots or dice was treated by theologians not as a matter of chance but as a revelation of divine will.[38] For moralists writing at the time, the "science" of probability was irrelevant, since providence determined whether one's venture was going to be successful. When lots were cast, it was God who controlled the result. The use of lots in England was used with this context in mind: as in the practice of casting lots for making political decisions (considered to be sanctioned by God). Throughout the sixteenth century, borough officers in England were sometimes chosen by lot, and in 1583 the Chapter of Wells Cathedral apportioned patronage this way.[39] Lots were used for condemned men, and the lucky ticket was labeled "life given by God."[40]

But sometimes that spirit of the practice was broken, as when Queen Elizabeth employed lotteries for less serious matters, as when she chartered one in 1569 for a drawing of prizes in goods as well as money.[41] One prize awarded the winner £5,000, and another protected the buyer from arrest for seven days, excepting a major crime. The Virginia Company also used lotteries for funding in subsequent years. But by 1621 Parliament halted lotteries until, they wrote, "we shall be more fully informed of the inconveniences and evils [of lotteries] . . . and may ordaine due remedy to the same."[42] The use of lottery for profit, Queen Elizabeth's and the Virginia Company's activities notwithstanding, was generally condemned. In 1593 James Balmford wrote a "Black Letter" tract on cards, in the form of a dialogue between a Professor and a Preacher. The Preacher proclaims dice as wholly evil, but distinguishes that game from a lot, in which "prayer is expressed, or to be understood (I Sam. xiv. 41)."[43] He continues, "the use of Lots, directly of itself, and in a special manner, tendeth to the advancing of the name of God, in attributing to His special Providence in the whole and immediate disposing of the Lot, and expecting the event (Pro. xvi. 33; Acts i. 24, 26)."[44] He condemns using lotteries for recreation or profit alone: "lots, (as oaths) are not to be used for profit or pleasure, but only to end a controversy."[45] Combining chance with wit in gaming, the Preacher says, is a sin: "For as calling God to witness by vain swearing, is a sin, so making God an umpire, by playing with lottery, must needs be a sin."[46] "Hazard" or chance is differentiated from providence, the former determining human lotteries for recreation, and the latter manifested in the lot delivered to mankind by God.

When Andrewes referred to the divine providence in the "lot" of King James I and of the people of England during the Gunpowder Plot, in his November 5, 1618 sermon preached before James at Whitehall, he remarked that "the Lord hath maintained our lott."[47] This distinction between chances taken in human affairs, be they in gaming or in mercantile activity, and providence delivered by God, was one that hinged upon actual risk-taking as opposed to the attempt to control an outcome. The immoral action lay in chance-taking for mere recreation, or in "making God an umpire," in James Balmford's words.

Risk-taking in business ventures began to be legitimized because of this difference between gaming chance and work-related chance. Labor was the crucial factor that distinguished the two: gambling was associated with risks taken without real labor, while in merchant adventuring, labor was considered inherent in the undertaking. This distinction recalls the original difference drawn between money-lending and usury, the latter involving money-making without any "work" or risk. As the sixteenth century came to a close, discussion on the continent and in England centered around the distinction between insurance, usury, and other forms of investment on the basis of risk, dividing those where gains were obtained with labor from those obtained without labor.

It is the product of that labor, however, that holds the key to the ethical legitimization of risk. The requirements of commerce demanded risk, and the common wealth prospered with rises in national productivity. The impetus for merchants' insurance, for example, lay in the government's interest in encouraging merchants' hazardous ventures. When marine insurance developed in England, statutes licensing it recognized the need for merchants to have "assurance" in their dangerous voyages and risky commercial ventures. The 1601 "Act Concerning Matters of Assurances, Amongst Merchants" spoke of the "policy of this realm" . . . "to comfort and encourage the merchant," recognizing that "when they make any great adventure (specially into remote parts)" that it is necessary for them to have "assurance made of their goodes merchandizes ships and things adventured."[48] The purpose of this "assurance," the statute goes on to say, is so that merchants, "specially of the younger sort, are allured to venture more willingly and more freely."[49] This argument reiterates the moral approval of hazard or "venture," as a defense of profit-taking (as Andrewes had set out), but it also recognizes the need to inspire or encourage young merchants to become risk-takers in business, or to "venture more willingly." At the same time, it speaks to the increasing commercial need for an instrument to measure risk, here in terms of knowing how much money should be laid out for each venture in order to insure the "things adventured."

This commercial insurance was a new version of the function that family, kin, and community charity had served in the preceding century. As insurance became more widespread in the eighteenth century, Adam Smith would call it a "precise, scientific, and at the same time practical form of that unconscious solidarity that unites men."[50] As a form of "solidarity," insurance for merchant adventurers can be seen as an extension of the associative spirit of the "club" discussed in Chapter One. Economists and legal historians have in fact applied the "theory of clubs" in examining usury laws as an early form of insurance, to consider how the Talmudic prohibition of lending at interest to fellow Jews helps the group attain economic advantage.[51] While the period that we have examined relied most heavily on credit networks to supply the needs that usury supplied earlier, and that insurance would later supply, it is crucial to understand that the justifications for insurance relied heavily on approval of merchants' "hazard" and "adventure." The acceptance of these risk-taking behaviors went hand in hand with the acceptance of a measure of self-interest, because both were understood to serve the interests of the common wealth.

Notes

NOTES TO CHAPTER ONE

1. William Shakespeare, *Shakespeare's Sonnets*, ed. Stephen Booth (New Haven, CT, 1977), 74.1–4, 64.
2. Anon., *Britannia Languens or a Discourse of Trade: shewing the grounds and reasons of the increase and decay of land-rents, national wealth and strength* (London, 1680), reprinted in *Early English Tracts on Commerce*, ed. J. R. McCulloch (Cambridge, 1952), pp. 287–88. We now assume the author to be William Petyt.
3. Thomas Wilson, *Arte of Rhetorique* (London, 1553), p. 69.
4. Traino Boccalini, *I raggvagli of Parnasso, or Advertisements from Parnassus: in two centuries: with the politick touchstone/written originally in Italian by Trajano Bocalini, and now put into English by Henry Earl of Monmouth*, trans. Henry Carey, 3rd edn. (London, 1674), I. XI.14.
5. John Fitzherbert, *Here begynneth aryght frutefull mater: and hath to name The Boke of Surveying and improumentes* (London, 1523), p. bii.
6. William Shakespeare, *2 Henry VI*. *The Norton Shakespeare*, eds. Stephen Greenblatt, Walter Cohen, Jean E. Howard, and Katharine Eisaman Maus (New York, 1997), 3.1.84.
7. The word held a relation to the older French term "interesse," the legal term Edward Coke glossed as "*Interesse* . . . in legal understanding extendeth to estates, rights and titles, that a man hath of, in, to, or out of lands, for he is truly said to have an interest in them." Edward Coke, *The First Part of the Institutes off the lawes of England. Or, a commentarie upon Littleton* (London, 1628), p. 345b.
8. Sir Geoffrey Fenton, *The historie of Guicciardini Conteining the vvares of italie, and other parts* (London, 1579), III, p. 129.
9. See, for instance, Peter Lake and Michael Questier, *The Antichrist's Lewd Hat: Protestants, Papists and Players in Post-Reformation England* (New Haven, CT, 2002), esp. pp. 477–79, and Kristen Poole, *Radical Religion: Figures of Nonconformity from Shakespeare to Milton* (Cambridge, 2000).

10. Jane J. Mansbridge, "The Rise and Fall of Self-Interest in the Explanation of Political Life," ed. Jane Mansbridge, *Beyond Self-Interest* (Chicago, 1990), pp. 3–22 elucidates the promotion of self-interest as a "natural" pursuit only in the second half of the seventeenth century. Milton L. Myers, *The Soul of Modern Economic Man: Ideas of Self-Interest, Thomas Hobbes to Adam Smith* (Chicago, 1983) and Albert O. Hirschman, *The Passions and the Interests: Political Arguments for Capitalism Before its Triumph* (Princeton, 1977) most thoroughly examined the flowering of economic self-interest in the eighteenth century.
11. Mark Kishlansky, *Parliamentary Selection: Social and Political Choice in Early Modern England* (Cambridge, 1986). See also, Paul D. Halliday, *Dismembering the body politic : partisan politics in England's towns, 1650–1730* (Cambridge, 1998).
12. Andrew McRae, *God Speed the Plough: The Representation of Agrarian England, 1500–1660* (Cambridge, 1996).
13. J.A.W. Gunn, *Politics and the Public Interest in the Seventeenth Century* (London, 1969), p. 20; C. B. Macpherson, *The Political Theory of Possessive Individualism* (Oxford, 1962); Eric Hobsbawm, "The Seventeenth Century in the Development of Capitalism," *Science and Society* 24 (1960); Joyce Appleby, *Economic Thought and Ideology in Seventeenth-Century England* (Princeton, 1978) exemplify historians' thought regarding economic self-interest. The line of literary critics seeing private interest as individualistic and harmful to communal interests includes L. C. Knights in *Drama and Society in the Age of Jonson* (London, 1937), p. 117; Douglas Bruster, *Drama and the Market in the Age of Shakespeare* (Cambridge, 1992), p. 117; Walter Cohen, *Drama of a Nation* (Ithaca, NY, 1985), p. 290; and Richard Halpern, *The Poetics of Primitive Accumulation: English Renaissance Culture and the Genealogy of Capital* (Ithaca, NY, 1991).
14. Marcus Tullius Cicero, *De finibus bonorum et malorum*, trans. H. Rackham (Cambridge, MA, 1931) v. 24.
15. Francesco Guicciardini, *Maxims and Reflections of a Renaissance Statesman*, ed. Nicolai Rubinstein, trans. Mario Domandi (New York, 1965), p. 121.
16. Malvezzi, Virgilio, *Discorsi sopra Cornelio Tacito* (Venice, 1635), trans. R. Baker as *Discourses Upon Cornelius Tacitus* (London, 1642).
17. J.A.W. Gunn, "'Interest Will Not Lie': A Seventeenth-Century Political Maxim," *Journal of the History of Ideas* (1968), pp. 551–64, at p. 557 outlines the various interpretations of the word "interest" in the context of the political maxim "interest will not lie," a misinterpretation of the phrase first coined in 1628 by the Huguenot statesman and general the Duke of Rohan, "l'interest seul ne peut jamais manquer." Marchamont Nedham's *Interest Will Not Lie* (1659) picked up the maxim and extended

its meaning from Rohan's more purely political sense of states' interest to a more social understanding that humans base decisions on their own self-interest.

18. Thomas Tusser, *Fiue hundred pointes of good Husbandrie* (London, 1580), which went through nearly two dozen editions by the 1640s.
19. McRae, *God Speed*, p. 147. I am indebted to McRae for this close reading of Tusser's manual (see pp. 145–52).
20. Tusser as quoted by McRae, *God Speed*, p. 148.
21. William Scott, *An Essay of Drapery*, int. Sylvia Thrupp (Cambridge, MA, 1953), p. 17.
22. Theodore Leinwand, *The City Staged: Jacobean Comedy, 1603–1613* (Madison, WI, 1986), p. 31.
23. Lewes Roberts, *The Treasure of Traffike* (1641), p. 1. He was quoting from Nicholas Grimalde's 1558 translation of Cicero, *De Officiis*.
24. John Wheeler, *A Treatise of Commerce* (Middleburgh, 1601), p. B2v.
25. The minister Joseph Lee argued for individual gain and profit as a rationale for enclosures, in his *Considerations concerning common fields and inclosures* (London, 1653).
26. Joseph Lee, *A vindication of a regulated enclosure* (London, 1656), p. 9: "Whensoever there is the least want of corn, and men's Land is fit to bear corn, men will plow up their enclosed land for their own profit" exemplifies the maxim, "That every one by the light of nature and reason will do that which makes for his greatest advantage . . . ."
27. Ibid., pp. 22–23.
28. See for instance Thomas Fuller's *The Holy State* (London, 1642), for his essay on 'The Good Landlord' which teaches industry and the value of economic stimulus, and his essay on 'The Good Yeoman' who pursues the "surplusage of estate" (pp. 99, 116).
29. Edward Misselden, *The Circle of Commerce, or the balance of trade* (London, 1623), p. 17.
30. Sir Thomas Smith, *A Discourse of the Commonweal of this Realm of England*, ed. Mary Dewar (Charlottesville, VA, 1969). I follow Mary Dewar's attribution of the *Discourse* to Smith, and her dating of the text to 1549, which was printed in 1581, four years after Smith's death. All references to the text are to this edition and hereafter will be cited parenthetically.
31. Ibid., p. 35.
32. Ibid., p. 53.
33. For an elaborated version of this argument, see McRae, *God Speed*, esp. pp. 52–57. Regarding Smith, McRae concludes: "As he draws together the representations of complaint and moves beyond these statements toward a conception of economic process grounded on an acceptance of self-interest, Smith places his *Discourse* at the very centre of the ideological

confrontation which would shape rival representations of agrarian England well into the seventeenth century" (p. 57).

34. Misselden, *The Circle of Commerce*, p. 17. Misselden's tract was one of a series of hostile exchanges with Gerard de Malynes over England's foreign trade balance. Misselden viewed the solution to obtaining a favorable balance of trade in leaving the province of trade essentially free and uncontrolled by the state. Malynes had accused English merchants of seeking their private gain and it was this objection to which Misselden replied.
35. Adam Smith, *The Wealth of Nations*, introduction by Edwin R. A. Seligman (London, 1954), p. 12; and *Lectures on Jurisprudence*, eds. R. L. Meek, D. D. Raphael, and P. G. Stein (Oxford, 1978), pp. 526–27.
36. Max Weber, *General Economic History*, trans. F. H. Knight (New York, 1927), chapters. 22, 30; idem, *The Protestant Ethic and the Spirit of Capitalism*, trans. Talcott Parsons (London, 1930); R. H. Tawney, *Religion and the Rise of Capitalism* (London, 1936), pp. 175–85, chapter. 5. Laura Caroline Stevenson, *Praise and Parodox: Merchants and Craftsmen in Elizabethan Popular Literature* (Cambridge, 1984), pp. 132–37 counters Weber's thesis that Puritanism gave rise to the work ethic and the "spirit" of capitalism. Instead, she argues, using Elizabethan discussions of diligence, thrift, and prosperity, that personal gain was considered unethical until the seventeenth century. Among the historians Stevenson takes to task are Christopher Hill and Louise Wright. Arguing against their general point that Elizabethan literature offers lessons in diligence and thrift and thus concluding that bourgeois values flourished in the late sixteenth century, Stevenson counters that puritan notions of the "calling" imparted an ethical duty upon notions of money-making so that the bourgeois acceptance of profit-seeking for personal gain did not become current until the seventeenth century.
37. Christopher Hill, *The World Turned Upside Down: Radical Ideas During the English Revolution* (1982), pp. 107–50. Hill, "Individuals and Communities," in idem, *Society and Puritanism in Pre-Revolutionary England* (London, 1969), pp. 467–71 argues that early modern markets broke down village communities based on local custom and led to a "spirit of individualism." Alan Macfarlane finds that from the thirteenth century, workers in England were "economically 'rational,' market-oriented, and acquisitive," in *The Origins of English Individualism: The Family, Property and Social Transition* (London, 1978), p. 163.
38. See Joyce Appleby, *Economic Thought and Ideology in Seventeenth-Century England* (Princeton, 1978), pp. 3–23, 93–95, 183–84, 245–47, 271–79; Jean-Christophe Agnew, *Worlds Apart: The Market and the Theater in Anglo-American Thought, 1550–1750* (Cambridge, 1986), pp. 1–52.
39. C.B. Macpherson, *The Political Theory of Possessive Individualism* (Oxford, 1962), pp. 53–55, 61–62.

40. Craig Muldrew, "Interpreting the Market," *Social History* 18:2 (1993) pp. 163–83, at p. 172.
41. Richard Grassby, *The Business Community of Seventeenth-Century England* (Cambridge, 1995), p. 177 argues that "indebtedness . . . far from creating a subordinate relationship, reinforced connections . . . ."
42. Muldrew, "Interpreting," p. 169.
43. Craig Muldrew, *The Economy of Obligation: The Culture of Credit and Social Relations in Early Modern England* (New York, 1998).
44. Muldrew, *Economy*, p. 318.
45. Muldrew, *Economy*, p. 328.
46. Ibid.
47. Elizabeth Hanson, *Discovering the Subject in Renaissance England* (Cambridge, 1998). Hanson bases her claims on Foucault's theory of epistemic shifts in *The Order of Things*, and finds an exemplary instance of the construction of "interiority" in acts of concealment on the part of tortured Catholics but also finds them in actions by Elizabethan bureaucrats. An earlier and influential study is Katharine Eisaman Maus, *Inwardness and Theatre in the English Renaissance* (Chicago, 1995) which examines inwardness without equating it to what traditional new historicist methodology terms "subjectivity." That methodology, as Maus points out, is based upon philosophical positions that deny subjectivity independent from social determination.
48. J.G.A. Pocock, *Politics, Language and Time: Essays on Political Thought and History* (Chicago, 1989), at p. 25. See also, Quentin Skinner, *Visions of Politics, Vol. I: Regarding Method* (Cambridge, 2002); James Tully, *Meaning and Context: Skinner and His Critics* (Princeton, NJ, 1988).
49. Bruster, *Drama and the Market,* p. 37 integrates economic and psychoanalytic modes of reading social and aesthetic phenomena and argues that in drama (especially that employing farce), human subjectivity comes to be invested in commodified objects in a commodity fetishism. What our approaches share is a conclusion that such processes, rather than alienating the subject in a traditional Marxist account, construct and manipulate subjectivity. Such criticism falls broadly within the tradition of linking English literature and the market system that Knights, *Drama and Society in the Age of Jonson* initiated.
50. Theodore B. Leinwand, *Theatre, Finance and Society in Early Modern England* (Cambridge, 1999). Leinwand and others have built upon the seminal examinations of city comedy in its formal and generic contexts (such as Roman New Comedy and morality plays) by Brian Gibbons in *Jacobean City Comedy* (London, 1968) and Alexander Leggatt, *Citizen Comedy in the Age of Shakespeare* (Toronto: University of Toronto Press, 1973).
51. J.L. Austin, *How to Do Things With Words* (Cambridge, MA, 1975), pp. 109–20.
52. Skinner, *Visions of Politics*, I, p. 157.

53. Ibid., p. 154. Skinner cites Wheeler, *A treatise of commerce* (1601), ed. G. B. Hotchkiss (New York, 1931), pp. 179–80: "the ideal of acting religiously began to be invoked simply to refer to instances of diligent and punctilious behavior. We encounter this usage as early as John Wheeler's *Treatise of Commerce,* in which he praises the freedom of trade originally permitted to the English in the Low Countries. These 'ancient freedomes, and liberties of the Empire,' he remarks, were 'freelie yielded, and so longer Religiouslie mainteyned.'"
54. Skinner, *Visions*, I, p. 182.
55. Quoted in Quentin Skinner, *Visions* I, pp. 183.
56. Ian Archer, *The Pursuit of Stability: Social Relations in Elizabethan London* (Cambridge, 1991), p. 258.
57. For critics who see the prodigals as marginalized and troubling the social fabric, see Margot Heinemann, "Drama and Opinion in the 1620s: Middleton and Massinger," in *Theatre and Government under the Early Stuarts*, eds. J. R. Mulryn and Margaret Shewring (Cambridge, 1993), pp. 258, 260. Keith Lindley, "Noble Scarlet vs. London Blue," in *The Theatrical City: Culture, Theatre and Politics in London, 1576–1649*, eds. David L. Smith, Richard Strier and David Bevington (Cambridge University Press, 1995), p.183 see a conflict between "established landed elites" and a "social parvenu." Leonard Tennenhouse, *Power On Display: The Politics of Shakespeare's Genres* (London, 1986), p. 161 sees city comedy as a genre in which these strict dichotomies operate, in which "one is either predator or prey." See also Gail Kern Paster, *The Idea of the City in the Age of Shakespeare* (Athens, GA, 1988), chapter 6. The critic who sees the outsider as insider is Martin Butler, "The Outsider as Insider," in *The Theatrical City*, p. 205.
58. Lawrence Manley, *Literature and Culture in Early Modern London* (Cambridge, 1995), esp. pp. 431–78.
59. For a discussion of the literature of paternalism, see below (Chapter Two).
60. See reviews of injunctions for women in Ian Maclean, *The Renaissance Notion of Woman* (Cambridge, 1980); Suzanne Hall, *Chaste, Silent, and Obedient: English Books for Women, 1475–1640* (San Marino, CA, 1982); Linda Woodbridge, *Women and the English Renaissance: Literature and the Nature of Womankind, 1540–1620* (Urbana, IL, 1984); Margaret R. Sommerville, *Sex and Subjection: Attitudes to Women in Early-Modern Society* (New York, 1995).
61. See Sylvia Brown (ed.), *Women's Writing in Stuart England: The Mother's Legacies of Dorothy Leigh, Elizabeth Joscelin, and Elizabeth Richardson* (Stroud, 1991), p. ix.
62. Lancelot Andrewes, *The pattern of catechistical doctrine at large, or, A learned and pious exposition of the Ten Commandments* (London, 1650).

63. "Act Concerning Matters of Assurances, Amongst Merchants" (London, 1601), quoted in John Ashton, *The History of Gambling in England* (Detroit, 1968), p. 13.

NOTES TO CHAPTER TWO

1. George Chapman, Ben Jonson, and John Marston, *Eastward Ho!*, ed. R.W. Van Fossen (Manchester, 1999). All references to the play derive from this edition.
2. Craig Muldrew, *The Economy of Obligation* (New York, 1998).
3. L.C. Knights, *Drama and Society in the Age of Jonson* (London, 1937), p. 117 contends that city comedies reflect a dislike of merchants, who, he claims, stand outside the traditions of the social hierarchy. Douglas Bruster, *Drama and the Market in the Age of Shakespeare* (Cambridge, 1992), p. 117 locates conflict in the "systemic" economic system represented in, for example, *Troilus and Cressida* "that apparently distorts human relationships and actively encourages the lapses in morality once ascribed to the machinations of abstract sins and commodities." Of course, Marxist critiques highlight class-driven conflicts most explicitly. Walter Cohen, *Drama of a Nation* (Ithaca, NY, 1985), p. 290 locates an "underlying ideology" in many city comedies in which gentry classes triumph over commercial ones.
4. Laura Caroline Stevenson, *Praise and Paradox: Merchants and Craftsmen in Elizabethan Popular Literature* (Cambridge, 1984), pp. 104–05 observes that Middleton and his contemporaries represent this attitude toward individualism: "the sin they objected to was not greed, but social ambition."
5. Brian Gibbons, *Jacobean City Comedy*, 2nd edn. (London, 1980), p. 34.
6. Andrew Gurr, *Playgoing in Shakespeare's London* (Cambridge, 1987), p. 159.
7. Jacques Le Goff, *Time, Work, and Culture in the Middle Ages* (Chicago, 1980), p. 29.
8. David Hawkes, *Idols of the Marketplace: Idolatry and Commodity Fetishism in English Literature 1580–1680* (New York, 2001), esp. pp. 95–114, discusses early modern conceptions of "usury," especially as it was seen as a type of "sodomy."
9. Aristotle believed that trading for gain was contrary to nature; that trade could only be natural in so far as it is a requirement for self-provisioning, and in this "natural economy," money produces no offspring. Thus prices should be set so as to exclude profit.
10. Jonathan P. Parry and Maurice Bloch, 'Introduction: money and the morality of exchange' in *Money and the Morality of Exchange*, eds. Jonathan P. Parry and Maurice Bloch (Cambridge, 1989), pp. 1–32 provides a valuable introduction to this shift. The collection, a series of essays concerning economic theory and economic anthropology, examines the ways in which money is symbolically represented in a range of societies. It compares the

moral evaluation of monetary and commercial exchanges against other forms of exchange.

11. Albert O. Hirschman, *The Passions and the Interests: Political Arguments for Capitalism before Its Triumph* (Princeton, 1977), pp. 36–42, examines the political basis for pro-capitalist arguments in the Early Modern market culture. He locates the vocabulary of "interest" (meaning primarily economic self-interest) as a new paradigm for human motivation as set against the "passions" (e.g., greed, lust, power, glory).
12. As quoted in David H. Wilson, ed. *The Parliamentary Diary of Robert Bowyer 1606–1607* (Minneapolis, 1931), p. 151.
13. Norman Jones, in *God and the Moneylenders: Usury and Law in Early Modern England* (Oxford, 1989), p. 178 comments, "In 1571 the arguments had been made from church councils and English law, but no one had made an argument from what we could call economics."
14. Ibid., p. 178.
15. Quoted in J. W. Gough, *The Rise of the Entrepreneur* (New York, 1969), p. 23.
16. Ibid., 17.
17. Thomas Powell, *Tom of All Trades, or The Plaine Pathway to Preferment* (London, 1631), p. E^3.
18. See Keith Wrightson, *Earthly Necessities: Economic Lives in Early Modern Britain* (New Haven, CT, 2000), pp. 168–171. Among the industries requiring substantial initial capitalization were iron production, and lead- and coal-mining.
19. Lawrence Stone, *The Crisis of the Aristocracy* (London, 1965).
20. Richard Grassby, *The Business Community of Seventeenth-Century England* (Cambridge, 1995), p. 112.
21. In early Stuart London, just 45% of the Goldsmiths, for example, took their freedom. Ibid., 139.
22. Powell, *Tom of All Trades*, p. E^3v.
23. See *Cicero, De Officiis*, 2.33, trans. Walter Miller, Loeb Classical Library (Cambridge, MA, 1985), pp. 202–03. Miller translates the phrase *ita fides habetur* as "confidence is reposed in men," which equates *fides* with "confidence," where Grimalde had previously given "credit." The *Oxford Latin Dictionary*, ed. P.G.W. Glare (Oxford, 1982), p. 698, lists this same phrase from Cicero as an example for *fides* as "trust": *fidem habere* (with dat.), "to place trust (in), give credence (to)." Also see Cicero, *Marcus Tullius Ciceroes thre bokes of duties*, trans. Nicholas Grimalde (London, 1556), p. K^4v.
24. Gerard Malynes, *Consuetudo or Lex Mercatoria* (London, 1622), p. B^3r-^{3}v.
25. On "neighborliness," see Keith Wrightson, *English Society, 1580–1680* (New Brunswick, NJ, 1982), pp. 51–57.
26. Thomas Powell, *The Art of Thriving* (London, 1635), p. A^5v.

27. Craig Muldrew, "Interpreting the market: the ethics of credit and community relations in early modern England," *Social History* 18:2 (1993), pp. 163–83, at p. 169.
28. John Wheeler, *A Treatise of Commerce*, ed. George B. Hotchkiss (New York, 1931), pp. 6–7.
29. Richard Hooker, *Of the Laws of Ecclesiastical Polity*, ed. Arthur Stephen McGrade (Cambridge, 1989), pp. 89, 91.
30. Ibid., (I.3.1).
31. The term "capitalism" has been the subject of considerable scrutiny recently by economic historians. Richard Grassby, *The Idea of Capitalism before the Industrial Revolution*, (Oxford, 1999) contends that capitalism is virtually indefinable, annoying many economic historians in the process. But Grassby has argued coherently that capitalism, defined by the existence of surplus commodities, capital investment, and the effort to maximize returns, was not unique to early modern England or Europe, but is as old as civilization itself (p. 21). He argues that other characteristics attributed to capitalism were a consequence of the industrial revolution (p. 63). One traditional argument holds that it was in the early modern period that capitalism began to expand so that its social force expanded to all levels of society. As Fernand Braudel *Civilization and Capitalism 15th-18th Century, Vol. II: The Wheels of Commerce* 1979, trans. Sian Reynolds (New York, 1982), p. 239 notes, "capitalism in the past (as distinct from capitalism today) only occupied a narrow platform of economic life. . . . It was nevertheless a world apart, different from and indeed foreign to the social and economic context surrounding it."
32. See Jonathan Barry, "Bourgeois Collectivism? Urban Association and the Middling Sort," in *The Middling Sort of People: Culture, Society and Politics in England, 1550–1800*, eds. Jonathan Barry and Christopher Brooks (New York, 1994), pp. 84–112.
33. Paul Seaver, "The Puritan Work Ethic Revisited," *Journal of British Studies* 19:2 (1980), p. 43.
34. Ibid, p. 47.
35. Max Weber, *The Protestant Ethic and the Spirit of Capitalism,* trans. Talcott Parsons (London, 1992). Weber turned to religion as the initiator of change, associating Calvinism with Capitalism.
36. See for instance, C.B. Macpherson in *The Political Theory of Possessive Individualism* (Oxford, 1962), and Eric Hobsbawm in *The Seventeenth Century in the Development of Capitalism*. For a review of theories of the market as a "depersonalizing mechanism," see Joyce Appleby, *Economic Thought and Ideology in Seventeenth Century England* (Princeton, 1978), pp. 13–15. For these theorists, the market mechanism is the force behind social change, but it is the leverage of those in power—the buyers, investors, and employers—that moves the rest of society, producing the Marxist alienation of land and labor. Where labor becomes a commodity, "market relations so shape

and permeate all social relations that it may properly be called a market society, not merely a market economy" (Macpherson, *The Political Theory of Possessive Individualism*, p. 48).

37. While Marx's dialectical materialism—the model whereby individuals are forced to assume roles in production and man's social being determines his consciousness—does not accurately describe the play's economic culture, neither really does classical economics. According to the latter school of thought, the economy is driven by impersonal forces, with individuals making economically rational choices based, among other things, on their natural propensity to truck and barter.
38. See Ian Archer, *The Pursuit of Stability: Social Relations in Elizabethan England*, (Cambridge, 1991), p. 259.
39. Ibid.
40. Ibid., pp. 163–82, 186–90.
41. See David Rollison, "The bourgeois soul of John Smyth of Nibley," *Social History* 12 (1987), pp. 309–30.
42. Ibid., p. 326.
43. Ibid., p. 328.
44. See Felicity Heal, "The idea of hospitality in early modern England," *Past and Present* 102 (1984), p. 67.
45. Andrew Gurr, *Playgoing in Shakespeare's London*, 2nd edn. (Cambridge, 1996), p. 165, notes that *Westward Ho* is not an anti-citizen play because it dramatizes the triumph of the citizen women in the fifth act.
46. J.A. Bastiaenen, *The Moral Tone of Jacobean and Caroline Drama* (New York, 1930), p. 172 found *Eastward Ho* "replete with moral and religious instruction." Later critics would complicate this formulation. Una Ellis-Fermor, *The Jacobean Drama*, rev. edn. (New York, 1964), p. 136 identified in the play "a sub-sardonic comment . . . on the citizen values of thrift and patience"; Richard Horwich, "*Hamlet* and *Eastward Ho*," *Studies in English Literature* (1971), pp. 224, 233 sees the play as a "demonstration of the homiletic ideals of its main character, Touchstone, who believes that thrift, industry, and sobriety—the citizen values—will triumph over ambition, prodigality, and radical innovation," but that "the audience . . . should regard Touchstone's sense of thrift . . . as a virtue too simple . . . to be taken seriously by men who understand the harsh realities of the world." But this line of criticism relegates the critique of "the citizen values" to a minor effect, maintaining that the play's main thrust implicates social climbing. Ralph A. Cohen, "The Function of Setting in *Eastward Ho*," *Renaissance Papers* (1973), p. 91 has written that "[t]he Thames acts in accordance with the play's moral that it is wrong to aspire to higher social status."
47. Theodore Leinwand, *Theatre, Finance, and Society* (Cambridge, 1999), p. 42.
48. E.H.C. Oliphant (ed.), *Shakespeare and His Fellow Dramatists* (New York, 1929), p. 1007, finds that "Mildred and Golding are somewhat sickening

prigs"; Bastiaenen, *Moral Tone*, p. 109, remarks that Golding and Mildred's love "displays an entire absence of passion"; Van Fossen, ed. *Eastward Ho*, pp. 28, 31 finds Golding "devoid of humor," and remarks that "[Quicksilver's changeableness is stressed] to emphasize . . . the contrast with Golding and to suggest by implication the deficiencies of the boring stability in Golding's character," and "Golding's uniform qualities . . . are not held up for admiration, especially as we see him juxtaposed to the lively Quicksilver and the whimsical Touchstone."

49. See Joseph Sigalas, "Sailing Against the Tide: Resistance to Pre-Colonial Constructs and Euphoria in *Eastward Ho!*," *Renaissance Papers* (1994), pp. 85–94, esp. pp. 89–90.
50. See Helen Ostovich, "Introduction," *Eastward Ho!* (London, 2002), xiii.
51. Craig Muldrew, "From a 'light cloak' to an 'iron cage': historical changes in the Relation between Community and Individualism," in *Communities in Early Modern England: Networks, Place, Rhetoric*, eds. Alexandra Shepard and Phil Withington (Manchester, 2000), pp. 166–67.
52. Robert Burton, *The Anatomy of Melancholy*, eds. Nicholas K. Kiessling, Thomas Faulkner, and Rhonda L. Blair (Oxford, 1989), I, p. 348.
53. To "take up the freedom of the city," to become a citizen, meant to join one of the city Livery companies. All liverymen had votes in the Common Hall which was responsible for nominating the Lord Mayor, the City Chamberlain, and other officers. The whole structure was regulated by a Charter which set forth the relations between Crown and City.
54. For my comments on habeas corpus I am indebted to legal historian Paul D. Halliday, whose enlightening talk, "*Liberty of the Subject: Habeas Corpus and English Society, 1500–1800*," delivered at the Department of History Workshop, at the University of Virginia, October 2002, detailed the significance of subjects' uses of the writ.
55. Other prerogative writs include *mandamus*, prohibitions, *certiorari*, and *quo warranto*. The writs derived from the power of the King and were adjudicated largely in King's Bench. See Edward Jenks, "The Prerogative Writs in English Law," *Yale Law Journal* 32 (1923), pp. 523–34 and S. A. de Smith, *Judicial Review of Administrative Action*, 4th edn. (London, 1980), pp. 584–95.
56. Susan Wells, "Jacobean City Comedy and the Ideology of the City," *English Literary History* 48 (1981), p. 49.
57. Muldrew, "From a 'light cloak' to an 'iron cage': historical changes in the relation between community and individualism," p. 162.
58. Ibid., p. 161 goes on to state: "I wish to dispense with the teleological notion that increasing market competition has created conflict which has dissolved communities . . . I would rather say that the exact opposite is true: that conflict exists where co-operative bonds are the *most* interpersonal. In such close relations there is the most scope for argument, misunderstanding, disagreement and disappointment. Thus spousal or sexual relations now

lead to more disruptive conflict than banking, politics, or even labour relations. . . ."

NOTES TO CHAPTER THREE

1. Quoted in Keith Wrightson, *English Society, 1580–1680* (New Brunswick, NJ, 1982), pp. 58–59.
2. Keith Wrightson, *Earthly Necessities: Economic Lives in Early Modern Britain* (New Haven, CT, 2000), p. 322; Wrightson, *English Society,* pp. 57–61, 63–65, 179; and Peter Laslett, *The World We Have Lost* (London, 1965) review the general practice and theory of paternalism in sixteenth- and seventeenth-century England. For more detailed discussions, especially regarding agrarian paternalism, see Mervyn James, *Family, Lineage, and Civil Society: a Study of Society, Politics and Mentality in the Durham Region, 1500–1640* (Oxford, 1974) and G. E. Mingay, *The Gentry: The Rise and Fall of a Ruling Class* (London, 1976). *The Deferential Worker: A Study of Farm Workers in East Anglia* (London, 1977) is excellent regarding deferential relationships.
3. Charles Webster, *The Great Instauration: Science, Medicine, and Reform, 1626–1660* (London, 1975), pp. 25, 447–48 notes the connection between the new economic theorists such as William Petty and the Baconian natural philosophers, arguing that it is "only a slight exaggeration to regard Baconianism as the official philosophy of the [Puritan] Revolution." See also Timothy Reiss, *The Discourse of Modernism* (Ithaca, NY, 1985), p. 136: "There is nothing new in [Bacon's] statement of identity between the politics of possessive individualism and the scientific stance of experimentalism: "we do publish such profitable inventions as *we* think good" p. 194 [emphasis in the original]. Elizabeth Hanson, *Discovering the Subject in Renaissance England* (Cambridge, 1998), p. 136 finds that "There is, in fact, a persistent conjunction in Bacon's writing of pecuniary self-interest, potential subversiveness, and the work of thinking the 'totally new'."
4. Markku Peltonen, "Bacon's Political Philosophy," in *The Cambridge Companion to Bacon*, ed. Markku Peltonen (Cambridge, 1996), p. 290 poses this question. Julian Martin, *Francis Bacon, the State and the Reform of Natural Philosophy* (Cambridge, 1992), p. 134 invokes the oft-cited frontispiece of Bacon's *Instauratio magna* (1620) as an "unequivocal declaration that natural philosophy would contribute to empire." Ian Box, "Bacon's Moral Philosophy," in *The Cambridge Companion to Bacon,* p. 275 says, of Bacon's *Instauration*, "The politicization of knowledge which subordinates inquiry to 'the benefit and use of life' (IV, 21) has its counterpart in the political organization of investigation." David Colclough, "Ethics and politics in the New Atlantis," in *Francis Bacon's New Atlantis: New Interdisciplinary Essays*, ed. Bronwen Price (Manchester, 2002), pp. 60–81 at p. 75 finds the *New Atlantis* to be "an extended reflection on

the ethics and politics of the philosopher's relations with past authorities. . . ."

5. Ian Box, "Politics and Philosophy: Bacon on the values of peace and war," *The Seventeenth Century* 7:2 (1992), pp. 113–27 ascribes the gap between political and ethical thought in the *New Atlantis* to a fundamental contradiction between Bacon's identities as a "scientist" and a "statesman."
6. See Markku Peltonen, "Politics and science: Francis Bacon and the true greatness of states," *Historical Journal* 35:2 (1992), pp. 279–305; idem, *Classical Humanism and Republicanism in English Political Thought 1570–1640* (Cambridge, 1995), pp. 190–228 at p. 195.
7. Francis Bacon, *New Atlantis and The Great Instauration*, ed. Jerry Weinberger (Arlington Heights, IL, 1989), p. 36 [hereinafter: *TNAGI*]. All references to the *New Atlantis* are to this edition and will subsequently be noted in parentheses.
8. On the Atlantis myth, see Plato, *The Collected Dialogues*, ed. Edith Hamilton and Huntington Cairns (Princeton, 1961) at *Timaeus*, trans. Benjamin Jowett, pp. 1151–211; and *Critias*, trans. A. E. Taylor, pp. 1212–24.
9. Bacon refers to More's *Utopia* in the phrase "a book of one of your men, of a Feigned Commonwealth" at p. 68. On links between Andreae, Campanella, and Bacon, see Joyce L. Hertzler, *The History of Utopian Thought* (New York, 1965), pp. 146–65; and Eleanor Dickinson Blodgett, "Bacon's New Atlantis and Campanella's *Civitas Solis*: A Study in Relationships," *PMLA* 46:3 (1931), pp. 763–80.
10. *TNAGI*, p. 36.
11. Simon Wortham, "Censorship and the institution of knowledge in Bacon's *New Atlantis*," in *Francis Bacon's New Atlantis: New Interdisciplinary Essays*, pp. 180–98 at p. 195.
12. Ibid.
13. Recent analyses of utopian literature can be found in Glenn Negley and J. Max Patrick, *The Quest for Utopia: An Anthology* (New York, 1952); Joyce Hertzler, *The History of Utopian Thought* (New York, 1965); Frank E. Manuel (ed.), *Utopias and Utopian Thought* (Boston, 1966); J.C. Davis, *Utopia and the Ideal Society: A Study of English Utopian Writing 1516–1700* (Cambridge, 1981); Theodore Olson, *Millennialism, Utopianism, and Progress* (Toronto, 1982); Krishan Kumar, *Utopia and Anti-Utopia in Modern Times* (Oxford, 1987); idem, *Utopianism* (Minneapolis, 1991); Marina Leslie, *Renaissance Utopias and the Problem of History* (Ithaca, NY, 1998); and Mary Baine Campbell, *Wonder and Science: Imagining Worlds in Early Modern Europe* (Ithaca, NY, 1999).
14. John Michael Archer, *Sovereignty and Intelligence: Spying and Court Culture in the English Renaissance* (Stanford, CA, 1993), p. 144.
15. See Amy Boesky, "Bacon's *New Atlantis* and the laboratory of prose," in *The Project of Prose in Early Modern Europe and the New World*, eds. Elizabeth Fowler and Roland Greene (Cambridge, 1997), pp. 138–53; Robert K.

Faulkner, *Francis Bacon and the Project of Progress* (Lanham, MD, 1993), p. 248 , which argues "the order that orders . . . is hidden"; and Charles Whitney, "Merchants of Light: science as colonization in the *New Atlantis*," in *Francis Bacon's Legacy of Texts*, ed. William Sessions (New York, 1990), pp. 255–68, which reads the *New Atlantis* as a colonialist narrative.

16. *TNAGI*, p. xxxi.
17. See Peter Donaldson, *Machiavelli and Mystery of State* (Cambridge, 1988) for the origins of "mystery of state" (*arcana imperii*), and its development in fifteenth- and sixteenth-century political thought in England. I am also indebted to Richard McCoy and his discussion of sacred kingship and the *arcana* in James I's rituals at court, in the seminar, "Political Thought at the Tudor and Stuart Courts," Folger Shakespeare Library Institute, Fall 2000.
18. Leslie, *Renaissance Utopias and the Problem of History*, p. 105 comments that "Bacon's utopian fantasy suggests that the *arcana imperii* could themselves be anatomized and reproduced at will."
19. As Jerry Weinberger notes, "in the absence of [a safeguard against excessive desire] Bensalemite science might be said to base human endeavor on the very foundation of moral excess: the human body and the myriad desires that bring one body into conflict with others": *TNAGI*, pp. xxx-xxxi.
20. I see a "patriarchy" represented here as weakened under the larger control of the paternalistic state control: my reading contrasts with those critics such as Susan Bruce, who claims that Bacon's is a patriarchal system to be contrasted with the society of, for example, Margaret Cavendish's *Blazing World*, where the Emperor is a cipher who allows the Empress complete domination over his world. Susan Bruce, "Virgins of the world and feasts of the family: sex and the social order in two renaissance utopias," in *English Renaissance Prose: History, Language and Politics*, ed. Neil Rhodes (Tempe, 1997), pp. 139–46.
21. For a recent discussion of Bacon's legal arguments including those in Chudleigh's Case, see Daniel R. Coquillette, *Francis Bacon* (Stanford, CA, 1992), pp. 56–58, 134.
22. See L. B. Curzon, *English Legal History*, 2nd edn. (Estover, 1979), pp. 120–21; J. H. Baker, *An Introduction to English Legal History*, 4th edn. (London, 2002), pp. 255–57.
23. *Dillon v. Freine*, 1594, I Co. Rep. 1136, 76 Eng. Rep. 261 (KB 1594), as translated from the law French by Spedding *et. al* and reprinted in *The Works of Francis Bacon*, ed. Basil Montagu (London, 1827), VII, p. 625 [hereinafter: *WFB*].
24. Ibid., p. 634.
25. Ibid., p. 634
26. Ibid., pp. 634–35.
27. Francis Bacon, *Novum Organum, with other parts of The Great Instauration*, eds. Peter Urbach and John Gibson (Chicago, 1994), p. 131 [hereinafter: *NO*].

28. Ibid.
29. Francis Bacon, *Valerius Terminus of the Interpretation of Nature, with the annotations of Hermes Stella*, (*WFB*, III, p. 215).
30. *WFB*, III, p. 222.
31. Davis, *Utopia*, p. 125.
32. Kumar, *Utopia and Anti-Utopia*, p. 29. Kumar goes on to quote Christopher Hill in support of his point: "Christopher Hill points up admirably the significance for utopia of this Baconian achievement. 'Though Bacon accepted a Fall of Man, he rejected the full Calvinist doctrine of human depravity.'" It would seem instead that Bacon's drive for the improvement of mankind through learning appreciates fully its tendency toward depravity.
33. Ibid. p. 430, n. 60.
34. Box, "Bacon's Moral Philosophy," p. 279.
35. *WFB*, I, p. 64.
36. Virgil K. Whitaker, *Francis Bacon's Intellectual Milieu* (Los Angeles, CA, 1962), p. 22.
37. *NO*, p. 38.
38. Whitaker, *Francis Bacon's Intellectual Milieu*, p. 23.
39. *WFB*, III, p. 231.
40. *WFB*, (1872) XIII, pp. 35, 37, 46, 49.
41. *WFB*, XIV, pp. 70–71.
42. Ibid.
43. *WFB*, XIV, p. 72.
44. *WFB*, XI, p. 249
45. Martin, *Francis Bacon, the State and the Reform of Natural Philosophy*, pp. 134–40 finds that Bacon adapted Tudor strategies of state management and the common law into his method for the sciences. Hanson, *Discovering the Subject in Renaissance England*, p. 135 concludes that "His writing forges positive ideological links between the state, knowledge production, and the control of information."
46. Julie Robin Solomon, *Objectivity in the Making* (Baltimore, 1998), p. 10.
47. Ibid., p. 13.
48. Hanson, p. 135.
49. *WFB*, VII, (1827), p. 267.
50. For an excellent argument of this point, see Solomon, *Objectivity in the Making*, pp. 63–88.
51. *TNAGI*, p. 1.
52. In 1621 Bacon was accused of accepting bribes and other dishonesties, he admitted the charges, and was dismissed from his office of Lord Chancellor. Sentenced to a fine of £40,000 and life imprisonment, he was relieved of punishment by the King. He then retired to his country home at Gorhambury. For a detailed account of the case, the decision against Bacon, and Bacon's ultimate denial of any wrongdoing, see Lisa Jardine and Alan

Stewart, *Hostage to Fortune: The Troubled Life of Francis Bacon* (New York, 1998), pp. 449–69.

53. William Shakespeare, *Timon of Athens*, ed. H.J. Oliver (London, 1997). All subsequent citations refer to this edition and will be given in parentheses.
54. Most scholars believe the play was written between 1605 and 1608, several years after James I's accession to the English throne. Many argue the play was left unfinished and un-produced, and we have no proof of its performance during James's lifetime. William Shakespeare, *The Norton Shakespeare*, eds. Stephen Greenblatt, Walter Cohen, Jean Howard, Katharine Maus (New York, 1997), p. 2247.
55. For instance see Philip Caesar, *A General Discourse against the Damnable Sect of Usurers* (London, 1578); Henry Smith, *The Examination of Usury* (London, 1591); Miles Mosse, *The Arraignment and Conviction to Usurie* (London, 1595), p. 101; Roger Fenton, *A Treatise of Usurie* (London, 1611); John Blaxton (compiler), *The English Usurer; or Usury condemned, by the most learned and famous Divines of the Church of England*, 2nd edn. (London, 1634).
56. See Richard Tuck, *Philosophy and Government 1572–1651* (Cambridge, 1993); Peter Burke, "Tacitism," in *Tacitus*, ed. T.A. Dorey (London, 1969), pp. 149–71; Burke, "Tacitism, Scepticism, and Reason of State," in *The Cambridge History of Political Thought 1450–1700*, ed. J. H. Burns (Cambridge, 1991), pp. 479–98; J.H.M. Salmon, "Seneca and Tacitus in Jacobean England," *Journal of the History of Ideas* 50 (1989), pp. 199–225.
57. Sir Thomas Elyot, *The Book Named the Governor*, ed. S.E. Lehmberg (New York, 1962), p. 81.
58. A.D. Nuttall, *Timon of Athens* (Boston, 1989), p. 72.
59. Not every critic accepts Alcibiades' sincerity in this instance. Rolf Soellner doubts the value of his settlement at the play's conclusion, in *Timon of Athens: Shakespeare's Pessimistic Tragedy* (Columbus, OH, 1979), pp. 53–63. William O. Scott, "The Paradox of Timon's Self-Cursing," *Shakespeare Quarterly* 35 (1984), p. 300, too, wonders "whether such an opportunist as Alcibiades really cares about the evils that were the matter of Timon's curses." It seems that the communal and civic value of Alcibiades' participations in "public laws" is the valuable social contract here, not necessarily his inner sincerity. The Senators are not asking Alcibiades to swear an oath or reveal his conscience in this instance, just to behave in alignment with civil laws and codes of behavior.
60. E.K. Chambers, *Shakespeare: A Survey* (London, 1925), p. 269. E. H. Wright, *The Authorship of Timon of Athens* (New York, 1910), p. 44 contends that Alcibiades' banishment "has not the slightest reference to Timon"; and Hardin Craig, *An Interpretation of Shakespeare* (New York, 1948), p. 253 writes of the "inconsistent Alcibiades."
61. Mervyn James, *Society, Politics, and Culture: Studies in Early Modern England* (Cambridge, 1986), p. 465 notes that a few decades after Timon was written, "the dissidents of the Long Parliament gave precedence not to the

language of honor, but of law and religion; the terminology of Tudor conformity and social wholeness had been adapted to the needs of dissidence."

62. Pauline Croft, paper given at the seminar, "Political Thought at the Tudor and Stuart Courts," Folger Institute Seminar, October 27, 2000.
63. I am indebted to Pauline Croft for this insight into Cecil's political activities, see above.
64. Anna Bryson, *From Courtesy to Civility: Changing Codes of Conduct in Early Modern England* (Oxford, 1998) examines pre-eighteenth century political thought as an aspect of "manners" and Pocock's civic humanism. She locates a "changing mentality of aristocracy . . . values and practices which identified their interests more closely with the universalizing claims of the state." (p. 24).
65. Quentin Skinner, *The Foundations of Modern Political Thought*, 2 vols. (Cambridge, 1978); idem, *Visions of Politics, Vol. I: Regarding Method* (Cambridge, 2002); J.G.A. Pocock, *The Ancient Constitution and the Feudal Law* (Cambridge, 1987); idem, *The Machiavellian Moment* (Princeton, NJ, 1975); Pocock, *Virtue, Commerce, and History* (Cambridge, 1985).
66. Elyot, *The Book Named the Governor*, p. 82.
67. Ibid.
68. Ibid.
69. Geoffrey Bullough, *Narrative and Dramatic Sources of Shakespeare* (London, 1966), VI, p. 237 does not mention Elyot as a source for *Timon of Athens,* focusing instead on Plutarch: "The introduction of Alcibiades was suggested by Plutarch's account of Timon."
70. Richard Fly, *Shakespeare's Mediated World* (Amherst, MA, 1976), pp. 141–42 has commented on Alcibiades' behavior as "civil" at the play's end, without explicitly noting his shift with the Senators. Nuttall comments, that with the Senators, "Alcibiades perceives at once that a civic (civilised) response has simply ruled out his fundamentally martial assumptions": *Timon*, p. 74.
71. Aristotle condemns interest as "unnatural" in his *Politics*: "this term 'interest,' which means the birth of money from money, is applied to the breeding of money because the offspring resembles the parent. Wherefore of all modes of getting wealth this is the most unnatural" in *Politics*, trans. Benjamin Jowett (New York, 1943), I.10, 1258.
72. Bullough, *Narrative and Dramatic Sources of Shakespeare* ("The Dialogue of Timon"), VI, p. 265.
73. C.L. Barber and Richard Wheeler, *The Whole Journey: Shakespeare's Power of Development* (Berkeley, CA, 1986), p. 306 employs a psychoanalytic approach in some of its sections: "Shakespeare shows Timon trying to make up for insecurity about maternal nurturance by doing the nurturing himself"; and Coppelia Kahn, "'Magic of Bounty': *Timon of Athens*, Jacobean Patronage, and Maternal Power," *Shakespeare Quarterly* 38 (1987), pp. 34–57 at p. 57 extends this approach to include the Stuart court as well: "It seems possible

that the extreme dependency created by patronage, in which advancement or obscurity, prosperity or ruin, hung on the granting of a suit, could have reawakened anxieties stemming from infantile dependency on the mother who, it seems to the child, can give or take away all."

74. See R. Malcolm Smuts, *Court Culture and the Origins of the Royalist Tradition in Early Modern England* (Philadelphia, 1987), p. 260. On the relation of this notion to sacral kingship, see Debora K. Shuger, *Political Theologies in Shakespeare's England* (New York, 2001), esp. 54–62.
75. For an early modern expression of this common dictum, see Edward Forset, *A Comparative Discourse of the Bodies Natural and Politique* (London, 1606), p. 10.
76. See Paul S. Seaver, *Wallington's World: A Puritan Artisan in Seventeenth-Century London* (Stanford, CA, 1985), pp. 114–15.
77. Caroline Bingham, *James I of England* (London, 1981), p. 93.
78. Lawrence Stone, *Family and Fortune: Studies of Aristocratic Finance in the Sixteenth and Seventeenth Centuries* (Oxford, 1973), p. 25.
79. See, for example, Michael Chorost, "Biological Finance in Shakespeare's *Timon of Athens*," *ELR* 21 (1991), pp. 349–70; Coppelia Kahn, "Magic"; and Katharine Maus, intro., "The Life of Timon of Athens," *The Norton Shakespeare* (New York: Norton, 1997), p. 2246.
80. Marcel Mauss, *The Gift: Forms and Functions of Exchange in Archaic Societies,* trans. Ian Cunnison (New York, 1925).
81. Wrightson, *Earthly Necessities,* p. 322.
82. The famous phrase is from John Donne's "An Anatomy of the World: The First Anniversary," l. 213, from *The Norton Anthology of English Literature,* ed. M.H. Abrams, 6th edn. (New York, 1993), I, p. 1113.
83. The 1549 catechism of the Church of England: quoted in Laslett, *The World We Have Lost*, p. 176.
84. James, *Family, Lineage, and Civil Society*, p. 27.
85. On the gentry's attitude of superiority, see Mingay, *The Gentry*, p. 164.
86. Lawrence Stone, "Patriarchy and Paternalism in Tudor England: The Earl of Arundel and The Peasants' Revolt of 1549," *Journal of British Studies* 13 (1974), pp. 19–23.
87. Ibid., p. 21.
88. Anonymous landlord, as quoted in Mingay, *The Gentry,* p. 119.
89. Wrightson, *English Society*, pp. 61–62.
90. Theodore Leinwand, *Theatre, finance, and society in early modern England* (Cambridge, 1999) p. 41 does not mention paternalism in his chapter on Timon, but he concludes his chapter with an observation along these lines, regarding changes in "commonwealth and political economy": "What had been conceived of as reciprocity (common wealth) between one person and another, between sovereign and subject, is increasingly understood in terms of *quid pro quo* (contract)."

NOTES TO CHAPTER FOUR

1. See for example Margaret Patterson Hannay (ed.), *Silent But for the Word: Tudor Women as Patrons, Translators, and Writers of Religious Works* (Kent, OH, 1985); Margaret W. Ferguson, Maureen Quilligan, and Nancy Vickers, eds., *Rewriting the Renaissance: The Discourses of Sexual Difference in Early Modern Europe* (Chicago, 1986); Elaine V. Beilen, *Redeeming Eve: Women Writers of the English Renaissance* (Princeton, 1987); Ann Rosalind Jones, *The Currency of Eros: Women's Love Lyric in Europe 1540–1620* (Bloomington, 1990); Barbara Kiefer Lewalski, *Writing Women in Jacobean England* (Cambridge, MA, 1993); Ilona Bell, *Elizabethan Women and the Poetry of Courtship* (Cambridge, 1998); and Lynette McGrath, *Subjectivity*.
2. Isabella Whitney, "Wyll and Testament," in *Isabella Whitney, Mary Sidney and Aemilia Lanyer: Renaissance Women Poets*, ed. Danielle Clarke (London, 2000) pp. 18–28, ll. 225–28.
3. All quotes from Whitney's "Wyll and Testament" are taken from Clarke; hereafter line numbers will be cited parenthetically. The poem includes a preface titled "A comunication which the Auctor had to London, before she made her Wyll," numbered separately, and will be cited parenthetically as "comunication." I distinguish between the speaker of the poem and Isabella Whitney: we should not conflate the speaker's fate with Whitney's or assume autobiography, as some critics have done. Betty Travitsky, whose invaluable work introduced the poem to the modern reader in "The 'Wyll and Testament' of Isabella Whitney," *ELR* 10 (1980), pp. 76–94, at p. 78 nonetheless assumes that the poetic persona offers biographical information about Whitney; Tina Krontiris, in *Oppositional Voices: Women as Writers and Translators of Literature in the English Renaissance* (London, 1992), p. 28 assumes that Whitney was a maid employed in London, but we have no direct evidence of this. The headnote to the Norton Seventh Edition more reasonably suggests, "She writes in the voice of an impoverished gentlewoman who is compelled by her circumstances to leave the city": *Norton Anthology of English Literature*, ed. M.H. Abrams 7th edn. (New York, 1999), I, p. 606. Lynette McGrath, *Subjectivity and Women's Poetry in Early Modern England* (Aldershot, 2002), p. 145 identifies the speaker as a "persona," as does Kim Walker, *Women Writers of the English Renaissance* (New York, 1996), p. 157. In drawing connections between the challenges facing female writers producing printed texts in London's market economy and Whitney's speaker's conundrums and descriptions, I emphasize the literariness of one author's response to this situation.
4. See Betty Travitsky (ed.), *The Paradise of Women: Writings by Englishwomen of the Renaissance* (Westport, CT, 1981); Mary Beth Rose, "Where are the Mothers in Shakespeare?" *Shakespeare Quarterly* 42 (1991), pp. 291–314; Susan Dwyer Amussen, *An Ordered Society: Gender and Class in Early*

Modern England (New York, 1988), pp. 81–85, 91–93, 119–23; Wendy Wall, *The Imprint of Gender: Authorship and Publication in the English Renaissance* (Ithaca, NY, 1993), pp. 284–306; and Randall Martin (ed.) *Women Writers in Renaissance England* (London, 1997), pp. 279–281.

5. See Betty S. Travitsky, 'Whitney, Isabella (fl. 1566–1573),' *Oxford Dictionary of National Biography* (Oxford, 2004). Commentators believe that Whitney was fairly young when she published the poems and so was probably born in the mid-sixteenth century.
6. For biographical details about Whitney, much of it speculative, see R. J. Fehrenbach, "Isabella Whitney, Siir Hugh Plat, Geffrey Whitney, and 'Sister Eldershae,'" *ELN* 21 (1983), pp. 7–11; Richard Panofsky (ed.), *The Floures of Philosophie (1572) by Hugh Plat and A Sweet Nosgay (1573) and The Copy of a Letter (1567) by Isabella Whitney* (Delmar, NY, 1982) intro.; Henry Green (ed.), *Geffrey Whitney, A Choice of Emblemes* (New York, 1967) intro., and Martin (ed.), *Woman Writers,* p. 280.
7. Clarke, "A modest meane for Maides In order prescribed, by Is. W. to two of her yonger Sisters servinge in London," "To her Sister Misteris. A.B." pp. 10–13; "IS. W. being wery of writyng, sendeth this for Answere," p. 17.
8. Christopher Brooks, "Apprenticeship, Social Mobility and the Middling Sort, 1550–1800," in *The Middling Sort of People: Culture, Society and Politics in England, 1550–1800,* eds. Jonathan Barry and Christopher Brooks (New York, 1994), p. 53.
9. Whitney is pathetically fallacious here, according to Ruskin, because she is ascribing human feeling to the Fleet prison, who will feel so bitter, she suggests, that he will "curse" her if she gives "him nought," (l. 167; 166). Ruskin's explanation of the "pathetic fallacy" appears in *Modern Painters* (Boston, 1851) III, pp. 200–18.
10. Since Ruskin applied his term "pathetic fallacy" in a derogatory sense because it applied not to the actual appearance or state of things but to false appearances described by a writer under the influence of emotion, here I distinguish between true pathetic fallacy and Whitney's description of prisons that actually were crowded with criminals and debtors. In other words, while the personification of the prisons was a literary trope, the description of them was not.
11. *Geneva Bible* (London, 1579) Matthew 6:12, p. B7^{v}.
12. Thomas Tusser outlined the elements of honest trade in *Five hundred pointes of good Husbandrie* (London, 1580); Sir Thomas Smith recognized self-interest as an acceptable force in *A Discourse of the Commonweal of this Realm of England,* asserting that men naturally "seek where their advantage is": Sir Thomas Smith, *A Discourse of the Commonweal of this Realm of England,* ed. Mary Dewar (Charlottesville, VA, 1969), p. 35; John Wheeler emphasized merchants' communication skills in *A Treatise of Commerce* (Middleburgh, 1601); William Scott asserted the importance of some self-interest

in business dealings, claiming that "honesty without wisdome is unprofitable" in *An Essay on Drapery* (Cambridge, MA, 1953), p. 17. In addition, seventeenth-century casuistry manuals took up "cases of conscience" concerning economic issues in great detail, including those concerning "profit" and "traffique." (Some were delivered as sermons beginning in the sixteenth century.) Among the topics explored were the legality of monopolies, the morality of profit margins, pursuing debtors, and even the retrieval of goods from robbers. On this last topic, Joseph Hall would write in 1650, "if . . . in hot chase [you] so strike him . . . and if hereupon his death shall follow . . . God and [your] own heart would acquit [you]," Joseph Hall, *Resolutions and decisions of divers practical cases of conscience* (London, 1650), p. E4.; William Perkins, *The Whole Treatise of the Cases of Conscience* (Cambridge, 1604); and William Ames, *Conscience with the Power and Cases Thereof* (Leyden and London, 1639). Among other common topics were the negotiation of contracts, and the use of riches. The puritan divine Ames, p. 253, would write that "riches" "are usefull and profitable, and . . . rightly called the gifts and blessings of God."

13. *The Norton Shakespeare*, eds. Stephen Greenblatt, Walter Cohen, Jean E. Howard, Katharine Eisaman Maus (New York, 1997) *The Tragedy of Coriolanus* (3.3.127), p. 2841.
14. On this topic see Arthur F. Marotti, "Patronage, Poetry, and Print," in *Patronage, Politics, and Literary Traditions In England, 1558–1658*, ed. Cedric C. Brown (Detroit, 1993), p. 24.
15. Wall, *Imprint,* p. 297.
16. Elizabeth Eisenstein, *The Printing Press as an Agent of Change: Communication and Cultural Transformation in Early Modern Europe*, (Cambridge, 1979) I, p. 121.
17. A small number of authors secured patents in the sale of their works. Royal printing patents supervened upon the institution of guild copyright by which the stationers regulated with own competitive practices. Patents gave authors a direct financial interest in the sale of their printed work. See Joseph Loewenstein, "Wither and Professional Work," in *Print, Manuscript and Performance: The Changing Relations of the Media in Early Modern England,* eds. Arthur F. Marotti and Michael D. Bristol (Columbus, OH, 2000), p. 107.
18. For a review of the establishment of literary publishing and the growth in reading publics, see *The Cambridge History of the Book in Britain, Vol. 4, 1557–1695*, eds. John Barnard and D.F. McKenzie (Cambridge, 2002).
19. The study of counterfactuals is a methodology traditionally employed by military historians, engaging "what if" questions of speculative history. It has re-emerged most recently in the work of the historian Niall Ferguson who, as editor of and contributor to the collection *Virtual History: Alternatives and Counterfactuals* (New York, 1997), explores with other historians

the implications of a series of historical scenarios that might have turned out differently.

20. Alexandra Halasz, "Pamphlet Surplus: John Taylor and Subscription Publication," in *Print, Manuscript and Performance*, pp. 90–102.
21. "An Acte for the Punishement of Vacabondes, and for Relief of the Poore and Impotent" (14 Elizabeth, c. 5), 1572. Reprinted in *Tudor Economic Documents*, eds. R. H. Tawney and Eileen Power (London, 1924), II, p. 328–29.
22. Ibid.
23. As cited above, among the critics who have placed her poem in the tradition are Travitsky, *Paradise*; Rose, "Where are the Mothers?"; Amussen, *Ordered*; Wall, *Imprint*; and Martin, *Women Writers*.
24. Wall, *Imprint*, 340.
25. Among the influential proscriptions on women's learning and writing were those forwarded by Juan Luis Vives, whose *De Institutione Feminiae Christianae* (1523) was translated by Richard Hyrde in 1540 as *Instruction of a Christian Woman*. Vives argued for the limitations of the uses to which women might apply their humanist learning; and Richard Brathwaite, *The English Gentlewoman* (1631), p. 39 tells us that "bashfull silence is an ornament to their sex." Of course we find a slightly different version of feminine conduct for women at court, who could look to more liberal models in continental courtesy books like Castiglione's *The Book of the Courtier* (1561) and Guazzo's *Civil Conversation* (1581). Ladies in waiting, for instance, were often encouraged to take part in conversations and contests. However, Whitney, a woman of the middling sort, was overstepping what might be considered "proper" behavior for women in their writing. See reviews of injunctions for women in Ian Maclean, *The Renaissance Notion of Woman* (Cambridge, 1980); Suzanne Hall, *Chaste, Silent, and Obedient: English Books for Women, 1475–1640* (San Marino, CA, 1982); Linda Woodbridge, *Women and the English Renaissance: Literature and the Nature of Womankind, 1540–1620* (Urbana, IL, 1984); M. R. Sommerville, *Sex and Subjection: Attitudes to Women in Early-Modern Society* (London, 1995).
26. See Sylvia Brown (ed.), *Women's Writing in Stuart England: The Mother's Legacies of Dorothy Leigh, Elizabeth Joscelin, and Elizabeth Richardson* (Stroud, 1991), p. ix.
27. See Margaret P. Hannay, "'So May I With the Psalmist truly Say': Early Modern Englishwomen's Psalm Discourse," in *Write or Be Written: Early Modern Women Poets and Cultural Constraints*, eds. Barbara Smith and Ursula Appelt (Aldershot, 2001), pp. 105–27. In this article Hannay points out that Anne Lock's 1560 Sonnets were presented as a socially sanctioned psalm "commentary" and "paraphrases," as her title suggests: "A Meditation of a Penitent Sinner: Written in Maner of a Paraphrase upon the 51 Psalm of David." Translations of non-religious works were also considered suspect:

Margaret Tyler goes to great lengths to defend her act of translating a secular piece of literature, Diego Ortunez de Calahorra's chivalric romance, *The Mirrour of Princely deedes and Knighthoood* (1578), in her preface, offering the novel assertion that "it is all one for a woman to pen a story as for a man to address his story to a woman," p. A3^{r}.

28. Wall, *Imprint*, p. 293.
29. Elizabeth Grymeston, *Miscelanea. Meditations. Memoratives.* (London, 1604), pp. A3^{v,} A3^{r}.
30. Dorothy Leigh, *The Mother's Blessing* (London, 1616), p. A11^{r}.
31. Testaments published as solitary texts, rather than as parts of larger texts, include Anonymous, *The Wyll of the Devyll, and Last Testament* (London, 1548); Robert Copland, *Jyl of Braintfords Testament, Newly Compiled* (London, 1535); and John Lacy, *Wyl Bucke his Testament* (London, 1560). Others were published within longer works, such as George Gascoigne's *Dan Bartholmew of Bathe*, "His last will and Testament," which appeared in Gascoigne's *Posies* (1575). Other anonymous solitary testaments include *The Testament of Andro Kennedy* (1508), *Hunting of the Hare with her last Wyll and Testament* (n.d.), and *Colyn Blowbols Testament,* (n.d.). William C. Hazlitt cites these last three in *Remains of the Early Popular Poetry of England* (London, 1864), p. 91.
32. Lorna Hutson, *The Usurer's Daughter: Male Friendship and Fictions of Women in Sixteenth-Century England* (London, 1994), p. 127.
33. Hutson had provided extensive analysis of the mock-testament genre in her earlier work on Nashe, *Thomas Nashe in Context* (Oxford, 1989), esp. chapter 7, "Nashe, Mock-Testament, and Menippean Dialogue," pp. 127–51. In *Usurer's Daughter*, she does refer to her earlier work in a footnote in the Whitney chapter. Her examination (in *Nashe*) of the backgrounds to early modern uses of the mock-testament is vigorous and illuminating.
34. Travitsky, "Whitney, Isabella," *ODNB*. The brief format of *ODNB* entries does not allow Travitsky the space to elaborate, so there is no discussion of the mock-testament tradition here, except for her point that "Gascoigne may have written his 'Last Will and Testament of Dan Bartholomew of Bath' in imitation."
35. Clarke, pp. xv.
36. Ibid.
37. See Charles Read Baskerville, *The Elizabethan Jig and Related Song Drama* (Chicago, 1929), pp. 23, 47.
38. Anonymous, *The Wyll of the Deuyll, and Last Testament* (London, 1548), reprinted in J. Payne Collier (ed.), *Illustrations of Early English Popular Literature* (London, 1966), I, pp. 4–14.
39. John Lacy, *Wyl Bucke his Testament* (London, 1560), pp. A3-B^{v}.
40. Winthrop Huntington Rice, *The European Ancestry of Villon's Satirical Testaments* (New York, 1941), pp. 210–11.

41. Francois Villon, *Le Testament Villon*, eds. J. Rychner and A. Henry (Geneva, 1974), p. 74, as quoted in Tony Hun, *Villon's Last Will* (Oxford, 1996), p. 8.
42. In his opening stanza, Villon writes of "the many penalties inflicted on me, all of them at the hands of Thibault d'Aussigny" ("maintes peines eues,/ Lesquelles j'ay toutes receues/Soubz la main Thibault d'Aucigny") Villon, *Testament*, pp. 4–6.
43. *The Works of Thomas Nashe*, ed. Ronald B. McKerrow, (Oxford, 1958), III, p. 272 (ln. 1235).
44. Robert Copland, *Jyl of Braintfords Testament, Newly Compiled* (London, 1535).
45. Mary Carpenter Erler (ed.), *Robert Copland, Poems* (Toronto, 1993), p. 177.
46. Copland, *Jyl of Braintfords Testament*, p. $A4^r$.
47. See Craig Muldrew, *The Economy of Obligation* (New York, 1998); Muldrew, "Interpreting the Market: The Ethics of Credit and Community Relations in Early Modern England," *Social History* 18:2 (1993), pp. 163–83; and Keith Wrightson, *Earthly Necessities: Economic Lives in Early Modern Britain* (New Haven, CT, 2000).
48. On economic "affect," see Theodore Leinwand, *Theatre, Finance, and Society in Early Modern England* (Cambridge, 1999), which examines emotional responses to socio-economic pressures as they are revealed in early modern English plays, historical narratives, and biographical accounts.
49. See David Underdown, "The Taming of the Scold: The Enforcement of Patriarchal Authority in Early Modern England," and Susan Amussen, "Gender, Family, and the Social Order, 1560–1725," both in *Order and Disorder in Early Modern England*, eds. Anthony Fletcher and J. Stevenson (Cambridge, 1985), pp. 116–36; 196–217; David Underdown, *Revel, Riot and Rebellion* (Oxford, 1985); and Laura Gowing, "Language, Power, and the Law: Women's Slander Litigation in Early Modern England," *Women, Crime, and the Courts in Early Modern England*, eds. Jennifer Kermode and Garthine Walker (Chapel Hill, NC, 1994), pp. 26–47.
50. While there is divergence among social historians and literary critics about how festival liberty functions, many recent theorists have argued for festival's inclusion of both normative and revisionary impulses. Mikhail Bakhtin argues that festival forms are completely separate from the official culture in *Rabelais and His World*, trans. Helene Iswolsky (Cambridge, MA, 1968), p. 255; responses countering that view and instead arguing that holiday "liberty" holds a more interactive relationship with the existing forms of political organization include Barbara A. Babcock (ed.), *The Reversible World: Symbolic Inversion in Art and Society* (Ithaca, NY, 1978), pp, 13–36; Natalie Zemon Davis, *Society and Culture in Early Modern France* (Stanford: Stanford UP, 1975); Clifford Geertz, "Ritual and Social Change," in *The*

Interpretation of Cultures (New York, 1973), pp. 142–69; and Leah S. Marcus, *The Politics of Mirth* (Chicago, 1986). As Michael Bristol has pointed out, a critical recognition of Carnival and misrule provides an alternative reading of such consolidation of authority. What Bristol terms "the political life of the plebeian culture" is expressed in the festive agon of the battle of Lent and Carnival, a battle in which there is no consolidation of rule. Michael Bristol, *Carnival and Theater: Plebeian Culture and the Structure of Authority in Renaissance England* (New York, 1985), p. 202.

51. Edward Wilson, "'The Testament of the Buck' and the sociology of the text," *Review of English Studies* 45:178 (1994), p. 182.
52. *The Goliard Poets*, trans. and ed. George F. Whicher (New York, 1949), pp. 4–5.
53. Karen Newman usefully points out Donne's rhetorical strategies by which he highlights his speaker's role as the outsider in *Satire I*, in her essay, "Walking Capitals: Donne's First Satyre," in *The Culture of Capital: Property, Cities, and Knowledge in Early Modern England*, ed. Henry S. Turner (New York, 2002), pp. 203–21. She ultimately locates Donne the satirist outside the city's dangers, as an onlooker. He protects himself from the threatening urban sear of trade by using, Newman asserts, a series of rhetorical distancing devices. For instance, the "needy broker" and the "cheape whore" appear only through simile in the poem, and the whore and prostitute boy "enter the poem interrogatively as an ethical opposition to virtue posed by the speake . . . ," p. 215. Donne used satire, Newman concludes, "to manage the burgeoning multitude of persons and behaviors that characterized early modern London and troubled its inhabitants and city government. . . . The satire protects the speaker rhetorically from peripatetic encounters and insists on his disconnection from the persons, sights, and things that people the city," p. 212. I am indebted to Margaret Ferguson for alerting me to this informative and enlightening essay.
54. Susan Amussen, *An Ordered Society*, p. 2 reviews some modern historians' claims that the two are blended.
55. James Cleland, *Hero-paideia, or the Institution of a young noble man* (Oxford, 1607), p. 181.
56. John Ferne, *The Blazon of Gentrie* (London, 1586), pp. 59–60. Ferne makes the case that these public office holders should be granted coats of arms.
57. Richard Brathwaite, *The English gentleman: containing sundry excellent rules . . . how to demeane or accommodate himselfe in the manage of publike or private affairs* (London, 1630), p. 136.
58. On women's domestic duties, see Robert Cleaver, *A Godlie Form of Household Government for the ordering of private families* . . . (London, 1598) and William Gouge, *Of Domesticall Duties* (London, 1622).
59. See for instance Margaret Hoby, *Diary of Lady Margaret Hoby 1599–1605*, ed. Dorothy M. Meads (London, 1930), pp. 136–39, 159, 167, 221.

60. Jones, *The Currency of Eros,* p. 43.
61. Retha Warnicke, "Private and Public: The Boundaries of Women's Lives in Early Stuart England," *Privileging Gender in Early Modern England,* ed. Jean R. Brink (Kirksville, MO, 1993), pp. 133–37.
62. Patricia Phillippy's critique, in "The maid's lawful liberty: service, the household, and "Mother B" in Isabella Whitney's 'A Sweet Nosegay,'" *Modern Philology* 95:4 (1998), p. 8, rests on the plight of maidservants in the marketplace: Whitney's persona in the poem is a writer seeking credit, but she also speaks for maidservants unable to find secure employment. Thus Whitney's mock-testament highlights the culture of service and itineracy. Domestic servants were not bound to contracts. Phillippy, p. 8, points out that maidservants were "both consumers and commodities."
63. Elaine Beilin, "Writing Public Poetry: Humanism and the Woman Writer," *Modern Language Quarterly* 51:2 (1990), p. 249. She finds a number of female authors who rewrite the "humanist concept of the learned lady" from the private into the public realm.
64. Ibid., pp. 249, 250.
65. Alvin Kernan, *The Cankered Muse: Satire of the English Renaissance* (New Haven, CT, 1959), p. 43, "[Piers] was a figure already associated with religious and social protest who had the characteristics needed for attacking vice and foolishness. Piers does not appear by name, of course, in the majority of medieval satires, but even in those cases where the speaker remains anonymous the Piers characteristics are evident: a plain man with plain morals addressing plain people in plain terms on plain matters. Piers Plowman is simply the most popular name for the medieval satirist, and although in the course of time the figure acquired many names he remained the same type. Colin Blowbol, Cock Lorel, Roderick Mors, Colin Clout, Jack Napes, and Jack Upland are all satiric personae who, as their plain, country names suggest, are proliferations of the Piers type."
66. Pamela Allen Brown, *Better A Shrew than a Sheep: Women, Drama, and the Culture of Jest in Early Modern England* (Ithaca, NY, 2003), p. 36.
67. Alastair Fowler, *Kinds of Literature: An Introduction to the Theory of Genres and Modes* (Cambridge, MA, 1982), p. 23 comments on this salient feature of genre: "Every literary work changes the genres it relates to . . . However a work relates to existing genres—by conformity, variation, innovation, or antagonism—it will tend, if it becomes known, to bring about new states of these genres."
68. W. Scott Blanchard, *Scholars' Bedlam: Menippean Satire in the Renaissance* (London, 1995), p. 17. I thank Anne Lake Prescott for this invaluable reference.
69. Ibid., p. 39: "As new social categories emerged, so, too, did the attention paid to less-valued social categories which now must be incorporated into the organization of social practices, as well as marginal types (courtesans,

pick pockets, etc.). Here the Menippean form shares the kind of urban crowding that we find in the Elizabethan "comicall satyre" play . . . ."

70. Lanyer had written "The Description of Cookeham" by early 1609, and it was published as the concluding poem of her *Salve Deus Rex Judaeorum* in October 1610. Cookeham was a royal manor in the possession of William Russel of Thornhaugh, Margaret's brother. Margaret was at Cookeham during periods from 1603 until sometime after the death of her estranged husband, George Clifford, in 1605. See Barbara K. Lewalski, "The Lady of the Country House Poem," in *The Fashioning and Functioning of the British Country-House*, ed. Gervase Jackson-Stops, *et. al* (Washington D.C., 1989), p. 265.
71. The opening dedication to Queen Anne recounts Lanyer's former favor under Elizabeth as contrasted with her lack of court acquaintance under James. The subsequent dedications claim no personal acquaintance with Princess Elizabeth, Mary (Sidney) Herbert, Countess of Pembroke, or Lucky (Harrington) Russell, Countess of Bedford. In addition she confesses that she is a stranger to the Countess of Suffolk, Katherine Howard. Nonetheless, she does admit that she did know Lady Arabella Stuart , first cousin of James I . . . and the Dowager Countess of Kent, Susan (Bertie) Wingfield.
72. Jonson's "To Penshurt" was written before the death of Prince Henry in 1612 but not published until Jonson's folio was printed in 1616. Lanyer's poem was written after Anne Clifford's marriage to Richard Sackville on Feb. 25, 1609 and before the volume was registered with the Stationer on October 2, 1610. These and other details are collected by Barbara K. Lewalski in "Of God and Good Women: The Poems of Aemilia Lanyer" in *Silent But for the Word*, p. 204.
73. This obvious point of comparison has been explored by, among others, Lewalski *Writing Women in Jacobean England*, p.235; Hugh Jenkins, *Feigned Commonwealths: The Country House Poem and the Fashioning of the Ideal Community* (Pittsburgh, 1998), p. 161; and Keri Boyd McBride, in *Country House Discourse in Early Modern England* (Aldershot, 2001), pp. 106–19.
74. Alastair Fowler, *The Country House Poem: A Cabinet of Seventeenth-Century Estate Poems and Related Items* (Edinburgh, 1994).
75. Eileen Spring, *Law, Land, and Family: Aristocratic Inheritance in England 1300 to 1800* (Chapel Hill, NC, 1993), p. 9.
76. Recent studies of Lanyer's life and writing include Lewalski, "Imagining Female Communities"; Susanne Woods (ed.), *The Poems of Aemilia Lanyer* (New York, 1993); Marshall Grossman (ed.), *Aemilia Lanyer: Gender, Genre, and the Canon* (Lexington, KY, 1998); Susanne Woods, *Lanyer: A Renaissance Woman Poet* (New York, 1999). A brief biographical sketch can also be found in Carol Levin, *et. al*, *Extraordinary Women of the Medieval and Renaissance World: A Biographical Dictionary* (Westport, CT, 2000).
77. In 1609 Alphonso was awarded a patent to take revenue from the weighing of hay and grain in London, and after his death in 1613 Aemilia was

involved in several lawsuits respecting her rights in this commission. *Calendar of State Papers, Domestic* (1634–35), pp. 516–17.

78. All references to Lanyer's poem are taken from Woods (ed.), *The Poems of Aemilia Lanyer*, and will hereafter be cited parenthetically.
79. Virgil, *I: Eclogues, Georgics, Aeneid I-VI*, Loeb Classical Library, rev. ed., tr. H. Rushton Fairclough (Cambridge, MA, 1986), 119.
80. Ibid., 205.
81. Georgic expressions in the Country House Poem genre has been most recently examined by Fowler, *The Country House Poem*, pp. 1–30.
82. For a review of the essential elements of the *beatus-ille* tradition, see Heather Dubrow, "The Country-House Poem: A Study in Generic Development," *Genre* 12 (1979), p. 158.
83. Woods (ed.), *The Poems of Amelia Lanyer*, p. 138 provides a note to "those rich chains" which identifies them as "of her virtues."
84. They would struggle to enforce an entail (in existence from the time of Edward II) which would allow the property to descend through the female line and thus prevent the customary passage of her husband's estate to collateral male heirs. See Barbara K. Lewalski, "Re-Writing Patriarchy and Patronage: Margaret Clifford, Anne Clifford, and Aemilia Lanyer," *The Yearbook of English Studies* 21 (1991), pp. 104–06.
85. Marshall Grossman writes, "the necessity of litigation to preserve rights of descent through the female line seems to have been a definitive feature in the landscape of feminine experience referenced in Lanyer's work," in "The Gendering of Genre: Literary History and the Canon," in *Aemilia Lanyer*, ed. Grossman 128–142; 139.
86. Among the historians who claim that property rights increasingly favored women in the period are H. J. Habakkuk, "Marriage Settlements in the Eighteenth Century," *Transactions of the Royal Historical Society*, Fourth Series, 32 (1950), pp. 15–30, who argues that portions for younger daughters rose with the development of the strict settlement; Lawrence Stone, *The Family, Sex and Marriage in England, 1500–1800* (New York, 1977), pp. 242–43, 380–81; Lloyd Bonfield, "Marriage, Property, and the 'Affective Family,'" *Law and History Review* 1 (1983), pp. 297–312; and idem, "Affective Families, Open Elites and Strict Family Settlements in Early Modern England," *Economic History Review*, 2nd series, 39 (1986), p. 349, as quoted in Spring, *Law, Land, and Family*, p. 2.
87. See Spring, *Law, Land, and Family;* Amy Louise Erickson, *Women and Property in Early Modern England* (New York, 1993); and Tim Stretton, *Women Waging Law in Elizabethan England* (Cambridge, 1998).
88. Spring, *Law, Land, and Family*,107.
89. A number of critics have reviewed the facts in this case, including Mary Ellen Lamb, in "The Agency of the Split Subject: Lady Anne Clifford and the Uses of Reading," *English Literary Renaissance* 22 (1992), pp. 347–68.

90. Carl Bridenbaugh, *Vexed and Troubled Englishmen* (New York, 1968) pp. 247–48; Roger Thompson, *Women in Stuart England and America* (London, 1974), p. 223.
91. Bernard Capp, "Separate Domains? Women and Authority in Early Modern England," in *The Experience of Authority in Early Modern England*, eds. Paul Griffiths, Adam Fox and Steve Hindle (London, 1996), p. 125.
92. As mentioned above, after Alphonse's death, Lanyer had to bring suit against his family regarding profits from her portion of his original grant for a patent to weigh hay and straw coming into London. She was receiving only £8 per annum and she sued for 50 *l.* per annum. As a result of her suit on February 19, 1635, the court granted her 20 *l.* per annum and after her death 10 *l.* per annum to two of her grandchildren. *Calendar of State Papers Domestic*, Charles I (1634–35) (Nendeln, Liechtenstein, 1967), 183, pp. 516–17.
93. Krontiris, *Oppositional Voices*, p. 13. She tempers this assertion in her admission that wealthy merchants imitated aristocratic trends and taught their daughters to read and write.

NOTES TO CHAPTER FIVE

1. William Shakespeare, *The Merchant of Venice*, ed. M. Lindsay Kaplan (Boston, 2002), 4.1.169, at p. 94. All references are to this edition and hereafter will be cited parenthetically.
2. While the comparison of usurers with "creditors" generally across the drama has not received critical attention, the much more studied question has been the comparison of usurer and merchant in this play. Many critics have commented upon the equivalence of merchant and usurer in the play and in English society at large: See Walter Cohen, *Drama of a Nation: Public Theater in Renaissance England and Spain* (Ithaca, NY, 1985); Walter Cohen, "*The Merchant of Venice* and the Possibilities of Historical Criticism," *ELH* 49:4 (1982), pp. 765–89. Cohen, in *Drama of a Nation*, p. 199 points out that "merchants were the leading usurers," after reviewing the anti-usury literature still popular in England in the late sixteenth and early seventeenth centuries: "the distinction between merchants and usurers . . . of medieval origin, could be drawn on the grounds that only the former operated for mutual benefit, as opposed to self-interest" (p. 198).
3. See Karen Newman, "Portia's Ring: Unruly Women and Structures of Exchange in *The Merchant of Venice*," *Shakespeare Quarterly* 38:1 (1987), pp. 19–33; Marc Shell, "The Wether and the Ewe: Verbal Usury in *The Merchant of Venice*," *Kenyon Review* 1:4 (1979), pp. 65–92; and Leonard Tennenhouse, "The Counterfeit Order in *The Merchant of Venice*," in *Representing Shakespeare: New Psychoanalytic Essays*, eds. Murray M. Schwartz and Coppelia Kahn (Baltimore, 1972), pp. 54–69.

4. See Lars Engle, *Shakespearean Pragmatism* (Chicago, 1993) esp. pp. 77–106. Engle, p. 100 examines the constitutive "moral luck," a term he borrows from Bernard Williams, that makes it possible "not only for Portia and Bassanio to be happy, but to be morally exemplary in their happiness"—such moral luck "denies the practical possibility of morality as a fixed system and suggests the substitution of a pragmatic economic for it" (98). In the pragmatic economy of *The Merchant of Venice*, Engle points out, "the morally attractive are blessed . . . by privileges which they exploit" (p. 106).
5. The Athenian Theophrastus (373–284 B.C.) wrote sketches that examined cases in which men vary from the ideal in terms of their habitual conduct. His essays begin by describing a specific quality, such as avarice, or boorishness, and then illustrate the definition with a number of characteristic actions. See J.M. Edmonds (ed.), *The Characters of Theophrastus* (Cambridge, MA, 1967). The seventeenth-century Theophrastian character sketch, such as Joseph Hall, *Characters of Virtues and Vices* (1608) and John Stephens, *Satyrical Essays* (1615) more specifically condemn vices at court by caricaturing court corruption and depravity.
6. Craig Muldrew, *The Economy of Obligation: The Culture of Credit and Social Relations in Early Modern England* (New York, 1998), p. 2 finds that in early seventeenth-century England, "credit was a public means of . . . circulating judgment about the value of other members of communities. . . ." He locates "a reordering of notions of community relations towards a . . . mobile . . . language of judgment about the creditworthiness of households. . . ." Further, he notes "the culture of credit was generated through a process whereby the nature of the community was redefined as a conglomeration of competing but interdependent households which had to trust one another" (p. 4).
7. *OED*, Credit, n.: 1. Belief, credence, faith, trust. To give credit to: to believe, put faith in, credit (1542 Brinklow *Lament.*). 9. Comm. a. Trust or confidence in a buyer's ability and intention to pay at some future time, exhibited by entrusting him with goods, etc., without present payment. (first listed use 1542; next listed use 1576, then 1627). b. Reputation of solvency and probity in business, enabling a person or body to be trusted with goods or money in expectation of future payment. (first use at 1573, Tusser; next 1576, *Merchant*).
8. Cicero, *Marcus Tullius Ciceroes thre bokes of duties,* trans. Nicholas Grimalde (London, 1556), p. K^4v.
9. Daniel Price, *The Merchant: A Sermon Preached at Paul's Cross on Sunday the 14th of August Being the Day before Bartholomew Fair, 1607* (Oxford, 1608).
10. Sir Thomas Wyatt, *The Complete Poems*, ed. R.A. Rebholz (London, 1978), Sonnet 19, ll 1, 3, p. 81.
11. Thomas Heywood, *A Critical Edition of* The Faire Maide of The Exchange, Ed. Karl E. Snyder (New York, 1980), 5.1.176 at p. 173. Moll tells the

Cripple that she will love Barnard in order that her father will discharge the debt, and she attests to the fact that the canceling of bonds is proof that she loves him. Barnard, the gentleman in debt, agrees to marry Moll because he needs her money.

12. Thomas Heywood, *If You Know Not Me, You Know Nobody, Part II* (Oxford, 1934) 16.2527–2528, at I3r. The dissolute Jack Gresham (the famous John Gresham's nephew), acknowledges in an aside that he "rose by Lady Ramsies kisse" (16.2534). All references are to this edition and hereafter will be cited parenthetically.
13. Thomas Heywood, *A Woman Killed With Kindness*, ed. Brian Scobie (London, 1985), Scene 14.88–89, p. 75.
14. Diana E. Henderson, "The Theater and Domestic Culture," in John D. Cox and David Scott Kastan, eds. *A New History of Early English Drama* (New York, 1997), p. 187. Henderson, p. 180 acknowledges the problem that Heywood "mutes" any notion of a woman's independent will, but she seems to discount Susan's role altogether by neglecting the fact that Mountford does ultimately rely on "kin"—his own sister, to save him economically: Henderson writes, p. 187, "In a world in which kin—or at least "cousins"—can no longer be relied upon for kindness, economic self-sufficiency becomes all the more crucial." I suggest that Susan willingly (though with much regret) saves her brother by sacrificing her honor in order to prevent him from descending into the "hell" of debtors' prison. In other words, Susan accepts the role that Isabel in *Measure for Measure* refuses.
15. Philip Henslowe, *Henslowe's Diary*, ed. R.A. Foakes (Cambridge, 2002), p. 170. Henslowe notes, "Lent unto Robert Shaw and Mr. Jube the 19 of May 1601 to buy divers things for the Jew of Malta the some of . . . £5/lent more to the little tailor the same day for more things for the Jew of Malta the sum of . . . xs."
16. Mark Eccles, "Elizabethan Actors I: A-D," *Notes and Queries* (1991), p. 40. Also, Thomas Greene of Queen Anne's Men and John Duke gave bail for A. Rogers of Whitechapel on 14 May, 1608 (Eccles, "Elizabethan Actors II: E-G," *Notes and Queries* (Dec. 1991), 455–461; 456). Robert Browne gave bail (Eccles, "A-D," 41). Henry Clay gave bond for John Newton on 25 June 1614 (Eccles, "A-D," 44). Clay would be with the King's Men in 1624 and Newton with Prince Charles's Men.
17. Eccles, "Eliz. Actors I: A-D," p. 46.
18. For his brother Edmund's son John, Henslowe paid for two shirts, a hat, a cloak for bad weather, and the cost of altering to fit them (some 28s 4d). Cited in Andrew Gurr, *The Shakespeare Company, 1594–1642* (Cambridge, 2004), p. 104.
19. This was in 1614. Mark Eccles, "Elizabethan Actors III: K-R," *Notes and Queries* (1992), pp. 293–303; 298.
20. *Fair Maid*, 2.2.139.

21. Mark Eccles, "Elizabethan Actors IV: S to End," *Notes and Queries* (1993), p. 167.
22. Theatre managers often wanted players to sign bonds forcing them to stay at a specific playhouse for a period of time. Francis Langley tried to force his players in the Earl of Pembroke's Company to sign bonds forfeiting £100 if they left his Swan, and The Admiral's Company players would forfeit 100 marks to £40 to Henslowe if they left his theatre within three years. In 1624 Richard Gunnell, manager of The Fortune theatre tried to do the same thing to hold together Palsgrave's Company by convincing six of the sharers to sign a bond to continue playing together at the Fortune. But the players left for Henslowe's Rose Theatre. In addition, seven principal sharers wrote to Edward Alleyn in 1616–17 explaining why they were deserting the Hope Theatre (blaming it on the theatre owner). See C.W. Wallace, "The Swan Theatre and the Earl of Pembroke's Servants," *Englische Studien* 43 (1911), pp. 345–55, supplemented by William Ingram, *A London Life in the Brazen Age: Francis Langley, 1548*–1602 (Cambridge, MA, 1978); E.K. Chambers, *The Elizabethan Stage* (Oxford, 1923), II, pp. 151–55; G.E. Bentley, *The Profession of Dramatist and Player in Shakespeare's Time, 1590–1642* (Princeton, NJ, 1986); G.E. Bentley, *The Jacobean and Caroline Stage* (Oxford, 1941–68), I, pp. 200–201; *JCS* VI, pp. 207–09; Philip Henslowe, *The Henslowe Papers*, ed. R. A. Foakes (New York, 1977), p. 93.
23. Anonymous, *A Yorkshire Tragedy* (London, 1608), p. 16. All references are to this edition and hereafter will be cited parenthetically.
24. Ben Jonson, *The Comedies: Volpone, The Alchemist, Bartholomew Fair*, ed. Michael Jamieson (New York, 1966. Quote from *The Alchemist* 1.1.43, p. 194. Subsequent references are to this edition and will be made parenthetically.
25. Also see M.M. Mahood's note to Cambridge edition of *The Merchant of Venice* at "squandered": "Shakespeare's only other use of the verb, 'squand'ring glances of the fool' in *AYLI* 2.7.57, implies folly; so Shylock may, from the viewpoint of a prudent financier, be glancing at the want of prudence in Antonio's undertakings," at *The Merchant of Venice*, ed. M. M. Mahood (Cambridge, 1987), 1.3.18, p. 83, n. 18.
26. George Chapman, *The Plays of George Chapman. The Tragedies: A Critical Edition,* ed. Allan Holaday (Cambridge, 1987), 1.1.124–27 at p. 282.
27. For def. of "purchase," see n. 127 in Chapman, p. 282.
28. Thomas Dekker, *The Shoemaker's Holiday*, ed. Anthony Parr (London, 1990) Scene 8.42–44. All references are to this edition and hereafter will be cited parenthetically.
29. Dekker's choice to make Eyre's transaction possible by this loan from Lacy departs from his source, Deloney's *The Gentle Craft*, in which Eyre's wife convinces her husband to disguise himself as an alderman in order to obtain credit.

30. Morris Palmer Tilley, *A Dictionary of Proverbs in England in the Sixteenth and Seventeenth Centuries* (Ann Arbor, 1950) N320, p. 507; cf. N319.
31. Miles Mosse, *The Arraignment and Conviction of Usury* (London, 1595), p. 57, as quoted in Eric Kerridge, *Trade and Banking in Early Modern England* (Manchester, 1988), p. 34.
32. Ben Jonson, *Every Man Out of His Humour*, ed. Helen Ostovich (Manchester, 2001), 1.2.108–110, at p. 143. All references to are to this edition and hereafter will be cited parenthetically.
33. George Chapman, *The Plays of George Chapman: The Comedies: A Critical Edition,* ed. Allan Holaday (Urbana, 1970) *An Humorous Day's Mirth*, 3.1.2–3, p. 92.
34. Thomas Nashe, *Pierce Penilesse his Supplication to the Devil* (London, 1592), p. 19.
35. Nashe, *Pierce*, 19.
36. Ibid., 19.
37. Douglas Bruster examines the Renaissance theater as an "institutionalized, profitable market" in *Drama and the Market in the Age of Shakespeare* (1992), p. 8.
38. Sir Philip Sidney, *The Defence of Poesy,* ed. Katherine Duncan-Jones (Oxford, 1989), p. 235.
39. William Rankins, *A Mirror of Monstors* (London, 1587), p. 9.
40. John Stephens, *Essays and Characters* (London, 1615), p. 9. All references are to this edition and hereafter will be cited parenthetically.
41. While it has been proven that Overbury, author of the popular 1614 poem *The Wife*, is not the author of the character sketches appended to later editions of that poem, his name is often associated with the "character," and since authorship of the characters printed in his name is still up for debate, I here attribute those characters to Overbury. Some of the characters were by John Webster; others have been ascribed, less certainly, to Thomas Dekker and John Ford, and one of them was later printed with the juvenilia of John Donne, though not likely to be his. See John Considine, 'Overbury, Sir Thomas (b. 1581, d. 1613),' *Oxford Dictionary of National Biography*, (Oxford, 2004).
42. Joseph Hall, *Characters of Virtues and Vices* (London, 1608). While some point to Nicholas Breton as the first English writer of characters, Hall provides the first complete work more consciously modeled on the Theophrastian example.
43. See *The Characters of Theophrastus, passim.*
44. Sir Thomas Overbury, *New and Choice Characters* (London, 1615) p. M.
45. Henry Fitzgeffrey, *Certain Elegies* (London, 1618). Fitzgeffrey, a Lincoln's Inn student, describes London life and theatrical circles in his satires, offering several references to debt.
46. Fitzgeffrey, *Certain Elegies*, F3.

47. Thomas Dekker, *The Seven Deadly Sins of London* (London, 16060) pp. 4–5.
48. Nashe, *Pierce,* p. 11.
49. John Day, William Rowley, and George Wilkins, *The Travels of the Three English Brothers* (1607) in Anthony Parr (ed.), *Three Renaissance Travel Plays* (Manchester, 1995), scene 9, 11. 58–59, at p. 104.
50. Jest books celebrate the wit of clever characters, and often feature jesting reversals of authority. Some popular examples were Dekker, *The Seven Deadly Sins of London*; idem, *Jests to Make you Merry with the Conjuring Up of Cock Watt* (London, 1607); Robert Armin, *A Nest of Ninnies* (London, 1608); and George Peele, *Merry Conceited Jests* (London, 1627).
51. Edward Sharpham, *A Critical Old Spelling Edition of The Works of Edward Sharpham*, ed. Christopher Gordon Petter (New York, 1986), 2.1.262–3, p. 269. All references are to this edition and hereafter will be cited parenthetically.
52. Muldrew emphasizes that "moral discipline and probity were increasingly stressed" from 1580 through the early seventeenth century, *Economy of Obligation*, p. 3
53. Lawrence Danson comments upon the play's "prominent series of binary relationships" in The Harmonies of *The Merchant of Venice* (New Haven, CT, 1978) p. 10; and Karen Newman points to the initial presentation of Belmont as different from Venice in terms of "love" talk vs. "economic motives," respectively, in "Portia's Ring," p. 19.
54. Sigurd Burckhardt, in "*The Merchant of Venice*: The Gentle Bond," *English Literary History* 29:3 (1962), pp. 239–62, explores how Shakespeare's departure from his source material, *Il Pecorone* and the *Gesta Romanorum*, emphasizes a circularity in the plot in which "the vicious circle of the bond's law can be transformed into the ring of love" (p. 243); Karen Newman comments upon the "structure of exchange . . . which characterizes both the economic transactions of Venice and the love relationships forged at Belmont" ("Portia's Ring," p. 19); Marc Shell notes that "the marriage bond cannot be concluded until the commercial bond is cancelled" in "The Wether and the Ewe," p. 75.
55. Edward Coke, *Institutes III* (London, 1648), c. 15, p. 165.
56. See John Spurr, "'The Strongest Bond of Conscience': Oaths and the Limits of Tolerance in Early Modern England," in *Contexts of Conscience in Early Modern Europe, 1500–1700*, eds. Harald E. Braun and Edward Vallance (New York, 2004), pp. 151–65.
57. Sir John Baker, *The Oxford History of the Laws of England, 1483–1558* (note 88, at 183); Brian P. Levack, *The Civil Lawyers in England, 1603–1641: A Political Study* 16–34 (Oxford, 1973); Amalia D. Kessler, "Our Inquisitorial Tradition: Equity Procedure, Due Process, and The Search for an Alternative to the Adversarial," *Cornell Law Review* 90:1181 (2005), p. 1185, 1201.

58. See B. J. Sokol, "*The Merchant of Venice* and the Law Merchant," *Renaissance Studies* 6:1 (1992), p. 62. J. H. Baker, "The Law Merchant and the common law before 1700," *Cambridge Law Journal* 38 (1979), pp. 295–332.
59. Many of the imperatives I have suggested—e.g. the celebration of the resourceful economic adventurer—have a connection to the imbroglios or "merry tales" of Italian comedy, in which plots of trickery and disguise reward the trickster and punish the miser.

NOTES TO CHAPTER SIX

1. As quoted in David H. Wilson, ed. *The Parliamentary Diary of Robert Bowyer 1606–1607* (Minneapolis, 1931), p. 151.
2. Francis Bacon, "Of Usury," *The Essays or Counsels, Civil and Moral, of Francis Bacon* (London, 1625), p. 241.
3. William Shakespeare, *The Merchant of Venice*, ed. Kaplan (Boston, 2002), at 2.9.21 (p. 64).
4. P.E. McCullough, 'Andrewes, Lancelot (1555–1626),' *Oxford Dictionary of National Biography* (Oxford, 2004); Nicholas Tyacke, 'Lancelot Andrewes and the Myth of Anglicanism,' in *Conformity and Orthodoxy in the English Church, c.1560–1660*, eds. Peter Lake and Michael C. Questier (Woodbridge, 2000), pp. 5–33.
5. Lancelot Andrewes, *The pattern of catechistical doctrine at large, or, A learned and pious exposition of the Ten Commandments* (London, 1650), p. 111.
6. Ibid.
7. Geoffrey Chaucer, *The Complete Poetry and Prose of Geoffrey Chaucer*, ed. John H. Fisher (New York, 1989), at "Canon's Yeoman's Tale," ll. 946–50, p. 326.
8. *OED*, "Adventure" 4. Chance of danger or loss; risk, jeopardy, peril. To put in adventure: to put in jeopardy, to imperil, to risk, to stake (p. 135).
9. Andrewes, *The pattern of catechistical doctrine at large*, p. 469.
10. Ibid., p. 470
11. Ibid.
12. Ibid.
13. Ibid.
14. Ibid.
15. Ibid., p. 490.
16. Ibid.
17. Ibid.
18. Ibid., p. 487.
19. See above, in Chapter One: Introduction (pp. X-Y).
20. Nicholas Breton, *The Good and the Bad* (London, 1616).
21. Breton, *The Good and the Bad*, p. 18.
22. Breton, p. 18.

23. Ibid.
24. Ibid.
25. Ibid.
26. Chaucer, *The Complete Poetry and Prose of Geoffrey Chaucer*, ed. Fisher, in "The Pardoner's Tale," l. 897, at p. 230.
27. Oystein Ore, *Cardano, The Gambling Scholar* (New York, 1965), p. 111; also see Gerda Reith, *The Age of Chance: Gambling in Western Culture* (London, 1999), p. 77.
28. Ore, *Cardano*, p. 111.
29. Both cited in John Ashton, *The History of Gambling in England* (Detroit, MI, 1968), p. 13.
30. Ibid.
31. As quoted in Bryan Reynolds, *Becoming Criminal: Transversal Performance and Cultural Dissidence in Early Modern England* (Baltimore: Johns Hopkins UP, 2002), 120.
32. Thomas Dekker, *Jests to Make you Merry* (London, 1607)
33. Reith, p. 23.
34. Ore, *Cardano*, pp. viii, 120.
35. Reith, 23.
36. As quoted in Ore, *Cardano*, p. 122.
37. Thomas Cooper, *The Art of Giving* (London, 1615), p. 104.
38. Reuven Brenner with Gabrielle A. Brenner, *Gambling and Speculation: A Theory, A History, and a Future of Some Human Decisions* (Cambridge, 1990), p. 51.
39. Ibid., p. 6.
40. Ibid.
41. John Samuel Ezell, *Fortune's Merry Wheel: The Lottery in America* (Cambridge, MA, 1960), p. 4.
42. Ibid., p. 8.
43. Ashton, *The History of Gambling in England*, p. 30.
44. Ibid.
45. Ibid., p. 31.
46. Ibid., p. 32.
47. Lancelot Andrewes, *A Sermon Preached Before the King's Majesty at Whitehall, on the V of November, Anno Domini, MDCXVIII.*
48. As quoted in Ashton, *The History of Gambling in England*, pp. 275–76.
49. Ibid., p. 276.
50. As quoted in Lorraine Daston, *Classical Probability in the Enlightenment* (Princeton, NJ, 1988), p. 253.
51. Richard Posner, Edward Glaeser, Jack Carr and Janet Landa have examined usury laws as a form of insurance in premodern societies. Carr and Landa, in "The Economics of Symbols, Clan Names, and Religion," *The Journal of Legal Studies* 12:1 (1983), pp. 135–56, use the "theory of clubs" to examine

the advantage gained by Jews with regard to usury laws. Usury laws were meant to apply to "consumption loans" rather than loans for normal commercial transactions. Because Jews engaging in normal commercial transactions could lend funds to one another at interest, the usury laws did not impede normal commerce. They were applied, however, when someone had a year of losses and was forced to borrow money. Here the rules imposed costs on lenders and yielded benefits to borrowers. In this sense the interest-free loan works like insurance, with the insurance scheme enforced by the club. The loan is not a cost of belonging to the club, but "an insurance premium paid by a club member" (p. 153). Usury laws, then, were a primitive means of social insurance. Richard Posner and Edward Glaeser offer similar findings: Glaeser, in "Neither a Borrower nor a Lender Be: An Economic Analysis of Interest Restrictions and Usury Laws," *Journal of Law and Economics* 41:1 (1998), pp. 1–36, explains "usury laws a primitive means of social insurance" (p. 3), as does Posner in "A Theory of Primitive Society with Special Reference to Law," *Journal of Law and Economics* 23:1 (1980), pp. 1–53.

Bibliography

1. PRINTED PRIMARY SOURCES

1.1 Contemporary Publications

Andrewes, Lancelot, *The pattern of catechistical doctrine at large, or, A learned and pious exposition of the Ten Commandments* (London, 1650).

Anonymous, *Britannia Languens or a Discourse of Trade* (1680). *Early English Tracts on Commerce,* ed. J. R. McCulloch (Cambridge: Economic History Society, 1952).

Anonymous, *CSPD*, Charles I (1634–35) Vol. 283. (Nendeln, Liechtenstein, 1967).

Aristotle, *Politics*, trans. Benjamin Jowett (New York, 1943).

Bacon, Francis, *The Essays or Counsels, Civil and Moral, of Francis Bacon* (London, 1625).

———, *The Essays,* ed. John Pitcher (New York, 1985).

Bacon, Francis, *New Atlantis and The Great Instauration*, ed. Jerry Weinberger (Arlington Heights, IL, 1989).

Bacon, Francis, *Novum Organum, with other parts of The Great Instauration*, eds. Peter Urbach and John Gibson (Chicago, 1994).

———, *Works*, eds. James Spedding, Robert Leslie Ellis, and Douglas Denon Heath (London, 1857–74).

Bowyer, Robert, *The Parliamentary Diary of Robert Bowyer,* ed. David H. Wilson (Minneapolis, 1931).

Breton, Nicholas, *The Good and the Bad* (London, 1616).

Burton, Robert, *The Anatomy of Melancholy* (Oxford, 1621).

Calvin, John, *Institutes of the Christian Religion*, ed. John T. McNeill, trans. Ford Lewis Battles, The Library of Christian Classics, 2 vols. (Philadelphia, 1960).

Cicero, Marcus Tullius, *De Officiis*, trans. Walter Miller, Loeb Classical Library, v. 21 (Cambridge, MA, 1921).

———, *De finibus bonorum et malorum*, trans. H. Rackham, Loeb Classical Library, v. 24 (Cambridge, MA, 1921).

Coke, Edward, *The First Part of the Institutes of the lawes of England. Or, a commentarie upon Littleton* (London, 1628).

Cooper, Thomas, *The Art of Giving* (London, 1615).
Copland, Robert, *Jyl of Braintfords Testament, Newly Compiled* (London, 1535).
Elyot, Sir Thomas, *The Book Named the Governor*, ed. S.E. Lehmberg (New York, 1962).
Fenton, Sir Geoffrey, *The historie of Guicciardini Conteining the vvares of italie, and other parts* (London, 1579).
Fitzgeffrey, Henry, *Certain Elegies* (London, 1618).
Fitzgerald, John, *Here begynneth aryght frutefull mater: and hath to name The Boke of Surveying and improumentes* (London, 1523).
Forset, Edward, *A Comparative Discourse of the Bodies Natural and Politique* (1606).
Foxe, John, *Foxe's Book of Martyrs: A Universal History of Christian Martyrdom*, v. I (Philadelphia, 1832).
Grymeston, Elizabeth, *Miscelanea. Meditations. Memoratives* (London, 1604).
Guicciardini, Francesco, *Maxims and Reflections of a Renaissance Statesman* (Ricordi), trans. Mario Domandi, Nicolai Rubinstein (New York, 1965).
Hall, Joseph, *Characters of Virtues and Vices* (London, 1608).
Harrington, James, *The Historical Works of James Harrington*, ed. J.G.A. Pocock (Cambridge, 1977).
Henslowe, Philip, *Henslowe's Diary*, ed. R.A. Foakes (Cambridge, 2002).
———, *The Henslowe Papers*, ed. R. A. Foakes (New York, 1977).
Hooker, Richard, *Of the Laws of Ecclesiastical Polity*, ed. Arthur Stephen McGrade, Bk. I (Cambridge, 1989).
Lacy, John, *Wyl Bucke his Testament* (London, 1560).
Lee, Joseph, *Considerations concerning common fields and inclosures* (London, 1653).
———, *A vindication of a regulated enclosure* (London, 1656).
Leigh, Dorothy, *The Mother's Blessing* (London, 1616).
Lipsius, Justus, *Two Books of Constancie*, trans. John Stradling, eds. Rudolf Kirk and Clayton Morris Hall (New Brunswick, NJ, 1939).
Malvezzi, Virgilio, *Discourses Upon Cornelius Tacitus*, trans. R. Baker (London, 1642).
Malynes, Gerard, *Consuetudo or Lex Mercatoria* (London, 1622).
Misselden, Edward, *The Circle of Commerce, or the balance of trade* (London, 1623).
de Montaigne, Michel, *The Complete Essays of Montaigne*, trans. Donald M. Frame (Stanford, 1958).
Nashe, Thomas, *The Works of Thomas Nashe*, ed. Ronald B. McKerrow (Oxford, 1958).
Plato, *The Collected Dialogues*, ed. Edith Hamilton and Huntington Cairns (Princeton, 1961).
Powell, Thomas, *Tom of All Trades, or The Plaine Pathway to Preferment* (London, 1631).
———, *The Art of Thriving* (London, 1635).
Price, Daniel, *The Merchant: A Sermon Preached at Paul's Cross on Sunday the 14th of August Being the Day before Bartholomew Fair, 1607* (Oxford, 1608).
Roberts, Lewes, *The Treasure of Traffike* (London, 1641).
Scott, William, *An Essay of Drapery*, intro. Sylvia Thrupp (Cambridge, MA, 1953).

Sharpham, Edward, *A Critical Old Spelling Edition of The Works of Edward Sharpham*, ed. Christopher Gordon Petter (New York, 1986).
Sidney, Sir Philip, *The Defence of Poesy*, ed. Katherine Duncan-Jones (Oxford, 1989).
Smith, Sir Thomas, *A Discourse of the Commonweal of this Realm of England*, ed. Mary Dewar (Charlottesville, VA, 1969).
Stephens, John, *Essays and Characters* (London, 1615).
Tusser, Thomas, *Fiue hundred pointes of good Husbandrie* (London, 1580).
Virgil, *Eclogues, Georgics, Aeneid I-VI*, trans. H. Rushton Fairclough, Loeb Classical Library (Cambridge, MA, 1986).
Wheeler, John, *A Treatise of Commerce* (Middleburgh, 1601).
Whitney, Geffrey, *A Choice of Emblemes*, ed. Henry Green (New York, 1967).
Wilson, Thomas, *Arte of Rhetorique* (London, 1553).

1.2 Poems and Plays

Chapman, George, *The Plays of George Chapman. The Tragedies: A Critical Edition*, ed. Allan Holaday (Cambridge, 1987).
———, *The Plays of George Chapman: The Comedies: A Critical Edition*, ed. Allan Holaday (Urbana, 1970).
Chapman, George, Ben Jonson, and John Marston, *Eastward Ho!*, ed. R.W. Van Fossen (New York, 1999).
Dekker, Thomas, *The Shoemaker's Holiday*, ed. Anthony Parr (London, 1990).
———, *The Seven Deadly Sins of London* (London, 1606).
———, *Jests to Make you Merry* (London, 1607).
Heywood, Thomas, *A Critical Edition of* The Faire Maide of The Exchange, ed. Karl E. Snyder (New York, 1980).
———, *A Woman Killed With Kindness*, ed. Brian Scobie (London, 1985).
———, *If You Know Not Me, You Know Nobody, Part II* (Oxford, 1934).
Jonson, Ben, *The Comedies: Volpone, The Alchemist, Bartholomew Fair*, ed. Michael Jamieson (New York, 1966).
———, *Every Man Out of His Humour*, ed. Helen Ostovich (Manchester, 2001).
Shakespeare, William, *The Merchant of Venice*, ed. M. Lindsay Kaplan (Boston, 2002).
———, *Shakespeare's Sonnets*, ed. Stephen Booth (New Haven, CT, 1977).
———, *Timon of Athens*, ed. H. J. Oliver, Arden ed. (1959; London, 1997).
———, *The Tragedy of Coriolanus. The Norton Shakespeare*, eds. Stephen Greenblatt, Walter Cohen, Jean E. Howard, and Katharine Eisaman Maus (New York, 1997), pp. 2785–872.

2. SECONDARY SOURCES

2.1 Reference Works

Cross, F.L. and E.A. Livingstone (eds.), *Oxford Dictionary of the Christian Church*, 3rd edn. (Oxford, 1997).

Oxford Dictionary of National Biography, eds. H.G.C. Matthew, *et. al* (Oxford, 2004).
Oxford Latin Dictionary, ed. P.G.W. Glare (Oxford, 1982).

2.2 Books

Abrams, M.H. (ed.), *The Norton Anthology of English Literature,* 6th edn., 2 vols., (New York, 1993).
Agnew, Jean-Christophe, *Worlds Apart: The Market and the Theater in Anglo-American Thought, 1550–1750* (Cambridge, 1986).
Andrews, Michael Cameron, *Action of Our Death: The Performance of Death in English Renaissance Drama* (Newark, DE, 1989).
Appleby, Joyce, *Economic Thought and Ideology in Seventeenth-Century England* (Princeton, 1978).
Archer, Ian, *The Pursuit of Stability: Social Relations in Elizabethan England* (Cambridge, 1991).
Archer, John Michael, *Sovereignty and Intelligence: Spying and Court Culture in the English Renaissance* (Stanford, 1993).
Austin, J.L., *How to Do Things With Words*, 2nd edn. (Cambridge, MA, 1975).
Babcock, Barbara A. (ed.), *The Reversible World: Symbolic Inversion in Art and Society* (Ithaca, NY, 1978).
Baker, J.H., *An Introduction to English Legal History*, 4th edn. (London, 2002).
Bakhtin, Mikhail, *Rabelais and His World*, trans. Helene Iswolsky (Cambridge, MA, 1968).
Barber, C.L. and Richard Wheeler, *The Whole Journey: Shakespeare's Power of Development* (Berkeley, CA, 1986).
Barry, Jonathan and Christopher Brooks (eds.), *The Middling Sort of People: Culture, Society and Politics in England, 1550–1800* (New York, 1994).
Baskerville, Charles Read, *The Elizabethan Jig and Related Song Drama* (Chicago, 1929).
Bastiaenen, J.A., *The Moral Tone of Jacobean and Caroline Drama* (Amsterdam, 1930).
Beilen, Elaine V., *Redeeming Eve: Women Writers of the English Renaissance* (Princeton, 1987).
Bell, Ilona, *Elizabethan Women and the Poetry of Courtship* (Cambridge, 1998).
Bingham, Caroline, *James I of England* (London, 1981).
Braudel, Fernand, *Civilization and Capitalism 15th-18th Century, Vol. II: The Wheels of Commerce.* trans. Sian Reynolds (New York, 1982).
Bridenbaugh, Carl, *Vexed and Troubled Englishmen*, 1590–1642 (Oxford, 1968).
Bristol, Michael, *Carnival and Theater: Plebeian Culture and the Structure of Authority in Renaissance England* (New York, 1985).
Brown, Sylvia (ed.), *Women's Writing in Stuart England: The Mother's Legacies of Dorothy Leigh, Elizabeth Joscelin, and Elizabeth Richardson* (Stroud, 1991).
Bruster, Douglas, *Drama and the Market in the Age of Shakespeare* (Cambridge, 1992).

Bryson, Anna, *From Courtesy to Civility: Changing Codes of Conduct in Early Modern England* (Oxford, 1998).
Bullough, Geoffrey, *Narrative and Dramatic Sources of Shakespeare*, Vol. VI (London, 1966).
Campbell, Mary Baine, *Wonder and Science: Imagining Worlds in Early Modern Europe* (Ithaca, NY, 1999).
Chambers, E.K., *Shakespeare: A Survey* (London, 1925).
Clarke, Danielle (ed.), *Isabella Whitney, Mary Sidney and Aemilia Lanyer: Renaissance Women Poets* (London, 2000).
Cohen, Walter, *Drama of a Nation: Public Theater in Renaissance England and Spain* (Ithaca, NY, 1985).
Collier, J. Payne (ed.), *Illustrations of Early English Popular Literature*, vol. I (London, 1966).
Collinson, Patrick, *The Elizabethan Puritan Movement* (London, 1967).
Coquillette, Daniel R., *Francis Bacon* (Stanford, 1992).
Craig, Hardin, *An Interpretation of Shakespeare* (New York, 1948).
Cross, Claire, *Church and People: England 1450–1660*, 2nd edn. (Oxford, 1999).
Curzon, L.B., *English Legal History*, 2nd edn. (Estover, Plymouth, 1979).
Danby, John F., *Shakespeare's Doctrine of Nature: A Study of King Lear* (London, 1948).
Davis, J.C., *Utopia and the Ideal Society: A Study of English Utopian Writing 1516–1700* (Cambridge, 1981).
Daston, Lorraine, *Classical Probability in the Enlightenment* (Princeton, NJ, 1988).
Davis, Natalie Zemon, *Society and Culture in Early Modern France* (Stanford, 1975).
Eisenstein, Elizabeth, *The Printing Press as an Agent of Change: Communication and Cultural Transformation in Early Modern Europe*, 2 vols. (Cambridge, 1979).
Engle, Lars, *Shakespearean Pragmatism* (Chicago, 1993).
Erickson, Amy Louise, *Women and Property in Early Modern England* (New York, 1993).
Erler, Mary Carpenter (ed.), *Robert Copland, Poems* (Toronto, 1993).
Faulkner, Robert K., *Francis Bacon and the Project of Progress* (Lanham, MD, 1993).
Ferguson, Margaret W., Maureen Quilligan, and Nancy Vickers (eds.), *Rewriting the Renaissance: The Discourses of Sexual Difference in Early Modern Europe* (Chicago, 1986).
Ellis-Fermor, Una, *The Jacobean Drama*, rev. ed. (New York, 1964).
Fletcher, Anthony and J. Stevenson (eds.), *Order and Disorder in Early Modern England* (Cambridge, 1985).
Fly, Richard, *Shakespeare's Mediated World* (Amherst, MA, 1976).
Fowler, Alastair, *The Country House Poem: A Cabinet of Seventeenth-Century Estate Poems and Related Items* (Edinburgh, 1994).
Gallagher, Lowell, *Medusa's Gaze: Conscience and Casuistry in the Renaissance* (Stanford, 1991).
Gibbons, Brian, *Jacobean City Comedy*, 2nd edn. (London, 1980).

Goldberg, Jonathan, *James I and the Politics of Literature* (Baltimore, 1983).
Gough, J.W., *The Rise of the Entrepreneur* (New York, 1969).
Grassby, Richard, *The Business Community of Seventeenth-Century England* (Cambridge, 1995).
———, *The Idea of Capitalism before the Industrial Revolution* (Oxford, 1999).
Green, Ian, *The Christian's ABC: Catechisms and Catechizing in England c. 1530–1740* (Oxford, 1996).
———, *Print and Protestantism in Early Modern England* (Oxford, 2000).
Gunn, J.A.W., *Politics and the Public Interest in the Seventeenth Century* (London: Routledge & Kegan Paul, 1969).
Gurr, Andrew, *Playgoing in Shakespeare's London* (Cambridge, 1987).
Hall, Suzanne, *Chaste, Silent, and Obedient: English Books for Women, 1475–1640* (San Marino, CA, 1982).
Halpern, Richard, *The Poetics of Primitive Accumulation: English Renaissance Culture and the Genealogy of Capital* (Ithaca, NY, 1991).
Hannay, Margaret Patterson (ed.), *Silent But for the Word: Tudor Women as Patrons, Translators, and Writers of Religious Works* (Kent, OH, 1985).
Hanson, Elizabeth, *Discovering the Subject in Renaissance England* (Cambridge, 1998).
Hawkes, David, *Idols of the Marketplace: Idolatry and Commodity Fetishism in English Literature 1580–1680* (New York, 2001).
Henson, H. H., *Studies in English Religion in the Seventeenth Century* (London, 1903).
Herndl, George C., *The High Design: English Renaissance Tragedy and The Natural Law* (Lexington: University of Kentucky Press, 1970).
Hertzler, Joyce L., *The History of Utopian Thought* (New York, 1965).
Hill, Christopher, *Society and Puritanism in Pre-Revolutionary England* (London, 1969).
Hirschman, Albert O., *The Passions and the Interests: Political Arguments for Capitalism Before its Triumph* (Princeton, 1977).
Holmes, Peter, *Resistance and Compromise: The Political Thought of Elizabethan Catholics* (Cambridge, 1982).
Hun, Tony, *Villon's Last Will* (Oxford, 1996).
Hunter, G.K., *English Drama 1586–1642: The Age of Shakespeare*, The Oxford History of English Literature 6 (Oxford, 1997).
Hutson, Lorna, *Thomas Nashe in Context* (Oxford, 1989).
———, *The Usurer's Daughter: Male Friendship and Fictions of Women in Sixteenth-Century England* (London, 1994).
James, Mervyn, *Family, Lineage, and Civil Society: a Study of Society, Politics and Mentality in the Durham Region, 1500–1640* (Oxford, 1974).
———(ed.), *Society, Politics, and Culture: Studies in Early Modern England* (Cambridge, 1986).
Jardine, Lisa, *Still Harping on Daughters: Women and Drama in the Age of Shakespeare* (Brighton, 1983).

Jardine, Lisa and Alan Stewart, *Hostage to Fortune: The Troubled Life of Francis Bacon* (New York, 1998).
Jenkins, Hugh, *Feigned Commonwealths: The Country House Poem and the Fashioning of the Ideal Community* (Pittsburgh, 1998).
Jones, Ann Rosalind, *The Currency of Eros: Women's Love Lyric in Europe 1540–1620* (Bloomington, 1990).
Jones, David Martin, *Conscience and Allegiance in Seventeenth Century England: The Political Significance of Oaths and Engagements* (Rochester, NY, 1999).
Kantorowicz, Ernst, *The King's Two Bodies: A Study in Mediaeval Political Theology* (Princeton, 1957).
Kerridge, Eric, *Trade and Banking in Early Modern England* (Manchester, 1988).
Kerrigan, John, *Motives of Woe: Shakespeare and 'Female Complaint': A Critical Anthology* (Oxford, 1991).
Knights, L.C., *Drama and Society in the Age of Jonson* (London, 1937).
Krontiris, Tina, *Oppositional Voices: Women as Writers and Translators of Literature in the English Renaissance* (London, 1992).
Kumar, Krishan, *Utopia and Anti-Utopia in Modern Times* (Oxford, 1987).
———, *Utopianism* (Minneapolis, 1991).
Lake, Peter and Michael Questier (eds.), *Conformity and Orthodoxy in the English Church, c. 1560–1660* (Woodbridge, 2000).
Lake, Peter and Michael Questier, *The Antichrist's Lewd Hat: Protestants, Papists and Players in Post-Reformation England* (New Haven, CT, 2002).
Laslett, Peter, *The World We Have Lost* (London, 1965).
Levack, Brian P., *The Civil Lawyers in England, 1603–1641: A Political Study* (Oxford, 1973).
Le Goff, J., *Time, Work, and Culture in the Middle Ages* (Chicago, 1980).
Leggatt, Alexander, *Citizen Comedy in the Age of Shakespeare* (Toronto, 1973).
Leinwand, Theodore, *The City Staged: Jacobean Comedy, 1603–1613* (Madison, WI, 1986).
———, *Theatre, Finance, and Society in Early Modern England* (Cambridge, 1999).
Leslie, Marina, *Renaissance Utopias and the Problem of History* (Ithaca, NY, 1998).
Lewalski, Barbara Kiefer, *Writing Women in Jacobean England* (Cambridge, MA, 1993).
Lewis, C. S., *Studies in Words* (Cambridge, 1966).
Macfarlane, Alan, *The Origins of English Individualism: The Family, Property and Social Transition* (Oxford, 1978).
Maclean, Ian, *The Renaissance Notion of Woman* (Cambridge, 1980).
Macpherson, C.B., *The Political Theory of Possessive Individualism* (Oxford, 1962).
Manley, Lawrence, *Literature and Culture in Early Modern London* (Cambridge, 1995).
Manuel, Frank E. (ed.), *Utopias and Utopian Thought* (Boston, 1966).
Marcus, Leah S., *The Politics of Mirth* (Chicago, 1986).
Marotti, Arthur F. and Michael D. Bristol (eds.), *Print, Manuscript and Performance: The Changing Relations of the Media in Early Modern England,* (Columbus, OH, 2000).

Martin, Julian, *Francis Bacon, the State and the Reform of Natural Philosophy* (Cambridge, 1992).
Martin, Randall (ed.), *Women Writers in Renaissance England* (London, 1997).
Mauss, Marcel, *The Gift: Forms and Functions of Exchange in Archaic Societies,* trans. Ian Cunnison (New York: Norton, 1925).
Maus, Katharine Eisaman, *Inwardness and Theatre in the English Renaissance* (Chicago, 1995).
McBride, Kari Boyd, *Country House Discourse in Early Modern England* (Aldershot, 2001).
McGrath, Lynette, *Subjectivity and Women's Poetry in Early Modern England* (Aldershot, 2002).
Mingay, G.E., *The Gentry: The Rise and Fall of a Ruling Class* (London, 1976).
Muldrew, Craig, *The Economy of Obligation: The Culture of Credit and Social Relations in Early Modern England* (New York, 1998).
Mulryn, J.R. and Margaret Shewring (eds.), *Theatre and Government under the Early Stuarts* (Cambridge, 1993).
Myers, Milton L., *The Soul of Modern Economic Man: Ideas of Self-Interest, Thomas Hobbes to Adam Smith* (Chicago, 1983).
Negley, Glenn and J. Max Patrick, *The Quest for Utopia: An Anthology* (New York, 1962).
Newby, Howard, *The Deferential Worker: A Study of Farm Workers in East Anglia* (London, 1977).
Nuttall, A. D., *A New Mimesis: Shakespeare and the Representation of Reality* (New York, 1983).
———, *Timon of Athens* (Boston, 1989).
Oliphant, E.H.C. (ed.), *Shakespeare and His Fellow Dramatists* (New York, 1929).
Olson, Theodore, *Millennialism, Utopianism, and Progress* (Toronto, 1982).
Ore, Oystein, *Cardano, The Gambling Scholar* (New York, 1965).
Ovid, *Metamorphoses*, trans. Rolfe Humphries (Bloomington, IN, 1955).
Panofsky, Richard (ed.), *The Floures of Philosophie (1572) by Hugh Plat and A Sweet Nosgay (1573) and The Copy of a Letter (1567) by Isabella Whitney* (Delmar, NY, 1982).
Parry, Jonathan and Maurice Block (eds.), *Money and the Morality of Exchange* (Cambridge, 1989).
Paster, Gail Kern, *The Idea of the City in the Age of Shakespeare* (Athens, GA, 1988).
Peltonen, Markku, *Classical Humanism and Republicanism in English Political Thought 1570–1640* (Cambridge, 1995).
———(ed.), *The Cambridge Companion to Bacon* (Cambridge, 1996).
Pocock, J.G.A., *The Machiavellian Moment* (Princeton, 1975).
———, *Virtue, Commerce, and History* (Cambridge, 1985).
———, *The Ancient Constitution and the Feudal Law*, 2nd edn. (Cambridge, 1987).
———, *Politics, Language and Time: Essays on Political Thought and History* (Chicago, 1989).

Poole, Kristen, *Radical Religion: Figures of Nonconformity from Shakespeare to Milton* (Cambridge, 2000).

Reith, Gerda, *The Age of Chance: Gambling in Western Culture* (London, 1999).

Reiss, Timothy, *The Discourse of Modernism* (Ithaca, NY, 1985).

Reynolds, Bryan, *Becoming Criminal: Transversal Performance and Cultural Dissidence in Early Modern England* (Baltimore, 2002).

Rhodes, Neil (ed.), *English Renaissance Prose: History, Language and Politics* (Tempe, 1997).

Rice, Winthrop Huntington, *The European Ancestry of Villon's Satirical Testaments* (New York, 1941).

Rowe, George E., Jr., *Thomas Middleton and the New Comedy Tradition* (Lincoln, NE, 1979).

Seaver, Paul S., *Wallington's World: A Puritan Artisan in Seventeenth-Century London* (Stanford, 1985).

Showalter, Elaine, *Speaking of Gender* (New York, 1985).

Shuger, Debora Kuller, *Political Theologies in Shakespeare's England* (New York, 2001).

Skinner, Quentin, *The Foundations of Modern Political Thought* 2 vols. (Cambridge, 1978).

———, *Visions of Politics, Vol. I: Regarding Method* (Cambridge, 2002).

Smith, Adam, *The Wealth of Nations,* into. Edwin R.A. Seligman (London, 1954).

———, *Lectures on Jurisprudence*, eds. R.L. Meek, D.D. Raphael, and P.G. Stein (Oxford, 1978).

Smith, David L., Richard Strier and David Bevington (eds.), *The Theatrical City: Culture, Theatre and Politics in London, 1576–1649* (Cambridge, 1995).

Smuts, R. Malcolm, *Court Culture and the Origins of the Royalist Tradition in Early Modern England* (Philadelphia, 1987).

Soellner, Rolf, *Timon of Athens: Shakespeare's Pessimistic Tragedy* (Columbus, OH, 1979).

Solomon, Julie Robin, *Objectivity in the Making* (Baltimore, 1998).

Sommerville, Margaret R., *Sex and Subjection: Attitudes to Women in Early-Modern Society* (New York, 1995).

Spring, Eileen, *Law, Land, and Family: Aristocratic Inheritance in England 1300 to 1800* (Chapel Hill, NC, 1993).

Stevenson, Laura Caroline, *Praise and Paradox: Merchants and Craftsmen in Elizabethan Popular Literature* (Cambridge, 1984).

Stone, Lawrence, *The Crisis of the Aristocracy* (Oxford, 1965).

———, *Family and Fortune: Studies of Aristocratic Finance in the Sixteenth and Seventeenth Centuries* (Oxford, 1973).

———, *The Family, Sex and Marriage in England, 1500–1800* (New York, 1977).

Stretton, Tim, *Women Waging Law in Elizabethan England* (Cambridge, 1998).

Sullivan, Ceri, *The Rhetoric of Credit: Merchants in Early Modern Writing* (London, 2002).

Tawney, R. H. and Eileen Power (eds.), *Tudor Economic Documents*, vol. 2 (London, 1924).

———, *Religion and the Rise of Capitalism* (London, 1936).

Tennenhouse, Leonard, *Power On Display: The Politics of Shakespeare's Genres* (London, 1986).

Thompson, Roger, *Women in Stuart England and America* (London, 1974).

Travitsky, Betty (ed.), *The Paradise of Women: Writings by Englishwomen of the Renaissance* (Westport, CT, 1981).

Tuck, Richard, *Philosophy and Government 1572–1651* (Cambridge, 1993).

Underdown, David, *Revel, Riot and Rebellion* (Oxford, 1985).

Villon, Francois, *Le Testament Villon*, eds. Jean Rychner and Albert Henry (Geneva, 1974).

Walker, Kim, *Women Writers of the English Renaissance* (New York, 1996).

Wall, Wendy, *The Imprint of Gender: Authorship and Publication in the English Renaissance* (Ithaca, NY, 1993).

Weber, Max, *General Economic History*, trans. F. H. Knight (New York, 1927).

———, *The Protestant Ethic and the Spirit of Capitalism*, trans. Talcott Parsons (London, 1992).

Webster, Charles, *The Great Instauration: Science, Medicine, and Reform, 1626–1660* (London, 1975).

Whigham, Frank, *Seizures of the Will in Early Modern English Drama* (Cambridge, 1996).

Whitaker, Virgil K., *Francis Bacon's Intellectual Milieu* (Los Angeles, CA, 1962).

Woodbridge, Linda, *Women and the English Renaissance: Literature and the Nature of Womankind, 1540–1620* (Urbana, IL, 1984).

Woods, Susanne (ed.), *The Poems of Aemilia Lanyer* (Oxford, 1993).

———, *Lanyer: A Renaissance Woman Poet* (Oxford, 1999).

Wright, E. H., *The Authorship of Timon of Athens* (New York, 1910).

Wright, Louis B., *Middle-Class Culture in Elizabethan England* (New York, 1980).

Wrightson, Keith, *English Society, 1580–1680* (New Brunswick, NJ, 1982).

———, *Earthly Necessities: Economic Lives in Early Modern Britain* (New Haven, CT, 2000).

2.3 Articles/Chapters

Amussen, Susan, "Gender, Family, and the Social Order, 1560–1725," in *Order and Disorder in Early Modern England*, pp. 196–217.

Baker, J. H., "The Law Merchant and the common law before 1700," *Cambridge Law Journal* 38 (1979), pp. 295–332.

Barry, Jonathan, "Bourgeois Collectivisim? Urban Association and the Middling Sort," in *The Middling Sort of People*, eds. Barry and Brooks, pp. 84–112.

Bevington, David, "*The Tempest* and the Jacobean Court Masque," in *The Politics of the Stuart Court Masque*, eds. David Bevington and Peter Holbrook (Cambridge, 1998), pp. 218–43.

Blodgett, Eleanor Dickinson, "Bacon's *New Atlantis* and Campanella's *Civitas Solis*: A Study in Relationships," *PMLA* 46:3 (1931), pp. 763–80.

Boesky, Amy, "Bacon's *New Atlantis* and the laboratory of prose," in *The Project of Prose in Early Modern Europe and the New World*, Elizabeth Fowler and Roland Greene (Cambridge, 1997), pp. 138–53.

Bonfield, Lloyd, "Marriage, Property, and the 'Affective Family,'" *Law and History Review* 1 (1983), pp. 297–312.

Box, Ian, "Politics and Philosophy: Bacon on the values of peace and war," *The Seventeenth Century* VII:2 (1992), pp. 113–27.

———, "Bacon's Moral Philosophy," in *The Cambridge Companion to Bacon,* ed. Peltonen, pp. 260–82.

Brooks, Christopher, "Apprenticeship, Social Mobility and the Middling Sort, 1550–1800," in *The Middling Sort of People,* eds. Barry and Brooks, pp. 52–83.

Bruce, Susan, "Virgins of the world and feasts of the family: sex and the social order in two renaissance utopias," in *English Renaissance Prose*, ed. Rhodes, pp. 139–46.

Burke, Peter, "Tacitism," in *Tacitus*, ed. T.A. Dorey (London, 1969), pp. 149–71.

———, "Tacitism, Scepticism, and Reason of State," in *The Cambridge History of Political Thought 1450–1700*, ed. J. H. Burns (Cambridge, 1991), pp. 479–98.

Butler, Martin, "The Outsider as Insider," in *The Theatrical City*, eds. Smith, Strier and Bevington, pp. 193–208.

Capp, Bernard, "Separate Domains? Women and Authority in Early Modern England," *The Experience of Authority in Early Modern England*, eds. Paul Griffiths, Adam Fox and Steve Hindle (London, 1996), pp. 117–45.

Chorost, Michael, "Biological Finance in Shakespeare's *Timon of Athens*," *English Literary Renaissance* 21 (1991), pp. 349–70.

Cohen, R. A., "The Function of Setting in *Eastward Ho!*," *Renaissance Papers* (1973), pp. 83–96.

Cohen, Walter, "*The Merchant of Venice* and the Possibilities of Historical Criticism," *ELH* 49:4 (1982), pp. 765–89.

Colclough, David, "Ethics and politics in the New Atlantis," in *Francis Bacon's New Atlantis: New Interdisciplinary Essays*, ed. Bronwen Price (Manchester, 2002), pp. 60–81.

Dubrow, Heather, "A Mirror for Complaints: Shakespeare's Lucrece and Generic Tradition," in *Renaissance Genres: Essays on Theory, History, and Interpretation*, ed. Barbara Kiefer Lewalski (Cambridge, MA, 1986), pp. 399–417.

Dubrow, Heather, "The Country-House Poem: A Study in Generic Development," *Genre* 12 (1979), pp. 145–79.

Fehrenbach, R. J., "Isabella Whitney, Sir Hugh Plat, Geffrey Whitney, and 'Sister Eldershae,'" *English Language Notes* 21 (Sept. 1983).

Fincham, Kenneth and Peter Lake, "The Ecclesiastical Policy of King James I," *Journal of British Studies* 24:2 (1985), pp. 169–207.

Geertz, Clifford, "Ritual and Social Change," in idem, *The Interpretation of Cultures* (New York, 1973), pp. 142–69.

Glaesar, Edward, "Neither a Borrower nor a Lender Be: An Economic Analysis of Interest Restrictions and Usury Laws," *Journal of Law and Economics* 41:1 (1998), pp. 1–36.

Gowing, Laura, "Language, Power, and the Law: Women's Slander Litigation is Early Modern England," in *Women, Crime, and the Courts*, eds. Jenny Kermode and Garthine Walker (London, 1994), pp. 26–47.

Grossman, Marshall, "The Gendering of Genre: Literary History and the Canon," in *Aemilia Lanyer: Gender, Genre, and the Canon*, ed. Marshall Grossman (Lexington, KY, 1998), pp. 128–42.

Gunn, J.A.W., "'Interest Will Not Lie': A Seventeenth-Century Political Maxim," *Journal of the History of Ideas* (1968), pp. 551–64.

Habakkuk, H. J., "Marriage Settlements in the Eighteenth Century," *Transactions of the Royal Historical Society*, Fourth series, 32 (1950), pp. 15–30.

Halasz, Alexandra, "Pamphlet Surplus: John Taylor and Subscription Publication," in *Print, Manuscript, and Performance*, eds. Marotti and Bristol, pp. 90–102.

Hannay, Margaret P., "'So May I With the Psalmist truly Say': Early Modern Englishwomen's Psalm Discourse," in *Write or Be Written: Early Modern Women Poets and Cultural Constraints*, eds. Barbara Smith and Ursula Appelt (Aldershot, 2001), pp. 105–27.

Heal, Felicity, "The idea of hospitality in early modern England," *Past and Present* 102 (1982), pp. 67–82.

Hobsbawm, Eric, "The Seventeenth Century in the Development of Capitalism," *Science and Society* 24 (1960).

Horwich, Richard, "Hamlet and Eastward Ho!," *Studies in English Literature* (1971), pp. 223–33.

James, Mervyn, "At the crossroads of the political culture: the Essex revolt, 1601," in *Society, Politics, and Culture,* ed. James, pp. 416–65.

Kahn, Coppelia, "'Magic of Bounty': *Timon of Athens*, Jacobean Patronage, and Maternal Power," *Shakespeare Quarterly* 38 (1987), pp. 34–57.

Kishlansky, Mark, "Parliamentary Selection: the Emergence of Adversary Politics in the Long Parliament," *Journal of Modern History* 49:4 (1977), pp. 617–40.

Landa, Janet, "The Economics of Symbols, Clan Names, and Religion," *The Journal of Legal Studies* 12:1 (1983), pp. 135–56.

Lewalski, Barbara K. "Of God and Good Women: The Poems of Aemilia Lanyer," *Silent But for the Word: Tudor Women as Patrons, Translators, and Writers of Religious Works,* ed. Margaret Patterson Hanney (Kent, OH, 1985), pp. 203–04.

———, "The Lady of the Country House Poem," *The Fashioning and Functioning of the British Country House*, eds. Gervase Jackson-Stops, Gordon J. Schochet, Lena Cowen Orlin, and Elisabeth Blair McDougall (Hanover, 1989), pp. 261–75.

———, "Re-Writing Patriarchy and Patronage: Margaret Clifford, Anne Clifford, and Aemilia Lanyer," *The Yearbook of English Studies* 21 (1991), pp. 104–66.

Lamb, Mary Ellen, "The Agency of the Split Subject: Lady Anne Clifford and the Uses of Reading," *English Literary Renaissance* 22 (1992), pp. 347–68.

Lindley, Keith, "Philip Massinger's *A New Way to Pay Old Debts:* Noble Scarlet vs. London Blue," in *The Theatrical City*, eds. Smith, Strier and Bevington, pp. 183–192.

Loewenstein, Joseph, "Wither and Professional Work," in *Print, Manuscript and Performance,* eds. Marotti and Bristol, pp. 103–23.

Mansbridge, Jane J., "The Rise and Fall of Self-Interest in the Explanation of Political Life," in *Beyond Self-Interest*, ed. Jane J. Mansbridge (Chicago, 1990), pp. 3–22.

Marotti, Arthur F., "Patronage, Poetry, and Print," in *Patronage, Politics, and Literary Traditions In England, 1558–1658*, ed. Cedric C. Brown (Detroit, 1993), pp. 21–46.

Muldrew, Craig, "Interpreting the Market: the Ethics of Credit and Community Relations in Early Modern England," *Social History* 18:2 (1993), pp. 163–83.

———, "From a 'light cloak' to an 'iron cage': historical changes in the relation between community and individualism," in *Communities in Early Modern England: Networks, Place, Rhetoric*, eds. Alexandra Shepard and Phil Withington (Manchester, 2000), pp. 156–177.

Newman, Karen, "Portia's Ring: Unruly Women and Structures of Exchange in *The Merchant of Venice*," *Shakespeare Quarterly* 38:1 (1987), pp. 19–33.

Ostovich, Helen, "Introduction," *Eastward Ho!* (London, 2002).

Peltonen, Markku, "Politics and science: Francis Bacon and the true greatness of states," *Historical Journal* 35:2 (1992), 279–305.

———, "Bacon's Political Philosophy," in *The Cambridge Companion to Bacon*, ed. Peltonen, pp. 283–310.

Posner, Richard, "A Theory of Primitive Society with Special Reference to Law," *Journal of Law and Economics* 23:1 (1980), pp. 1–53.

Rex, Richard, "The Crisis of Obedience: God's Word and Henry's Reformation," *Historical Journal* 39:4 (1996), pp. 863–94.

Rollison, David, "The bourgeois soul of John Smyth of Nibley," *Social History* 12 (1987), pp. 309–30.

Rose, Mary Beth, "Where are the Mothers in Shakespeare?" *Shakespeare Quarterly* 42 (1991), pp. 291–314.

Russell, Conrad, "Divine Rights," in *Public Duty and Private Conscience in Seventeenth Century England*, eds. John Morrill, Paul Slack and Daniel Woolf (Oxford, 1993), pp. 101–20.

Salmon, J.H.M., "Seneca and Tacitus in Jacobean England," *Journal of the History of Ideas* 50 (1989), pp. 199–225.

Scott, William O., "The Paradox of Timon's Self-Cursing," *Shakespeare Quarterly* 35 (1984), pp. 290–304.

Seaver, Paul, "The Puritan Work Ethic Revisited," *Journal of British Studies* 19:2 (1980), pp. 35–53.

Shell, Marc, "The Wether and the Ewe: Verbal Usury in *The Merchant of Venice*," *Kenyon Review* 1:4 (1979), pp. 65–92.

Sigalas, Joseph, "Sailing Against the Tide: Resistance to Pre-Colonial Constructs and Euphoria in *Eastward Ho!*," *Renaissance Papers* (1994), pp. 85–94.

Stone, Lawrence, "Patriarchy and Paternalism in Tudor England: The Earl of Arundel and The Peasants' Revolt of 1549," *Journal of British Studies* 13 (1974), pp. 19–23.

Tennenhouse, Leonard, "The Counterfeit Order in *The Merchant of Venice*," in *Representing Shakespeare: New Psychoanalytic Essays*, eds. Murray M. Schwartz and Coppelia Kahn (Baltimore, 1972), pp. 54–69.

Travitsky, Betty, "The 'Wyll and Testament' of Isabella Whitney," *English Literary Renaissance* 10 (1980), pp. 76–95.

Tyacke, Nicholas, 'Lancelot Andrewes and the Myth of Anglicanism,' in *Conformity and Orthodoxy in the English Church, c.1560–1660*, eds. Peter Lake and Michael C. Questier (Woodbridge, 2000), pp. 5–33.

Underdown, David, "The Taming of the Scold: The Enforcement of Patriarchal Authority in Early Modern England," in *Order and Disorder*, eds. Fletcher and Stevenson, pp. 116–36.

Vallance, Edward, "Oaths, Casuistry, and Equivocation: Anglican Responses to the Engagement Controversy," *Historical Journal* 44:1 (2001), pp. 59–77.

Wells, Susan, "Jacobean City Comedy and the Ideology of the City," *English Literary History* 48 (1981), pp. 37–60.

Whitney, Charles, "Merchants of Light: science as colonization in the *New Atlantis*," in *Francis Bacon's Legacy of Texts*, ed. William Sessions (New York, 1990), pp. 255–68.

Index

For Product Safety Concerns and Information please contact our EU representative GPSR@taylorandfrancis.com
Taylor & Francis Verlag GmbH, Kaufingerstraße 24, 80331 München, Germany

www.ingramcontent.com/pod-product-compliance
Ingram Content Group UK Ltd.
Pitfield, Milton Keynes, MK11 3LW, UK
UKHW022120190926
475702UK00013B/1547

9780415879392